Publication Information

The first edition of this book was published in the UK in 2009 by Green Umbrella Publishing
ISBN: 978-1906635336
A reprint edition was published in 2010 by G2 Entertainment
ISBN: 978-1907803314
An eBook version was first published in April 2012 by Barry Rhodes, 37 Cairn Hill, Dublin 18, Ireland
ISBN: 978-0-9572620-0-3
An updated version '999 Updated Questions on the Rules of Golf, Effective January 2016' was published in January 2016

Note that several questions and answers have been changed from the previous print edition of this book, mainly resulting from the changes to the Rules of Golf and Decisions on the Rules of Golf that became effective on 1st January 2016

Copyright ©2012, ©2013, ©2014, ©2015, ©2016, Barry Rhodes

The right of Barry Rhodes to be identified as the author of this book has been asserted by him in accordance with the Copyright Designs and Patents Act 1988.

All rights reserved. No part of this work may be reproduced or utilised in any form or by any means, electronic or mechanical, including photocopying, recording or by any information storage and retrieval system, without prior written permission of the publisher.

Acknowledgement:

The answers to questions in this book refer to; 1) Rules of Golf 2016 ©2015 R&A Rules Limited and The United States Golf Association. All rights reserved. 2) Decisions on the Rules of Golf 2016-2017 ©R&A Rules Limited 2015. All rights reserved.

The R&A and USGA review and make revisions to the Rules of Golf every four years. The last revision was effective 1st January 2016.

The questions, answers and explanations to the questions in this book are the author's interpretation and understanding of the 34 Rules of Golf and do not carry the official approval of either the R&A or USGA.

Whilst every attempt has been made to ensure the accuracy and reliability of these questions and answers on the Rules of Golf, I am human and have been known to be wrong! I shall not be held responsible for any loss or damage of any sort caused by reliance upon the accuracy or reliability of such information. Readers should refer to the full text of the Rules and Decisions, as published in the official publications of the R&A (www.randa.org) and the USGA (www.usga.org).

About the Author:

Barry Rhodes qualified as a Chartered Accountant but has spent most of his career in senior sales, marketing and management roles within the information and communication technology (ICT) sector. He is an enthusiastic, high handicap golfer who developed an interest, then a fascination, and now a passion for the Rules of Golf. He is resident in Dublin, Ireland, where he is an active member of Milltown Golf Club.

Barry's relationship with the Rules began in 2000 with his participation in the inter-club Rules of Golf quiz competitions, organised by the Royal & Ancient for Golf Clubs in Great Britain and Ireland. This progressed to him writing articles, running quizzes, and delivering presentations on the Rules at various Golf Clubs and corporate functions. He writes a weekly web blog, containing interesting content for anyone who wishes to improve their knowledge and understanding of the Rules of Golf, at www.BarryRhodes.com. In 2009 the first edition of '*999 Questions on the Rules of Golf*' was published in the UK and sold in over 50 countries. Later in the same year Barry launched the '*Rhodes Rules School*' series, weekly emails posing questions based around photographs and diagrams of Rules incidents that may be encountered by golfers whilst on the course. Barry is a guest contributor and answers questions on the Rules of Golf on various golfing web sites. On his www.RhodesRulesSchool.com web site he markets low-cost, downloadable eDocuments that are ideal for Golf Clubs to spread knowledge on the Rules of Golf to their members (quizzes, notice board content, newsletters, etc.).

In March 2008, Barry became the first person to achieve a 100% correct mark on the public Advanced Rules of Golf Course examination, run by the Professional Golfers Association (PGA) in their headquarters at The Belfry, West Midlands, UK. More recently, in April 2015, Barry received a 'pass with distinction' in the R&A's Level 3, Tournament Administrators and Referees School examination (TARS), the highest certification awarded.

Dedication:
To Sandy, my darling wife, who is always there for me.

999 Updated Questions on the Rules of Golf 2016 by Barry Rhodes

Note that several questions and answers have been changed from the original print edition of this book, incorporating all the amendments to Rules and Decisions, including those effective from 1st January 2016.

Section 1: 333 simple questions which every golfer should be familiar with

True or False?

Q.1
A ball is unfit for play if its surface is scratched or scraped. True or False?
Answer: False. Rule 5-3.
Note: A ball is unfit for play if it is visibly cut, cracked or out of shape. Scratches or scrapes do not render a ball unfit for play.

Q.2
In a four-ball stroke play competition a player may play the whole round without a partner. True or False?
Answer: True. Rule 31-2.
Note: A side may be represented by either partner for all or any part of a stipulated round.

Q.3
A Stableford competition is a form of stroke play. True or False?
Answer: True. Rule 32-1.
Note: Bogey, Par and Stableford competitions are forms of stroke play in which play is against a fixed score at each hole.

Q.4
The penalty for agreeing to waive the operation of any Rule is disqualification. True or False?
Answer: True. Rule 1-3.
Note: Players must not agree to exclude the operation of any Rule or to waive any penalty incurred.

Q.5
A player must stand within the teeing ground to play his tee shot. True or False?
Answer: False. Rule 11-1.
Note: A player may stand outside the teeing ground providing his ball is teed within it.

Q.6
When taking relief from an immovable obstruction a player may not clean his ball. True or False?

Answer: False. Rule 24-2.
Note: The ball may be cleaned when lifted under this Rule.

Q.7
The general penalty for a breach of a Rule in stroke play is one stroke. True or False?
Answer: False. The general penalty in stroke play is two strokes. Rule 3-5.
Note: The general penalty for a breach of Rule in match play is loss of hole.

Q.8
A player may brush aside sand in the area where he is about to drop his ball under the Rules. True or False?
Answer: False. Rule 13-2.
Note: A player is not permitted to improve the area in which he is to drop or place a ball by removing sand or loose soil, which are not loose impediments, unless they are on a putting green.

Q.9
A competitor is a player in a match play competition. True or False?
Answer: False. Definition of Competitor.
Note: A competitor is a player in a stroke play competition.

Q.10
A fellow competitor or spectator may not assist a competitor in removing a large loose impediment. True or False?
Answer: False. Decision 23-1/3.
Note: The player may seek help from anyone to remove a loose impediment, providing that there is no undue delay in play.

Q.11
Time spent in playing a wrong ball is not counted in the five minute period permitted for searching for a ball. True or False?
Answer: True. Definition of Lost Ball.

Q.12
A player who is naturally right-handed may carry a left-handed club to use for shots where she might otherwise have to turn a clubhead over, for example, where her ball is lying against a tree. True or False?
Answer: True. Rule 4-4.
Note: There is nothing in the Rules to prevent a player carrying both left and right-handed clubs, providing they do not start their stipulated round with more than 14 clubs.

Q.13
A ball is in a bunker when any part of it touches the bunker. True or False?
Answer: True. Definition of Bunker.

Q.14
In match play, if a player plays from outside the teeing ground when starting play of a hole her opponent may require the stroke to be cancelled and replayed from within the teeing ground. True or False?
Answer: True. Rule 11-4a.
Note: However, the opponent may also elect to let the stroke stand.

Q.15
A player's provisional ball may not be played if their original ball is neither lost nor out of bounds. True or False?

Answer: True. Rule 27-2c.
Note: The player must continue play with the original ball.

Q.16
In match play, if a player's ball at rest is moved by an outside agency he loses the hole. True or False?
Answer: False. Rule 18-1.
Note: If a ball at rest is moved by an outside agency, there is no penalty and the ball must be replaced.

Q.17
To assist a player as to the location of a hole on the putting green it is permissible for another player to mark the position of the hole with the grip end of their putter. True or False?
Answer: True. Decision 17-3/6.
Note: A club used in this matter must be treated as a flagstick in applying the Rules.

Q.18
Information such as the position of hazards or the flagstick on a putting green is advice. True or False?
Answer: False. Definition of Advice.
Note: Information on the Rules, distance or matters of public information such as the location of the flagstick on the putting green, is not advice.

Q.19
In four-ball match play, if both partners on a side are not on the 1st tee at the time set by the Committee they are disqualified. True or False?
Answer: False. Rule 30-3a.
Note: One partner may represent the side for any part or all of a match. An absent partner may join a match between holes, but not during the play of a hole.

Q.20
There are some foreign materials that may be applied to the club face for the purpose of influencing the movement of the ball. True or False?
Answer: False. Rule 4-2b.
Note: Foreign material must not be applied to the club face for the purpose of influencing the movement of the ball.

Q.21
A half-eaten banana may be removed from a bunker if it interferes with a player's stroke. True or False?
Answer: False. Decision 23/3.
Note: A banana is a natural object and is therefore a loose impediment, which may not be removed from a hazard by a player before he makes a stroke from that hazard.

Q.22
In stroke play, if a player's ball in motion is accidentally deflected by an outside agency (e.g. a spectator) he incurs a penalty of one stroke. True or False?
Answer: False. Rule 19-1.
Note: If a player's ball in motion is accidentally deflected or stopped by any outside agency, it is a rub of the green, there is no penalty.

Q.23
If her ball is overhanging the hole a player may wait for 20 seconds after arriving at the hole, to see whether it will drop, before she has to count another stroke if it does subsequently

drop into the hole. True or False?
Answer: False. Rule 16-2.
Note: A player is allowed enough time to reach the hole without unreasonable delay, and an additional 10 seconds to determine whether the ball is at rest. If the ball falls into the hole after this period the player has holed out but must add another stroke to her score.

Q.24
On the putting green a player may touch his line of putt to remove sand. True or False?
Answer: True. Rule 13-2.
Note: Removing sand or loose soil on the putting green is one of the exceptions to the general rule that a player must not improve or allow to be improved, his line of play or a reasonable extension of that line beyond the hole.

Q.25
A ball is deemed lost as soon as the player has dropped another ball under the Rules. True or False?
Answer: True. Decision 27-1/2.
Note: When a player drops a ball at the spot of his previous stroke, with the intent to play a ball under penalty of stroke and distance (Rule 27-1a), the original ball is lost.

Q.26
In taking relief from a water hazard a player need not proceed with the ball that entered the hazard. True or False?
Answer: True. Rule 26-1.
Note: Even if the player retrieves his original ball from the water hazard he may still substitute a different ball.

Q.27
A ball may be replaced during play of a hole if it is visibly cut or cracked. True or False?
Answer: True. Rule 5-3.
Note: A ball is unfit for play if it is visibly cut, cracked or out of shape. The player must follow the procedure in Rule 5-3 to replace it.

Q.28
When dropping a ball at the nearest point of relief from interference by an immovable obstruction, it may never be played from a point that is nearer to the hole than where it originally came to rest. True or False?
Answer: True. Definition of Nearest Point of Relief.
Note: The nearest point of relief is the point on the course nearest to where the ball lies that is not nearer the hole, and where, if the ball were so positioned, no interference by the condition from which relief is sought would exist, for the stroke the player would have made from the original position if the condition were not there.

Q.29
The ball may only be struck at with the head of the club. True or False?
Answer: True. Rule 14-1a.
Note: The ball must be fairly struck at with the head of the club and must not be pushed, scraped or spooned.

Q.30
In match play, If Maria plays when her opponent, Rita, should have played, Rita may ask her to take back her ball and play again in turn. True or False?
Answer: True. Rule 10-1c.
Note: Rita may let the stroke stand or require Maria to cancel the stroke so made and, when

it is her turn, play a ball as nearly as possible at the spot at which the original ball was last played.

Q.31
A coin used to mark the position of a ball is part of the player's equipment. True or False?
Answer: False. Definition of Equipment.
Note: Any small object used to mark a ball is specifically excluded in the definition of equipment.

Q.32
Alistair's drive rebounds off a tree back to a position at rest within the same teeing ground. Alistair may re-tee his ball without penalty. True or False?
Answer: False. Decision 18-2a/2.
Note: Once Alistair has made a stroke at his ball it is in play and cannot be re-teed.

Q.33
A player may remove a loose impediment lying out of bounds that interferes with his stance. True or False?
Answer: True. Decision 23-1/9.

Q.34
A player putts his ball from the fringe of the putting green and it strikes the unattended flagstick in the hole. In stroke play, there is a penalty of two strokes. True or False?
Answer: False. Rule 17-3.
Note: If a ball struck from anywhere off the putting green hits the flagstick there is no penalty, providing the flagstick is not being attended, removed or held up.

Q.35
A ball dropped under the Rules for the first time does not have to be re-dropped if it rolls and comes to rest nearer the hole than its original position. True or False?
Answer: False. Rule 20-2c(vii).
Note: A ball must be re-dropped, without penalty, if it rolls and comes to rest nearer the hole than its original position or estimated position (see Rule 20-2b) unless otherwise permitted by the Rules.

Q.36
A water hazard that dries up and has no water in it is no longer a water hazard. True or False?
Answer: False. Definition of Water Hazard.
Note: Water hazards are defined by stakes and/or lines and do not necessarily contain water.

Q.37
A player may remove an easily removable out of bounds stake from its hole if it interferes with their swing. True or False?
Answer: False. Decision 13-2/17.
Note: Objects defining out of bounds are deemed to be fixed and may not be moved.

Q.38
A player is not permitted to use his hand to bend a branch obscuring his ball after his stance has been taken. True or False?
Answer: True. Decision 13-2/1.

Note: A player is not necessarily entitled to see his ball when making a stroke and must not move anything growing other than is necessary to take his stance.

Q.39
A player may touch his line of putt when repairing ball marks on the putting green. True or False?
Answer: True. Rule 16-1c.
Note: This is one of seven exceptions to the Rule that the line of putt may not be touched.

Q.40
In match play, a player picks up his ball thinking that he has won the hole and then finds out that he hasn't. He loses the hole. True or False?
Answer: False. Decision 20-1/8.
Note: The player incurs a one stroke penalty and must replace his ball.

Q.41
James has only been playing golf for a few months. In his first stroke play competition he takes two practice swings in a water hazard, touching the ground each time. He incurs total penalties of four strokes for grounding his club in a hazard twice. True or False?
Answer: False. Decision 1-4/12(3).
Note: A single penalty is incurred when related acts result in one Rule being breached more than once.

Q.42
An artificially-surfaced road is an obstruction from which the player may take relief without penalty. True or False?
Answer: True. Definition of Obstructions.
Note: An obstruction is anything artificial, including the artificial surfaces and sides of roads and paths. A player may take relief from interference by an immovable obstruction.

Q.43
A player rotates his ball on the putting green to line-up the trademark with the hole. He does not lift the ball, mark its position or change its position. There is no penalty. True or False?
Answer: False. Decision 18-2a/33.
Note: If the player had marked the position of the ball before rotating it, there would have been no penalty.

Q.44
A player may drop a rake in the bunker beside him before he takes his stance to make his stroke. True or False?
Answer: True. Decision 13-4/21.
Note: The player would incur a penalty if, when he dropped the rake, it moved his ball or improved the lie of his ball.

Q.45
A player says to his fellow competitor, "You have no shot at all. If I were you, I would declare your ball unplayable." He is penalised two strokes. True or False?
Answer: True. Rule 8-1 Advice and Definition of Advice.
Note: Advice is any counsel or suggestion that could influence a player in determining their play. However, information on the Rules is not advice, so if the player had outlined the three options for an unplayable ball, without making a recommendation, no penalty would have been incurred.

Q.46
Fran removes a broken tee touching his ball on the putting green causing the ball to move. There is a penalty of one stroke and the ball must be replaced. True or False?
Answer: False. Rule 18-2.
Note: There is no penalty if a player accidentally causes his ball to move in removing a movable obstruction.

Q.47
A player may have the flagstick attended even if his ball is not on the putting green. True or False?
Answer: True. Rule 17-1.
Note: Before making a stroke from anywhere on the course, the player may have the flagstick attended, removed or held up.

Q.48
A wooden match is a loose impediment. True or False?
Answer: False. Definition of Loose Impediments.
Note: A wooden match is artificial and is therefore an obstruction.

Q.49
In stroke play, a player removes grass clippings and pine cones from the vicinity of his ball lying in the rough. He is penalised two strokes. True or False?
Answer: False. Rule 23-1.
Note: Any loose impediment may be removed without penalty, except when both the loose impediment and the ball lie in or touch the same hazard.

Q.50
If a player is not sure whether a long blade of grass, a divot, a twig or other such natural object growing through the green is loose or attached she may move the object to the extent necessary to be certain. True or False?
Answer: True. Decision 13-2/26.
Note: A player is entitled to move a natural object for the specific purpose of determining whether the object is loose, providing that in doing so the object does not then become detached and it is returned to its original position before the next stroke.

Q.51
A ball that is lifted because it is assisting or interfering with another player's ball must be dropped as near as possible to the place from which it was lifted. True or False?
Answer: False. Rule 22-1.
Note: A ball lifted in these situations must be replaced, not dropped.

Q.52
A player may not remove a blade of grass adhering to his ball. True or False?
Answer: True. Decision 21/2 and Definition of Loose Impediments.
Note: Anything adhering to the ball is not a loose impediment.

Q.53
In match play, the penalty for a player testing the condition of a bunker that their ball lies in is loss of hole. True or False?
Answer: True. Rule 13-4.
Note: The penalty in stroke play is two strokes.

Q.54
A player may use standard binoculars in order to see whether there are bunkers surrounding the green. True or False?

Answer: True. Decision 14-3/3.
Note: Neither standard spectacles nor field glasses that have no range-finder attachments are artificial devices within the meaning of the term in Rule 14-3.

Q.55
A player may wrap a towel around the grip of his club in order to assist him making a stroke. True or False?
Answer: True. Rule 14-3c(iii).
Note: A player may not use any artificial device or unusual equipment to assist him in gripping his club. However, the Rule permits plain gloves to be worn. Resin, powder and drying or moisturising agents may be used, and a towel or handkerchief may be wrapped around the grip.

Q.56
A player must not make a stroke anywhere on the course with his caddie standing on or near an extension of his line of play behind the ball. True or False?
Answer: True. Rule 14-2b.
Note: However, there is no penalty if a caddie or playing partner, inadvertently stands on an extension of the player's line of play or line of putt behind the ball and is not positioned there to assist him.

Q.57
In a four-ball match the playing partners in a side may play in whichever order they choose. True or False?
Answer: True. Rule 31-4.
Note: Balls belonging to the same side may be played in whichever order the side considers best.

Q.58
When out of bounds is defined by a line on the ground the line itself is out of bounds. True or False?
Answer: True. Definition of Out of Bounds.
Note: So, if a ball is lying between the outside edges of a white line delineating out of bounds the ball is out of bounds.

Q.59
On the putting green, a player may lift her ball, replace it and lift it a second time, providing she marks it first on each occasion. True or False?
Answer: True. Rule 16-1b.
Note: A ball may be lifted from the green for any reason, providing it is marked first.

Q.60
A practice putting green on the course is a wrong putting green. True or False?
Answer: True. Definition of Wrong Putting Green.
Note: This term includes a practice putting green or pitching green on the course.

Q.61
Ryan marks his ball on the green with a small coin placed in front of the ball. He is penalised one stroke. True or False?
Answer: False. Rule 20-1.
Note: The Rule states that the position of a ball to be lifted should be marked by placing a ball-marker, a small coin or other similar object immediately behind the ball. The player may place their marker at the side or in front of the ball, but it is not recommended.

Q.62

The maximum number of clubs a player may carry is 14 and a putter. True or False?
Answer: False. Rule 4-4a.
Note: The player must not start a round with more than 14 clubs, which includes a putter.

Q.63
A player's ball is deflected to a point farther away from the green than where he played it from when it hits a movable sign that the Committee has put on the course to direct players to the next teeing ground. The player may replay his ball without penalty. True or False?
Answer: False. Decision 19-1/1.
Note: The deflection is a rub of the green and the ball must be played as it lies, without penalty.

Q.64
A player who carries 14 clubs in his bag breaks a club in anger. He may replace the broken club with any other club during the round, providing he does not unduly delay play. True or False?
Answer: False. Rule 4-3b.
Note: If, during a stipulated round, a player's club is damaged other than in the normal course of play, rendering it non-conforming or changing its playing characteristics, the club must not subsequently be used or replaced during the round.

Q.65
An outside agency includes any person who is not part of the match or, in stroke play, not part of the competitor's side, including their caddies. True or False?
Answer: True. Definition of Outside Agency.

Q.66
In stroke play, a player may concede a fellow competitor's putt when it is at rest on the lip of the hole. True or False?
Answer: False. Rule 3-2.
Note: In stroke play, competitors must hole out at every hole in the stipulated round or they are disqualified.

Q.67
Once a player has commenced the forward movement of his club, with the intention of striking the ball, the stroke always counts. True or False?
Answer: False. Definition of Stroke.
Note: If a player checks his downswing voluntarily before the clubhead reaches the ball he has not made a stroke.

Q.68
A player may mark and lift his ball in a bunker for identification purposes. True or False?
Answer: True. Rule 12-2.
Note: Before marking and lifting the ball, the player must announce his intention to an opponent in match play or a fellow competitor in stroke play.

Q.69
One of the options for relief from a ball lost in a water hazard is to drop a ball anywhere on the line of flight from where the ball was last played to where it crossed the margin of the hazard. True or False?
Answer: False. Rule 26-1.
Note: A player may not drop a ball on the so-called "line of flight". The option for which this is commonly mistaken is to drop a ball behind the water hazard, keeping the point at which the original ball last crossed the margin of the water hazard directly between the hole and the

spot on which the ball is dropped, with no limit to how far behind the water hazard the ball may be dropped.

Q.70
In a singles stroke play competition a competitor is not the partner of his fellow competitor. True or False?
Answer: True. Definition of Competitor.

Q.71
Colin was a bag of nerves on the 1st tee and completely missed his ball with his first stroke. There is no stroke or penalty, as he had not yet put a ball into play in the stipulated round. True or False?
Answer: False. Definition of Stroke.
Note: Colin intended to strike and move his ball and the stroke must be counted.

Q.72
Ram is last to play from the teeing ground and thinks that his sliced, blind tee shot may be out of bounds. Without making any comment he tees another ball and plays it. Surprisingly, he does find his original ball, which must have hit a tree and rebounded back onto the course. He may now play his original ball. True or False?
Answer: False. Rule 27-2a.
Note: As Ram did not declare his second ball from the tee a provisional ball, it becomes his ball in play and the original ball is treated as lost. Ram has now played three strokes as his second ball was played under penalty of stroke and distance.

Q.73
A player may remove a loose impediment at any time without incurring a penalty. True or False?
Answer: False. Rule 23-1.
Note: Loose impediments may not be removed without penalty when both the loose impediment and the ball lie in or touch the same hazard.

Q.74
If a player intentionally distracts another player while he is making his stroke he may be disqualified. True or False?
Answer: True. Decision 33-7/8.
Note: Although a Committee may disqualify a player under Rule 33-7 for a single act that it considers to be a serious breach of etiquette, in most cases it is recommended that such a penalty should be imposed only in the event of a further serious breach.

Q.75
A ball is holed when it is at rest within the circumference of the hole. True or False?
Answer: False. Definition of Holed.
Note: All of the ball must also be below the level of the lip of the hole.

Q.76
In stroke play, if a player plays out of turn there is no penalty but they may be required to play their stroke again, in turn. True or False?
Answer: False. Rule 10-2c.
Note: If a competitor plays out of turn, there is no penalty and the ball is played as it lies, unless the Committee determines that competitors have agreed to play out of turn to give one of them an advantage, in which case they are disqualified.

Q.77
During a match Reid grounds his club in a bunker. He incurs a penalty of two strokes. True or False?
Answer: False. Rule 13-4b.
Note: There would have been a penalty of two strokes had the breach of Rule occurred during stroke play, but in match play the penalty is loss of hole.

Q.78
A player starting a round with 11 clubs may add up to three clubs during the round. True or False?
Answer: True. Rule 4-4a.
Note: Players are entitled to carry up to 14 clubs providing they do not unduly delay play in adding clubs during the round and they may not add a club that has been used by any other person playing on the course.

Q.79
If, while taking his normal stance in a bunker, a player digs his feet several inches into the sand he should be penalised for testing the conditions of the hazard. True or False?
Answer: False. Decision 13-4/0.5.
Note: Digging in with the feet for a normal stance in a hazard does not constitute testing the condition of the hazard.

Q.80
A foursome is a match in which two players play their better-ball against the better-ball of two other players. True or False?
Answer: False. Definition of Forms of Match Play.
Note: A foursome is a match in which two players play against two others, and each side plays one ball.

Q.81
When a ball touches the course side of a white line defining out of bounds the player must take a stroke and distance penalty. True or False?
Answer: False. Definition of Out of Bounds.
Note: A ball is not out of bounds when any of it is on, or overhangs the course.

Q.82
A player may not clean his ball by rubbing it on the putting green. True or False?
Answer: False. Decision 16-1d/5.
Note: Though it is to be discouraged, a player may clean his ball by rubbing it on the putting green, providing the act is not for the purpose of testing the surface of the putting green.

Q.83
When a side is required to drop a ball in foursomes either partner may drop the ball. True or False?
Answer: False. Decision 29/4.
Note: The member of the side whose turn it is to play next must drop the ball.

Q.84
If a ball, when not in play, is accidentally knocked off a tee, it may be re-teed without penalty. True or False?
Answer: True. Rule 11-3.
Note: When a ball is not yet in play on the teeing ground, and it moves without the player intending to make a stroke at it, it may be re-teed, without penalty. This applies even if the player moves it 100 yards down the fairway with a practice swing.

Q.85
On every golf course in the world the holes on the putting green must always be the same depth of four inches (101.6 millimetres). True or False?
Answer: False. Definition of Hole.
Note: The hole must be at least four inches (101.6 millimetres) deep.

Q.86
Sand spilling over the margin of a bunker is still part of the bunker. True or False?
Answer: False. Decision 13/1.
Note: A bunker is a prepared area of ground from which turf or soil has been removed and replaced with sand or the like. When sand spills over the prepared area it does not extend the margin of the bunker.

Q.87
In stroke play, a player who takes his stance within the teeing ground but plays his ball from just outside it is penalised two strokes and must play his ball from where it comes to rest. True or False?
Answer: False. Rule 11-4.
Note: The player does incur a penalty of two strokes for playing a ball from outside the teeing ground but his next stroke must be to play a ball from within the teeing ground.

Q.88
In stroke play, a player touches her ball with her putter as she grounds it in front of her ball as part of her pre-putt routine. She incurs a penalty of one stroke even if the ball did not move. True or False?
Answer: False. Rule 18-2.
Note: However, if the ball leaves its position and comes to rest in any other place then the player is penalised one stroke and the ball must be replaced.

Q.89
When identifying his ball in the rough a player does not have to mark his ball, providing he rotates it on its spot without lifting it. True or False?
Answer: False. Rule 12-2.
Note: Before touching his ball to identify it the player must announce his intention to his opponent or fellow competitor and mark the position of the ball. He incurs a penalty of one stroke if he fails to do so.

Q.90
A player is always entitled to see his ball when playing a stroke. True or False?
Answer: False. Rule 12-1.
Note: A player is not necessarily entitled to see his ball when making a stroke.

Q.91
A ball to be dropped under the Rules may be dropped by the player, his partner or his caddie. True or False?
Answer: False. Rule 20-2a.
Note: A ball to be dropped under the Rules may only be dropped by the player himself.

Q.92
An island of grass in the middle of a bunker is not part of the bunker. True or False?
Answer: True. Definition of Bunker.
Note: Grass-covered ground bordering or within a bunker is not part of the bunker.

Q.93
Ground under repair may not be located on the putting green. True or False?
Answer: False. Definition of Ground Under Repair.
Note: Ground under repair may be on any part of the course the Committee orders.

Q.94
The Rules for ground under repair are the same as for abnormal ground condition. True or False?
Answer: True. Definition of Abnormal Ground Conditions and Rule 25-1.
Note: Ground under repair is an abnormal ground condition, together with casual water and holes, casts or runways on the course made by a burrowing animal, a reptile or a bird.

Q.95
A loose impediment on the fairway may be removed by any means. True or False?
Answer: True. Decision 23-1/1.
Note: Loose impediments may be moved by any means, except that, in removing loose impediments on the line of putt, the player must not press anything down. Rule 16-1a.

Q.96
A player is entitled to take free relief from a power pylon that is 20 yards away but directly on his line of play. True or False?
Answer: False. Rule 24-2a.
Note: Intervention on a line of play by an immovable obstruction is not interference within the Rules, other than on the putting green.

Q.97
Nick's ball lies through the green on a piece of paper. He lifts the ball, removes the obstruction and replaces the ball on the ground exactly under the spot where it came to rest on the paper, unaware that Rule 24-1b states that he must drop the ball at that place. When this breach of Rules is explained to him two holes later he does not incur the penalty of two strokes because he was completely unaware that he had committed a breach and he did not receive any real benefit. True or False?
Answer: False. Rule 6-1.
Note: A player is responsible for knowing the Rules.

Q.98
A player's ball crosses the margin of a lateral water hazard and bounces off rocks coming to rest in a ditch within the hazard, 60 yards nearer to the hole. Because it is a lateral water hazard the player has the option, under penalty of one stroke, of picking his ball out of the ditch and dropping it within two club-lengths of the margin, alongside the point where the ball lay in the ditch, not nearer the hole. True or False?
Answer: False. Rule 26-1.
Note: The additional options for relief, under penalty of one stroke, for a ball in a lateral water hazard are to drop a ball within two club-lengths of and not nearer the hole than (i) the point where the original ball last crossed the margin of the lateral water hazard or (ii) a point on the opposite margin of the lateral water hazard equidistant from the hole.

Q.99
An apple core lying within the margin of a water hazard may be removed by a player if he considers that it interferes with his next stroke from that hazard, either physically or mentally. True or False?
Answer: False. Decision 23/3.
Note: An apple is a natural object and therefore a loose impediment, which cannot be moved by a player when his ball lies in the same hazard.

Q.100
If, after taking the honour at the teeing ground, a player thinks that his drive may be out of bounds he should immediately tee-up and play a provisional ball. True or False?
Answer: False. Rule 10-3.
Note: A provisional ball must be played after the other players in the group have made their tee shots.

Q.101
There is a penalty of one stroke if a player's ball in motion strikes himself, his partner, his caddie, his trolley or his club. True or False?
Answer: True. Rule 19-2.
Note: If a player's ball is accidentally deflected or stopped by himself, his partner or either of their caddies or equipment, the player incurs a penalty of one stroke.

Q.102
In stroke play, there is no penalty if a competitor plays out of turn and she must play her next stroke from where her ball lies. True or False?
Answer: True. Rule 10-2c.
Note: However, if the Committee determines that competitors in stroke play have agreed to play out of turn to give one of them an advantage, they are disqualified.

Q.103
On a par 3, both players have already played their tee shots to the green. One player's caddie asks the other caddie what club his player used. There is no penalty. True or False?
Answer: True. Decision 8-1/7.
Note: If the caddie asks the same question before his player has played, his player incurs a loss of hole penalty in match play or a penalty of two strokes in stroke play.

Q.104
Karen's ball comes to rest in an area of stinging nettles. In equity, she may take relief by claiming that it is a dangerous situation. True or False?
Answer: False. Decision 1-4/11.
Note: Within the Rules a dangerous situation is one which is unrelated to conditions normally encountered on the course. Unpleasant lies are a common occurrence which players must accept.

Q.105
If a player accidentally causes their ball to oscillate, without it moving from its original position, there is no penalty. True or False?
Answer: True. Definition of Move.
Note: A ball is only deemed to have moved if it leaves its position and comes to rest in any other place.

Q.106
A player may consider his ball in casual water as being either in an abnormal ground condition or in a water hazard. True or False?
Answer: False. Definition of Abnormal Ground Conditions.
Note: In the Rules casual water is an abnormal ground condition.

Q.107
A tee may be five inches (127 millimetres) long providing at least one inch of it is pressed into the ground. True or False?
Answer: False. Appendix IV – 1.
Note: A tee must not be longer than four inches (101.6 millimetres).

Q.108
In a match, a player is penalised if he treads on his ball and it moves while he is searching for it. True or False?
Answer: True. Rule 18-2.
Note: The player incurs a penalty of one stroke if he moves his ball, except as permitted by a Rule.

Q.109
In a four-ball stroke play event, a player may point out the line of putt to her partner. True or False?
Answer: True. Rule 8-2b.
Note: The partner may, before but not during the putt, point out the line of putt, but in doing so she must not touch the putting green.

Q.110
Loose impediments are natural objects such as stones, leaves, twigs and branches. True or False?
Answer: True. Definition of Loose Impediments.

Q.111
Jorma, a young golfer, is playing in his first competitive tournament. While taking practice swings preparing to putt he moves his ball by mistake. Jorma incurs a penalty of one stroke and must replace the ball to where it was before he accidentally hit it. True or False?
Answer: True. Rule 18-2(ii).
Note: Although Jorma did not intend to strike the ball, and has not therefore made a stroke, he does incur a penalty for causing the ball to move except as permitted by a Rule.

Q.112
A player is penalised for asking for advice which may affect how he plays his next stroke but not for giving advice that may affect another player's next stroke. True or False?
Answer: False. Rule 8-1.
Note: A player must not give advice to anyone in the competition playing on the course other than his partner or ask for advice from anyone other than his partner or either of their caddies. The penalty is loss of hole in match play or two strokes in stroke play.

Q.113
In stroke play, Jenny, in lifting a ball for the purpose of identification, fails to give her fellow competitors an opportunity to observe the lifting. Jenny is penalised one stroke. True or False?
Answer: True. Rule 12-2.
Note: Jenny must announce her intention to lift her ball to her fellow competitors and mark the position of the ball. She may then lift the ball and identify it, providing that she gives her opponents an opportunity to observe the lifting and then the replacement.

Q.114
A player, whose ball is lying through the green, may remove an insect crawling on his ball with his fingers, without penalty. True or False?
Answer: True. Decision 23-1/5.
Note: A live insect is not considered to be adhering to the ball and therefore is a loose impediment. For this reason an insect may not be removed with the fingers if the ball lies in a hazard.

Q.115
A path with a wood chip surface is an obstruction. True or False?
Answer: True. Definition of Obstructions.

Note: The status of anything artificial is an obstruction. Although wood is a natural object, the process it goes through to make it into wood chips transforms it into an obstruction.

Q.116
Foursome or four-ball partners may share clubs, providing they do not have more than 14 clubs between them. True or False?
Answer: True. Rule 4-4b.

Q.117
In stroke play, if a player returns a score higher than was actually taken he will be disqualified. True or False?
Answer: False. Rule 6-6d.
Note: If a player returns a score for any hole higher than was actually taken, the score as returned stands.

Q.118
A player cannot address their ball that lies in a bunker. True or False?
Answer: True. Definition of Addressing the Ball.
Note: A player has addressed the ball when they have grounded their club immediately in front of or immediately behind the ball, whether or not they have taken their stance. As a player is not permitted to ground their club in a bunker they cannot address a ball that is at rest in one.

Q.119
Partners in a four-ball match are allowed to give each other help on what they perceive to be swing faults. True or False?
Answer: True. Rule 8-1a.
Note: During a stipulated round, the only person that a player may give advice to is his partner.

Q.120
A ball is in play as soon as a player makes a stroke at it on the teeing ground, even if he completely misses the ball. True or False?
Answer: True. Definition of Ball in Play.

Q.121
Within the Rules of Golf a hazard is any bunker, water hazard or area marked as ground under repair. True or False?
Answer: False. Definition of Hazards.
Note: A hazard is any bunker or water hazard.

Q.122
A closely-mown area means any area of the course, including paths through the rough, cut to fairway height or less. True or False?
Answer: True. Rule 25-2. Appendix I, Part B, 4c.

Q.123
A lateral water hazard is a water hazard that is situated laterally between two holes on the course. True or False?
Answer: False. Definition of Lateral Water Hazard.
Note: A lateral water hazard is a water hazard or part of a water hazard, that is so situated that it is not possible or is impracticable, to drop a ball behind the water hazard in accordance with Rule 26-1b.

Q.124
A player may not touch the water in a water hazard with his club before playing his stroke. True or False?
Answer: True. Rule 13-4b.
Note: The player must not touch the ground in a hazard or water in a water hazard with his hand or club before making a stroke at a ball that lies within the water hazard.

Q.125
An empty cigarette packet is a movable obstruction. True or False?
Answer: True. Definition of Obstructions.
Note: A cigarette packet is artificial and is therefore an obstruction.

Q.126
A ball lying on an obstruction in a bunker is not considered to lie in the bunker since the margin of the bunker does not extend vertically upwards. True or False?
Answer: False. The ball is in the bunker. Decision 13/5.
Note: The ball may be lifted and the obstruction removed. The ball must be dropped as near as possible to the spot directly under the place where the ball lay in or on the obstruction, but not nearer the hole.

Q.127
A player may remove a pine cone lying next to their ball in a bunker without penalty. True or False?
Answer: False. Rule 13-4c and Definition of Loose Impediments.
Note: If a player's ball lies in a hazard he may touch or remove obstructions (anything artificial) from that hazard, without penalty, but not loose impediments (natural objects).

Q.128
A player is not entitled to relief from interference by a burrowing animal hole when his ball is in a water hazard. True or False?
Answer: True. Rule 25-1b.
Note: There is no relief from an abnormal ground condition when the ball lies in a water hazard.

Q.129
A tee may be designed so as to indicate the line of play. True or False?
Answer: False. Appendix IV – 1.
Note: A tee must not be designed or manufactured in such a way that it could indicate the line of play or influence the movement of the ball.

Q.130
Shane puts everything into his final drive on the 18th hole and as a result overbalances and kicks over one of the tee-markers. After dusting himself down his fellow competitor tells him that he has incurred a penalty for moving a fixed tee-marker. True or False?
Answer: False. Decision 11-2/2.
Note: There is no penalty for accidentally moving the tee-marker, which should be replaced.

Q.131
On the teeing ground a player may build a mound with loose soil to place his ball on, rather than using a tee. True or False?
Answer: True. Rule 11-1.
Note: When teeing his ball the player may create an irregularity of surface with sand or other natural substance.

Q.132
A ball is deemed to be on the putting green only when all of it lies on the putting green. True or False?
Answer: False. Definition of Putting Green.
Note: A ball is on the putting green when any part of it touches the putting green.

Q.133
There is no line of play relief for immovable obstructions located through the green. True or False?
Answer: True. Rule 24-2a.
Note: Intervention on a line of play by an immovable obstruction is not interference within the Rules, other than on the putting green.

Q.134
In stroke play, the penalty for playing a wrong ball is two strokes and the competitor must correct the error. True or False?
Answer: True. Rule 15-3b.
Note: If the player fails to correct his mistake before making a stroke on the next teeing ground or, in the case of the last hole of the round, fails to declare his intention to correct his mistake before leaving the putting green, he is disqualified.

Q.135
A player may take free relief from interference by an out of bounds fence. True or False?
Answer: False. Definition of Obstructions and Out of Bounds.
Note: Objects defining out of bounds, such as walls, fences, stakes and railings are considered fixed and therefore are not obstructions, so there is no relief.

Q.136
A player may move aside a bramble growing next to his ball, without penalty, providing he does not move his ball in doing so. True or False?
Answer: False. Rule 13-2 and Definition of Loose Impediments.
Note: A player must not improve the lie of his ball, the area of his intended stance or swing or his line of play by moving, bending or breaking anything growing or fixed.

Q.137
A cast made by a lizard, crocodile, tortoise or snake is an abnormal ground condition. True or False?
Answer: True. Definition of Abnormal Ground Conditions.
Note: Relief may be taken from a cast or runway made by a burrowing animal, reptile or a bird.

Q.138
In stroke play, a player searches for his ball for more than eight minutes. He incurs a penalty of two strokes. True or False?
Answer: True. Decision 6-7/2.
Note: The player incurs the penalty for undue delay, as he should know that the maximum time permitted by the Rules to search for a lost ball is five minutes. He is still not permitted to play his ball if he finds it after five minutes has passed.

Q.139
A person attending a flagstick must stand to the side of the hole and not immediately behind it. True or False?
Answer: False. Decision 17-1/4.
Note: There is no direction as to where the flagstick attendant has to stand. He might have to stand behind the hole to avoid standing on the line of putt of another player.

Q.140
A player concedes his opponent's next stroke and knocks his ball back to him across the green with his putter. The player only did so to return the opponent's ball to him. No penalty has been incurred. True or False?
Answer: True. Decision 16-1d/1.
Note: Such an action is not considered to be a breach of the Rule, which prohibits testing the surface of a putting green.

Q.141
In playing a ball from the teeing ground a player need not place her ball on a tee. True or False?
Answer: True. Rule 11-1.
Note: The ball may be played from the surface of the teeing ground.

Q.142
When a cart is being moved by one of the players sharing it, the cart and everything in it are deemed to be that player's equipment. True or False?
Answer: True. Definition of Equipment.
Note: Equipment includes a golf cart, whether motorised or not.

Q.143
Tractor ruts at the side of the fairway are an abnormal ground condition, from which free relief may be taken under the Rules. True or False?
Answer: False. There is no relief from tractor ruts unless they are clearly marked as ground under repair or there is a Local Rule permitting relief. Decision 25/16.
Note: However, a player would be justified in requesting the Committee to declare the rut to be ground under repair.

Q.144
Players may take relief without penalty from any young tree that has been staked. True or False?
Answer: False. Rule 33-8.
Note: There is nothing in the Rules of Golf granting relief, without penalty, from staked trees. However, a Committee may establish Local Rules to deal with local abnormal conditions, in this situation to protect newly planted trees from damage. See Appendix I, Part B, 3 for a specimen Local Rule for the Protection of Young Trees.

Q.145
A player accidentally touches his ball with his wedge as he prepares to take his stroke. He incurs a penalty of one stroke. True or False?
Answer: False. Rule 18-2(i).
Note: A player may touch his ball with his club in the act of addressing it, providing the ball does not move off its spot.

Q.146
Hale's putt slows down and stops just short of the hole. In his exasperation he strides up to his ball and casually tries to tap it in, missing the ball completely. The stroke still counts. True or False?
Answer: True. Definition of Stroke.
Note: Hale's intention was to move his ball with the club and therefore it counts as a stroke.

Q.147
A player or her caddie may not bend long grass, rushes, bushes, creepers or brambles when searching for her ball. True or False?

Answer: False. Rule 12-1.
Note: A player may move growing things to the extent necessary to find and identify a ball, providing this does not improve the lie, the area of intended stance or swing or line of play.

Q.148
There is nothing in the Rules to stop a player purposely standing in a position so that his shadow shields his four-ball partner from the sun while he is playing a stroke. True or False?
Answer: False. Decision 14-2/3.
Note: A player must not accept physical assistance or protection from the elements.

Q.149
In match play, if a player plays a ball dropped in a wrong place, the penalty is loss of hole. True or False?
Answer: True. Rule 20-7b.
Note: In match play, if a player makes a stroke from a wrong place, he loses the hole. In stroke play, the penalty is two strokes and the Committee must later determine whether the player has gained a significant advantage as a result of playing from a wrong place and should therefore be disqualified.

Q.150
A ball to be dropped under the Rules may be dropped by the player or someone authorised by the player. True or False?
Answer: False. Rule 20-2a.
Note: A ball to be dropped under the Rules must only be dropped by the player.

Q.151
Before commencing a round a player must put an identification mark on his ball. If he fails to do so, he incurs a penalty. True or False?
Answer: False. Rule 6-5.
Note: The wording of the Rule states that a player should put an identification mark on his ball, not must.

Q.152
A player removes a broken tee touching her ball on the putting green causing the ball to move. There is a penalty of one stroke and the ball must be replaced. True or False?
Answer: False. Rule 24-1a.
Note: If the movement of the ball is directly attributable to the removal of an obstruction there is no penalty.

Q.153
In match play, the side that wins a hole shall always take the honour at the next teeing ground. True or False?
Answer: True. Rule 10-1a.

Q.154
If a player pushes the ball into the hole with the head of his club, it has been fairly struck. True or False?
Answer: False. Rule 14-1a.
Note: In making a stroke the ball must not be pushed, scraped or spooned.

Q.155
In stroke play, a player who is acting as a marker must, between the putting green and the next teeing ground, check the score with the player concerned and record it on the score card. True or False?
Answer: False. Rule 6-6a.

Note: The wording of the Rule says that after each hole the marker <u>should</u> check the score with the competitor and record it, but it does not make it mandatory. However, all players should ensure that they follow this recommendation.

Q.156
A player must determine his nearest point of relief by using the club with which he expects to play his next stroke. True or False?
Answer: False. Definition of Nearest Point of Relief.
Note: The definition states that a player <u>should</u> use the same club with which he expects to make his next shot, it does not say <u>shall</u> use it.

Q.157
The Committee may stipulate that the round for a stroke play competition may start on the 5th hole and finish on the 4th hole. True or False?
Answer: True. Definition of Stipulated Round.
Note: The stipulated round consists of playing the holes of the course in their correct sequence, unless otherwise authorised by the Committee.

Q.158
The line of putt includes a reasonable distance beyond the hole. True or False?
Answer: False. Definition of Line of Putt.
Note: The line of putt includes a reasonable distance on either side of the intended line. The line of putt does not extend beyond the hole.

Q.159
Except when a ball is in motion, a movable obstruction may be removed at any time, without penalty. True or False?
Answer: True. Rule 24-1.
Note: If the ball moves as a result of the obstruction being removed, it must be replaced, and there is no penalty.

Q.160
During a stroke play competition James's golf balls seem magnetically drawn into the water and he runs out of balls. He may borrow one or more balls from another player. True or False?
Answer: True. Decision 5-1/5.
Note: Rule 4-4a prohibits a player from borrowing a club from another player playing on the course, but the Rules do not prevent a player from borrowing other items of equipment (balls, towels, gloves, tees, etc.) from another player or from an outside agency.

Q.161
A ball is in play as soon as it is teed. True or False?
Answer: False. Definition of Ball in Play.
Note: A ball is in play as soon as the player has made a stroke at it on the teeing ground.

Q.162
A provisional ball is one that is played in stroke play when the player is unsure as to whether the Rules permit him to play his original ball. True or False?
Answer: False. Definition of Provisional Ball.
Note: A provisional ball is a ball played under Rule 27-2 for a ball that may be lost outside a water hazard or may be out of bounds.

Q.163
In stroke play, if a competitor plays from the wrong teeing ground he incurs a penalty of two strokes and must then play a ball from within the correct teeing ground. True or False?
Answer: True. Rule 11-5.
Note: The stroke from the wrong teeing ground, and any subsequent strokes made prior to the correction of the mistake, do not count in the player's score.

Q.164
There is nothing in the Rules to stop a player chalking the face of his pitching wedge to achieve more backspin. True or False?
Answer: False. Rule 4-2b.
Note: Foreign material must not be applied to the club face for the purpose of influencing the movement of the ball.

Q.165
In a four-ball stroke play competition a player aligns his partner's putter to the line of putt and then steps a few paces aside before his partner plays. He incurs a penalty of two strokes. True or False?
Answer: False. Decision 14-2/1.
Note: A caddie or partner, may assist in determining a player's line of play prior to the stroke being made, but must move from the extension of the line of play before the stroke is made.

Q.166
A player is always entitled to see at least half of his ball when playing a stroke. True or False?
Answer: False. Rule 12-1.
Note: A player is not necessarily entitled to see his ball when making a stroke.

Q.167
A person who gives occasional advice on how a player should make his stroke is a caddie. True or False?
Answer: True. Definition of Caddie.
Note: A caddie is one who assists a player in accordance with the Rules, which may include carrying or handling the player's clubs during play.

Q.168
When a player strikes his ball twice with a single stroke he has to count the stroke and add a penalty stroke. True or False?
Answer: True. Rule 14-4.
Note: The ball must be played from where it comes to rest.

Q.169
Mike moves aside a creeper growing next to where his ball is at rest without moving his ball in doing so. He incurs a penalty of loss of hole in match play or two strokes in stroke play. True or False?
Answer: True. Rule 13-2.
Note: A player must not improve his lie, area of intended stance or swing or line of play by moving, bending or breaking anything growing or fixed.

Q.170
A ball is lost if a player has played a provisional ball from a point nearer the hole than where the original ball is likely to be. True or False?
Answer: True. Definition of Lost Ball.
Note: This is one of the five situations when a ball is deemed lost.

Q.171
During a stroke play competition a player tells a fellow competitor that he is over-swinging. He incurs a penalty of two strokes. True or False?
Answer: True. Decision 8-1/13.
Note: Advice is any suggestion that could influence a player in determining his play, the choice of club or the method of making a stroke.

Q.172
A, B & C are playing together in a singles stroke play competition. They are partners. True or False?
Answer: False. Definition of partner.
Note: They are fellow competitors. A partner is a player associated with another player on the same side.

Q.173
When a player is replacing his ball on the putting green, it is permissible for him to carefully position the ball so that the trademark is aimed so as to indicate his line of putt. True or False?
Answer: True. Decision 20-3a/2.
Note: A player may also draw a line on his ball in order to assist him to line-up his putts.

Q.174
The Rules of Golf as published by R&A Rules are effective worldwide. True or False?
Answer: True.
Note: The USGA (USA and Mexico) and R&A Rules (over 120 countries in Europe, Africa, Asia-Pacific, and The Americas, except USA and Mexico) meet regularly and agree any changes, so that there is only one set of Rules worldwide.

Q.175
Lateral water hazards must be defined by red stakes. True or False?
Answer: False. Definition of Lateral Water Hazard.
Note: Lateral water hazards may also be defined by red lines.

Q.176
A player may not enter the clubhouse to obtain refreshment between the play of two holes. True or False?
Answer: False. Note to Rule 6-8a.
Note: Leaving the course does not of itself constitute discontinuance of play. However, to avoid incurring a penalty under Rule 6-7 the player must not unduly delay either his own play, that of his opponent or any other competitor.

Q.177
When a player's ball lies in casual water he may choose which side of the abnormal ground condition to take relief on. True or False?
Answer: False. He must always take relief from the nearest point of relief. Definition of Nearest Point of Relief and Decision 25-1b/2.
Note: Very occasionally there may be two, equidistant nearest points of relief.

Q.178
A player may use a golf cart in both match play and stroke play competitions unless the use of golf carts is specifically prohibited in the conditions of competition. True or False?
Answer: True. Decision 33-1/8.
Note: The Committee must establish the conditions under which a competition is to be played.

Q.179
A ball that is stopped or deflected by an opponent or his caddie, may be replayed again without penalty. True or False?
Answer: True. Rule 19-3.
Note: The player who made the stroke may also choose to play his ball as it lies.

Q.180
A ball is out of bounds when any part of it lies out of bounds. True or False?
Answer: False. Definition of Out of Bounds.
Note: A ball is only out of bounds when all of it lies out of bounds.

Q.181
In match play, a player may not play a provisional ball. True or False?
Answer: False. Rule 27-2.
Note: A provisional ball may be played in all golf formats, and should be played for a ball that may be lost outside a water hazard or may be out of bounds, in order to save time.

Q.182
While walking down the fairway of the 16th hole Ludo flicks a range ball back towards the driving range with his 6-iron. He incurs a penalty of two strokes for practising during his round. True or False?
Answer: False. Decision 7-2/5.
Note: The casual flicking of a range ball for the purpose of tidying up the course is not a breach of the Rules.

Q.183
A player may declare his ball unplayable in a water hazard if it is embedded deep in mud. True or False?
Answer: False. Rule 28.
Note: A ball may not be declared unplayable in a water hazard.

Q.184
A player is permitted to carry a mat around with him, to stand on as he is making a stroke, when the underfoot conditions are wet. True or False?
Answer: False. Decision 13-3/1.
Note: The player would be building a stance in breach of Rule 13-3.

Q.185
Enrico takes four strokes on a par 5 hole, where he does not have a handicap stroke. He scores three points in a Stableford competition. True or False?
Answer: True. Rule 32-1b.
Note: The scoring in a Stableford competition is made by points awarded in relation to the par of the hole and the handicap strokes that a player may receive.

Q.186
A player must not move a water hazard stake when his ball is in a water hazard. True or False?
Answer: False. Definition of Water Hazard.
Note: The stakes used to define the margin of a water hazard are obstructions that are movable obstructions if they are easily moved or immovable obstructions if they cannot.

Q.187
Loose impediments are easily removable objects, such as score cards, pens, coins and abandoned balls. True or False?
Answer: False. Definition of Loose Impediments.

Note: These objects are all artificial and are therefore movable obstructions.

Q.188
Erik's ball lies against a fixed direction sign and he elects to take relief from it. Having properly taken relief, Erik's stance is on an artificial pathway. He is permitted to take further relief without penalty. True or False?
Answer: True. Decision 24-2b/9.
Note: A player is entitled to relief whenever there is interference by an immovable obstruction to his stance or area of intended swing.

Q.189
If a sprinkler head located close to the putting green does not interfere with the lie of a player's ball, stance or area of swing, she may still take relief under the Rule on obstructions for mental interference. True or False?
Answer: False. Decision 24-2a/1.
Note: Intervention by an immovable obstruction on the line of play is not interference affording relief. However, relief from sprinkler heads located within two club-lengths of the putting green and within two club-lengths of the ball is often provided for in a Club's Local Rules.

Q.190
If a player's ball is known to be lost in a water hazard he must always play his next stroke from where the ball was last played, under penalty of stroke and distance. True or False?
Answer: False. Rule 26-1.
Note: The player may also, under penalty of one stroke, drop a ball behind the water hazard, keeping the point at which the original ball last crossed the margin of the water hazard directly between the hole and the spot on which the ball is dropped, with no limit to how far behind the water hazard the ball may be dropped.

Q.191
Where the margin of a water hazard is defined by a line on the ground, the line itself is in the water hazard. True or False?
Answer: True. Definition of Water Hazard.
Note: Stakes or lines used to define the margin of a water hazard must be yellow.

Q.192
A player may make a stroke at her ball lying on a putting green other than that of the hole being played. True or False?
Answer: False. Rule 25-3.
Note: If a player's ball lies on a wrong putting green, she must lift it and take relief according to the Rules, without penalty.

Q.193
During a round a player must not give advice on club selection to anyone in the competition except his partner. True or False?
Answer: True. Rule 8-1.
Note: Advice is any counsel or suggestion that could influence a player in determining his play, the choice of a club or the method of making a stroke.

Q.194
In stroke play, if a competitor's ball in motion after a stroke strikes and rebounds off his own equipment, the competitor incurs a penalty of two strokes. True or False?
Answer: False. Rule 19-2.
Note: The player incurs a penalty of one stroke and the ball must be played as it lies.

Q.195
If a player is carrying less than 14 clubs he may borrow a club from one of his playing partners. True or False?
Answer: False. Rule 4-4a.
Note: A player may not borrow any club selected for play by any other person playing on the course, even if he is not carrying 14 clubs.

Q.196
Frank's ball lies out of sight in deep casual water and he kicks it accidentally while he is searching for it. Frank incurs a penalty of one stroke for moving his ball at rest. True or False?
Answer: False. Rule 12-1d.
Note: There is no penalty for moving a ball in an abnormal ground condition during search.

Q.197
A player may clean her ball when taking relief from a runway made by a mole. True or False?
Answer: True. Rule 21.
Note: A ball may be cleaned when lifted, except when it has been lifted to determine whether it is unfit for play, for identification or because it is assisting or interfering with play.

Q.198
A player may not use drying or moisturising agents to assist him in gripping the club. True or False?
Answer: False. Rule 14-3c(ii).
Note: Resin, powder and drying or moisturising agents may be used to assist the player to grip the club.

Open Answer

Q.199
Ravi's ball is on the green, a short distance from the hole. Ravi cannot find his ball-marker so he marks his ball's position with the end of his putter while he lifts it to wipe away some grass that is adhering to it. Does he incur a penalty?
Answer: No. Decision 20-1/16.
Note: The Note to Rule 20-1 states that the ball should be marked by placing a ball-marker, a small coin or other similar object immediately behind the ball. This is a recommendation of best practice, but there is no penalty for failing to comply, providing the ball is physically marked and not with reference to something like a blemish on the putting green.

Q.200
Fred has never had a hole-in-one as he strikes his tee shot on the short par 3. He sees his ball bounce once on the putting green and roll right up to the hole. He runs down to the hole and sees his ball resting against the flagstick, inside the circumference of the hole. "Yesssss" he shouts as he picks up his ball and kisses it. Was it Fred's first hole-in-one?
Answer: Unfortunately, no. Rule 17-4.
Note: Jim should have removed the flagstick carefully, letting his ball fall below the level of the lip of the hole. Since Jim did not hole out he is penalised one stroke under Rule 20-1 for lifting his ball without marking its position. He must then replace the ball against the flagstick and carefully remove it so that the ball drops into the hole. He will then have scored a hole in two!

Q.201
In taking relief from ground under repair, Roly purposely puts spin on his ball when dropping it from shoulder height at arm's length. His fellow competitor, Liam, advises him that he has incurred a penalty. Roly picks up his ball and drops it again within the Rules. Does Roly incur a penalty?
Answer: No. Rule 20-6.
Note: A ball that has not been dropped in accordance with the Rules, but has not been played, may be lifted without penalty, and the player must then proceed correctly.

Q.202
In what way may a player remove loose impediments from their line of putt?
Answer: By any means, providing nothing is pressed down. Rule 16-1a(i).
Note: This is one of the seven exceptions to the Rule that a player must not touch his line of putt.

Q.203
During the play of a hole is it always permissible for a player to repair damage to a putting green, whether or not his ball is on the putting green?
Answer: No. Rule 16-1c.
Note: During play of a hole a player may only repair an old hole plug or damage to the putting green made by the impact of a ball, whether or not their ball lies on the putting green. However, there is nothing to stop players repairing obvious damage to a putting green (e.g. spike marks or flagstick scrapes) as soon as their group has finished putting out.

Q.204
Miles has been searching for his ball in thick undergrowth for three minutes. He informs his fellow competitor, René that he will go back to play a provisional ball while he continues searching. René says that Miles may not play a provisional ball in these circumstances. Who is correct Miles or René?
Answer: René is correct. Rule 27-2.

Note: If a player chooses to play a provisional ball he must play it before he or his partner, goes forward to search for the original ball.

Q.205
In stroke play, what is the penalty if a ball putted from on the green hits another ball, in play and at rest that is also on the green?
Answer: A penalty of two strokes. Rule 19-5a.
Note: In match play, there is no penalty. The ball that was at rest must be replaced.

Q.206
In stroke play, if a competitor marks his ball with a tee that he used on the teeing ground, what is the penalty?
Answer: There is no penalty. Note to Rule 20-1.
Note: However, this Rule advises that players should use a small coin or other similar object.

Q.207
As Gerhardt is shaping up to drive his ball from the 14th teeing ground, by mistake he knocks his ball off the tee with the head of his club. Is he penalised and may he re-tee his ball before playing again?
Answer: There is no penalty and Gerhardt may re-tee his ball. Rule 11-3.
Note: The ball on the tee is not in play, so if it falls off the tee or is knocked off by the player in addressing it, it may be re-teed, without penalty.

Q.208
Trixie's drive lands in an area of large puddles and deep rough, which are not visible from the tee. If Trixie cannot find her ball may she assume that it is lost in the casual water?
Answer: No. Decision 25-1c/1.
Note: It has to be known or virtually certain that the ball is in casual water before relief from the abnormal ground condition may be taken.

Q.209
In stroke play, Rose places her golf bag close to her line of putt so as to shield her ball from the wind while she putts. Does she incur a penalty?
Answer: Yes. Rose incurs a penalty of two strokes. Decision 1-2/2.
Note: A player must not take any action with the intent to influence the movement of their ball.

Q.210
Is there any restriction on the clubhead size of a driver?
Answer: Yes. Rule 4-1.
Note: Players' clubs must conform to the provisions, specifications and interpretations set forth in Appendix II. The volume of the clubhead must not exceed 460 cubic centimetres (28.06 cubic inches), plus a tolerance of 10 cubic centimetres, otherwise it is a non-conforming club, the use of which would automatically disqualify the player that used it.

Q.211
In match play, Maggie's ball is on the putting green about 20 yards from the flagstick. Karla's ball is in a greenside bunker about 12 yards from the flagstick. Who must play first?
Answer: Maggie must play first. Rule 10-1b.
Note: The ball farther from the hole is played first.

Q.212
Mags and her fellow competitors see her ball land in an area of deep casual water through the green and they cannot find it. What is the correct procedure?
Answer: There is no penalty and Mags must drop a ball, under the Rules, within one club-

length of, and not nearer the hole, than the nearest point of relief to where the ball last crossed the outermost limits of the casual water. Rule 25-1c.

Q.213
What is the maximum number of clubs that a player may start a round with?
Answer: 14. Rule 4-4a.
Note: If a player starts with less than 14 clubs he may add any number, providing his total number does not exceed 14. A player may not borrow any club used by any other person playing on the course, even if he is not carrying 14 clubs.

Q.214
Bennie has a habit of tapping down the ground in front of his ball as part of his routine in setting himself up for a stroke. Should he be penalised?
Answer: Probably! It is a very bad habit and sooner or later he will be adjudged to have improved his line of play. Rule 13-2.
Note: A player must not improve his line of play by pressing a club on the ground.

Q.215
If a player's ball lies in a bunker is there anything that she is permitted to remove from a bunker before making her stroke?
Answer: Yes. A player may remove anything artificial (obstructions) but is not permitted to remove anything natural (loose impediments). Rule 13-4c.
Note: For safety reasons many Clubs have a Local Rule that stones may be removed from bunkers before playing a stroke.

Q.216
If a player's ball and one foot of his stance are inside the margin of a water hazard may the player's club be grounded outside the hazard?
Answer: Yes. Decision 13-4/29.
Note: The player may not touch the ground within the hazard with his hand or a club.

Q.217
In stroke play, Evan improves the area in which he is to drop a ball by clearing leaves, twigs, a paper cup and acorns. What is the penalty?
Answer: There is no penalty. Rules 23-1 & 24-1a.
Note: A player may always remove loose impediments, except when both the loose impediment and the ball lie in or touch the same hazard, and may always remove movable obstructions (e.g. a paper cup). However, sand and loose soil may not be removed other than on the putting green.

Q.218
During a match Nigel taps down scuff marks in the vicinity of the hole but not directly on his line of putt. What is the penalty?
Answer: Nigel loses the hole. Decision 16-1c/4.
Note: The repair of damage to the green in the vicinity of the hole, which was not made by the impact of a ball, might assist the player in his subsequent play of the hole. For example, if he putts wide of or past the hole.

Q.219
Ben is searching for his ball when he sees something white nestled in the very long, thick grass. In checking to see if it is his ball (which it is) he bends the grass aside and as he does so, the ball drops several inches from its resting position. What is the ruling?
Answer: Ben incurs a penalty of one stroke for causing his ball to move and he must replace it to where it was before he moved it. Rule 18-2.
Note: The same penalty applies for both match play and stroke play competitions.

Q.220
Is it within the Rules for a Committee to install markers on a hole to indicate distances to the green, thereby assisting players in their play of the hole?
Answer: Yes. Definition of Advice.
Note: Information on distance is not advice.

Q.221
When a player deems her ball unplayable what are her three options, under penalty of one stroke?
Answer: i) Proceed under the stroke and distance provision of Rule 27-1 by playing a ball as nearly as possible at the spot from which the original ball was last played (see Rule 20-5), ii) Drop a ball behind the point where the ball lies, keeping that point directly between the hole and the spot on which the ball is dropped, with no limit to how far behind that point the ball may be dropped. iii) Drop a ball within two club-lengths of the spot where the ball lies, but not nearer the hole. Rule 28.

Q.222
Rob shanks a fairway iron and his ball hits his opponent, Rory, on the knee. Fortunately, Rory soon recovers and is ready to continue the match. What are Rob's options?
Answer: There is no penalty and Rob may play his ball as it lies or he may elect to play a ball as nearly as possible at the spot from which his original ball was last played. Rule 19-3.

Q.223
In match play, Mary plays when Margaret's ball was farther away from the hole. What is her penalty?
Answer: Mary has not incurred any penalty. Rule 10-1c.
Note: Margaret may let Mary's stroke stand or she may immediately require Mary to cancel her stroke and, in correct order, play a ball as nearly as possible at the spot from which her original ball was last played.

Q.224
In match play, a player removes a bottle lying alongside his ball in a water hazard before playing from the hazard. What is the penalty?
Answer: There is no penalty. Rule 24-1.
Note: A player may move anything artificial in a hazard or anywhere else on the course, providing that their ball is at rest.

Q.225
Dave's ball is lying beside a cactus and he cannot take a proper stance or backswing. Do the Rules permit him to play his ball with the back of his clubhead?
Answer: Yes. Rule 14-1a.
Note: The Rule states that the ball must be struck at with the head of the club, it does not specify that it has to be the club face.

Q.226
Is a tree that has blown down in a storm a loose impediment?
Answer: No, if part of the tree is still attached to the stump, but yes, if no part of the fallen tree is attached to the stump. Decision 23/7.
Note: Natural objects are loose impediments, whatever their size, providing they are not fixed or growing, solidly embedded or adhering to the ball.

Q.227
In match play, a player plays a stroke in a hazard at a wrong ball. What is the penalty?
Answer: There is a penalty of loss of hole. Rule 15-3a.
Note: If a competitor makes a stroke at a wrong ball anywhere on the course, except a

wrong ball moving in water, they incur a penalty of loss of hole in match play or two strokes in stroke play.

Q.228
Does the location of each player's ball on the course, i.e. the apron, the rough, a hazard or the putting green, have any bearing on determining the order of play?
Answer: No. The order of play is determined solely by the distance from the hole of each ball. Rules 10-1 and 10-2.

Q.229
In stroke play, a player removes an acorn lying next to his ball in a bunker. What is the penalty?
Answer: There is a penalty of two strokes. Rule 13-4c and Definition of Loose Impediments.
Note: When a ball lies in a hazard a player may not remove any loose impediment (natural object) from the same hazard, without incurring a penalty.

Q.230
In a match, Ming's tee shot comes to rest 180 yards from the hole and the tee shot of her opponent, Kim, finishes 30 yards nearer the hole. Ming's approach shot heads towards the course boundary at the side of the green and she is not sure whether it has come to rest out of bounds. She announces her intention to play a provisional ball. What is the order of play for the provisional ball?
Answer: Ming must play her provisional ball before Kim makes her next stroke. Rule 10-1b.
Note: Ming must play from where her original ball was last played, which is farther away from the hole than Kim's ball. Therefore, Ming must play her provisional ball before Kim plays.

Q.231
In match play, a player whose ball lies in a bunker removes a cigarette packet lying in that bunker. What is the penalty?
Answer: There is no penalty. Rule 24-1.
Note: A player may remove, without penalty, any artificial object that can be moved.

Q.232
In stroke play, after completing play of the 7th hole Aisling drops a ball into a bunker and plays it out towards the next tee. Does she incur a penalty?
Answer: Yes. Aisling incurs a penalty of two strokes. Rule 7-2.
Note: Between holes a player may only practice putting or chipping between the hole of the last green played and the next tee.

Q.233
Audrey's ball comes to rest on a decorative, grass covered island in the centre of a greenside bunker. Is she permitted to ground her club in playing her next stroke?
Answer: Yes. Definition of Bunker.
Note: Grass covered ground bordering or within the bunker is not part of the bunker.

Q.234
In stroke play, a competitor uses a device to warm his golf ball during the round. What is the penalty?
Answer: Disqualification. Rule 14-3/13.5.
Note: However, an artificial device to warm the hands has traditionally been accepted, providing that it is not used to warm the ball during play.

Q.235
In stroke play, after finishing the 13th hole, Peter and Paul play from the teeing ground of the 17th hole instead of the 14th hole. They realise their error before completing the 17th hole,

return to the 14th tee and complete their round. What is the ruling?
Answer: Peter and Paul each incur a penalty of two strokes. Rule 11-5/4.
Note: Any strokes played at the 17th hole, when it was played out of order, do not count.

Q.236
If a dropped ball rolls to one of the seven places that require it to be re-dropped, how many more times may it be re-dropped within the Rules before the Rules require it to be placed?
Answer: One more time (twice in all). Rule 20-2c.
Note: If the first drop rolls into any of the places listed in this Rule, it must be re-dropped. If the second drop rolls into any of the places listed in this Rule it must then be placed as near as possible to the spot where it first struck a part of the course when re-dropped.

Q.237
In match play, what options does a player have when his opponent plays out of turn?
Answer: He may let the stroke stand (presumably, if his opponent's stroke was a poor one!) or he may require the opponent to cancel the stroke and, in correct order this time, play a ball as nearly as possible from the spot at which the stroke was played (if it was a good one!). Rule 10-1c.

Q.238
In match play, Paulo takes relief from a white, concrete post with letters OOB painted on it, saying that it is an immovable obstruction. He then plays his ball. Does Paulo incur any penalty?
Answer: Paulo loses the hole. Definition of Obstructions and Rule 18-2.
Note: The letters OOB denote that the white post is an out of bounds boundary. There is no relief from objects defining out of bounds, which are not obstructions and are deemed to be fixed.

Q.239
In stroke play, Jon reminds a fellow competitor that he is not permitted to touch the leaves lying across his ball in a bunker or he will incur a penalty. What is Jon's penalty?
Answer: Jon incurs no penalty. Definition of Advice.
Note: Information on the Rules is not advice.

Q.240
In match play, a player whose ball lies in a bunker moves a loose impediment lying in that bunker. What is the penalty?
Answer: Loss of hole. Rule 23-1.
Note: Any loose impediment may be removed without penalty, except when both the loose impediment and the ball lie in or touch the same hazard.

Q.241
On a Sunday afternoon, a group of competitors in a strokes competition go into their clubhouse after nine holes to watch an exciting final round of a golf tournament on television. An hour later the group resumes play. Do these players incur any penalty?
Answer: Yes. They should be disqualified. Decision 6-8a/1.
Note: Watching television is not a satisfactory reason for the Committee to waive the disqualification penalty for discontinuing play without permission.

Q.242
Juan and José are fellow competitors. José hits his second stroke and his ball hits Juan's ball, which was at rest on the fairway, knocking it forward several yards. José's own ball stops 50 yards short of where it would otherwise come to rest. Where do Juan and José play their next shots from?

Answer: Juan must replace his ball where it was before it was moved and José must play his ball from where it lies. Rule 18-5.
Note: A player is entitled to the lie that he had when his ball came to rest.

Q.243
In stroke play, who has the honour of playing first on the 1st tee if there is no draw?
Answer: In the absence of a draw, the honour should be decided by lot (e.g. tossing coins). Rule 10-2a.
Note: The convention that the lowest handicapper has the honour on the 1st tee is wrong and should be discouraged. It has flourished because there is no penalty for playing out of turn in stroke play.

Q.244
In stroke play, George was unable to find his ball after a big tee shot. He drops another ball in the area where his original ball was lost and plays that ball. What is the ruling?
Answer: George incurs a stroke and distance penalty and an additional penalty of two strokes for playing a ball from the wrong place. If he does not rectify the error before making a stroke at the next teeing ground he is disqualified. Decision 27-1/3.
Note: When a ball is lost the only options are to play the provisional ball, if one was played or return to the place where the original ball was last played from, under penalty of stroke and distance.

Q.245
Do the stakes or lines used to define the margins of water hazards and lateral water hazards have to be of a certain colour, and if so, what colours?
Answer: Yes, yellow for water hazards and red for lateral water hazards. Definition of Water Hazard and Lateral Water Hazard.

Q.246
In stroke play, Sid putts and his ball circles around the hole coming to rest an inch away. In his frustration Sid leans forward to tap the ball in with the toe of his putter. However, he is off balance and he misses the ball completely. Is there a penalty?
Answer: There is no penalty but the fresh air does count as a stroke. Definition of Stroke.
Note: A stroke is the forward movement of the club made with the intention of striking at and moving the ball.

Q.247
Mike's tee shot hits a tree. As he plays his second stroke he thinks that his ball does not sound right leaving his 3-iron. When he reaches his ball how should Mike proceed to ascertain whether it is damaged to the point where he may replace it?
Answer: Mike must announce his intention to his opponent or fellow competitor, mark the position of the ball and lift it without cleaning it. Rule 5-3.
Note: If it is agreed that his ball is damaged he may substitute another ball, placing it on the spot where the original ball was marked.

Q.248
Derek's Club has a Local Rule which says that players must take relief from staked trees. In a stroke play competition he thought that he had taken full relief from a staked tree but on the follow-through of his stroke his club hit some overhanging leaves. Did Derek incur a penalty?
Answer: Yes. Derek incurred a penalty of two strokes. Rule 33-8 and Decision 20-2c/6.
Note: The Committee may establish Local Rules for local abnormal conditions if they are consistent with the policy set forth in Appendix I. In this case the Local Rule said that players must take relief from staked trees. The fact that Derek subsequently hit part of the tree meant that he incurred a penalty for not fully complying with the Local Rule.

Q.249
In match play, Mario putts his ball and it strikes the flagstick, which his opponent has left lying on the putting green next to the hole. What is the penalty, if any?
Answer: Mario loses the hole. Rule 17-3.
Note: The player's ball must not strike the flagstick when it is attended, removed or held up.

Q.250
Marie starts a round with 14 clubs and loses her pitching wedge on the front nine. Is she permitted to add another club to her bag when she starts the 10th hole?
Answer: No. Decision 4-3/10.
Note: A player who is already carrying 14 clubs may not replace a lost club, only one which has become unfit for play in the normal course of play.

Q.251
Barbara hits her tee shot out of bounds. She begins to re-tee another ball when Carol, a fellow competitor, protests, saying that Barbara may not tee her ball when playing her third stroke from the tee. Who is correct?
Answer: Barbara is correct. Rule 20-5a.
Note: When a player is required to make her next stroke from where a previous stroke was made on a teeing ground the ball may be teed.

Q.252
During a stroke play event, Maryanne asks Betty where the flagstick is located on the putting green that they are playing into. Hilary, the third member of the three-ball, believes that Maryanne has broken the Rules by asking for advice. Has she?
Answer: No. Maryanne was asking for information, not advice. Definition of Advice.
Note: Information on the Rules, distance or matters of public information, such as the position of hazards or the flagstick on the putting green, is not advice.

Q.253
On the putting green a player holds his ball still with one finger and cleans grass from it with his other hand. He does not lift the ball, mark its position or change its position. What is the penalty?
Answer: He incurs a penalty of one stroke. Rule 18-2.
Note: If the player had marked the position of the ball on the putting green before touching it, there would have been no penalty.

Q.254
Describe the four-ball format for stroke play.
Answer: In a four-ball competition two competitors play as partners, each playing their own ball. The lower score of the partners is their score for the hole. Definition of Forms of Stroke Play.
Note: Only one partner has to complete a hole to record a score.

Q.255
In a singles stroke play competition, Kim's ball is at rest on the putting green on Chrissie's line of putt. As Kim has not yet reached the putting green Chrissie marks and lifts Kim's ball and then putts. Who is permitted to replace Kim's ball at the marker?
Answer: Either Kim or Chrissie must replace Kim's ball at the marker. Rule 20-3a.
Note: A ball to be replaced under the Rules must be placed at the marker by the player, her partner or the person who lifted it.

Q.256
Phyllis's third stroke to the putting green flies into a wooded area, and may be out of bounds. She says, "That might be lost. I am going to re-load", drops another ball according to the

Rules, and hits it onto the green. As she starts to walk to where she thinks her original ball might be, Stephanie, her fellow competitor, says that she has to play the ball on the green as the original ball is out of play. What is the ruling?
Answer: Stephanie is correct. Decision 27-2a/1.
Note: Phyllis did not specifically announce that she was going to play a provisional ball and therefore her second ball was in play as soon as she hit it and she was putting for a six.

Q.257
May a player remove a golf club, which has been left behind by a previous player, from a water hazard before playing his ball from within the same hazard?
Answer: Yes. Rule 24-1a.
Note: A golf club is artificial and is therefore a movable obstruction.

Q.258
Must a player take relief from an area marked as GUR?
Answer: No, the player may take relief. Rule 25-1b.
Note: GUR or ground under repair, is an abnormal ground condition defined by the Committee. The Rule states that a player may (not must) take relief from interference by an abnormal ground condition. However, Clubs' Local Rules often make it mandatory that the player must take relief from GUR.

Q.259
Toby's ball lies on the apron of the putting green. Gordon plays from the bunker behind and several lumps of wet sand land on and around Toby's ball. Is Toby permitted to remove this sand before making his next stroke?
Answer: Yes. Decision 13-2/8.5.
Note: Toby is entitled to the lie and line of play he had when his ball came to rest. Accordingly, in equity (Rule 1-4), he is entitled to remove the sand deposited by Gordon's stroke and lift his ball and clean it, without penalty.

Q.260
In stroke play, Randal misses a short putt and then holes the ball with the handle end of his club. What is the penalty?
Answer: Randal incurs a penalty of two strokes. Decision 14-1/3.
Note: The ball must be fairly struck at with the head of the club and must not be pushed, scraped or spooned. However the stroke with the club handle does count and Randal has completed play of the hole.

Q.261
A player's ball lies under a course maintenance trailer. What is the procedure?
Answer: If the trailer is easily movable, it should be treated as a movable obstruction and moved. Decision 24/8.
Note: If the trailer is not easily movable, it should be treated as an immovable obstruction and the player is entitled to relief.

Q.262
In foursome match play Claire and Ava are playing partners, Claire is teeing off at the odd numbered holes and Ava is teeing off at the evens. On the 16th, after an eventful 15th hole, Claire drives from the teeing ground by mistake. What is the penalty?
Answer: Claire and Ava lose the hole. Rule 29-2.
Note: In foursomes if a player plays when her partner should have played, her side loses the hole.

Q.263

Maurice plays a provisional ball from the tee into the same area as his original ball. The provisional ball is indistinguishable from his original ball. One ball is found in bounds and the other ball is lost or is found out of bounds. How does he proceed?
Answer: Maurice must presume that the ball found in bounds is his provisional ball. Decision 27/11.
Note: Maurice will be playing his fourth stroke from where he found the ball.

Q.264
In stroke play, what is the penalty if a player plays out of turn?
Answer: There is no penalty and the ball is played as it lies. Rule 10-2c.
Note: However, if the Committee determines that competitors have agreed to play out of turn to give one of them an advantage, they are disqualified.

Q.265
A player moves branches and leaves of a tree so that he may see his ball when playing his stroke. What is the penalty?
Answer: There is a penalty of two strokes for improving his intended area of swing or stance. Rule 12-1 and Rule 13-2.
Note: A player is not necessarily entitled to see his ball when making a stroke. However, he may touch or bend long grass to the extent necessary to find and identify the ball.

Q.266
May a player repair damage to a putting green caused by the impact of a ball when his ball lies off the putting surface?
Answer: Yes. Rule 16-1c.
Note: The only damage that may be repaired on a putting green is to an old hole plug or that made by the impact of a ball. It does not matter whether the player's ball lies on or off the putting green.

Q.267
In the Rules is ground under repair an abnormal ground condition?
Answer: Yes. Definition of Abnormal Ground Conditions.

Q.268
What constitutes addressing a ball outside of a hazard?
Answer: Outside of a hazard a player has addressed his ball when he has grounded his club immediately in front of or immediately behind the ball, whether or not he has taken his stance. Definition of Addressing the Ball.
Note: A player cannot address their ball in a hazard, as they are not permitted to ground their club when playing from it.

Q.269
In match play, a player uses a small telescope in order to see where the flagstick is positioned. What is the penalty?
Answer: There is no penalty. Decision 14-3/3.
Note: Neither standard spectacles nor field glasses which have no range-finder attachments are artificial devices within the meaning of the term in Rule 14-3.

Q.270
Roddie is taking relief from a staked tree under a Local Rule. He measures out his club-length from the nearest point of relief drops the ball over his shoulder and addresses his ball when his caddie says that he will be penalised if he makes the stroke. Is Roddie's caddie correct?
Answer: Yes. The caddie is correct. Rule 20-2c.

Note: Roddie must stand erect, hold the ball at shoulder height and arm's length and drop it without spin.

Q.271
May a player declare his ball lost?
Answer: No. Definition of Lost Ball.
Note: A ball is only deemed lost if it is not found or properly identified within five minutes of the search for it commencing or if another ball has been put in play within the Rules. Anything that the player says concerning his ball is not relevant.

Q.272
Monty plays a provisional ball from the teeing ground. He discovers his original ball out of bounds and cannot find the provisional ball. How does Monty proceed?
Answer: Monty must return to the tee where he will be playing his fifth stroke. Decision 27-2c/4.
Note: The provisional ball, Monty's third stroke off the tee, may not be disregarded.

Q.273
In a match, in the act of grounding her putter on the 18th putting green Heather accidentally moves her ball a fraction to the side. Is there a penalty?
Answer: Heather incurs a penalty of one stroke. Rule 18-2.
Note: There is no stroke unless the player intends to move her ball (Definition of Stroke) so Heather incurs a penalty stroke for moving her ball in play and it must be replaced.

Q.274
Donny's ball lies in a water hazard but not in water. Is he permitted to touch growing grass in the water hazard with his club in the process of preparing for his stroke?
Answer: Yes. Note to Rule 13-4.
Note: At any time, including at address or in the backward movement for the stroke, the player may touch, with a club or otherwise any grass, bush, tree or other growing thing.

Q.275
Pedro is not sure whether his handicap has been reduced following a good score in the previous week's competition. He starts his round intending to add his handicap to his score card at the end. However, he forgets and returns his signed score card with no handicap (which had not changed). What is the penalty?
Answer: Pedro is disqualified. Rule 6-2b.
Note: If no handicap is recorded on the score card before it is returned the player is disqualified.

Q.276
Is a player entitled to free relief from a hole made at the base of a tree by a dog?
Answer: No. Definition of Abnormal Ground Conditions and Rule 25-1a.
Note: A dog is not a burrowing animal.

Q.277
In stroke play, a competitor whose ball lies off the green has the flagstick attended. What is the penalty?
Answer: There is no penalty. Rule 17-1.
Note: Before making a stroke from anywhere on the course, the player may have the flagstick attended, removed or held up to indicate the position of the hole.

Q.278
Norm arrives at a green and discovers that he has left his new pitching wedge at a previous hole. He insists on returning back along the course to search for it, causing a delay in play.

Is Norm subject to a penalty?
Answer: Yes. Norm incurs a penalty of loss of hole in match play or two strokes in stroke play. Decision 6-7/1.
Note: Between completion of a hole and playing from the next teeing ground, the player must not unduly delay play.

Q.279
Raymond strikes a good 4-iron to the putting green but his ball hits a low-flying duck and drops straight to the ground, 100 yards short. What is the ruling?
Answer: It is a rub of the green, there is no penalty and the ball must be played as it lies. Rule 19-1.
Note: ... and the NSPCA or ASPCA should be notified!

Q.280
In match play, may a player withdraw a concession of a stroke or hole, providing he does so before his opponent lifts his ball?
Answer: No. Rule 2-4.
Note: A concession may not be declined or withdrawn.

Q.281
In match play, Angela's ball is in an area marked as ground under repair (GUR). The Rules state that a player may take relief from GUR but Angela's ball is sitting up and she decides to play it as it lies. After she has made her stroke her opponent, Margot, takes out her score card, sees that there is a Local Rule prohibiting play from GUR, and claims the hole. What is the ruling?
Answer: Margot is correct and wins the hole. Rule 33-8.
Note: The Committee may establish Local Rules for local abnormal conditions if they are consistent with the policy set forth in Appendix I. There is a specimen Local Rule in Appendix I, 2a, prohibiting play from GUR.

Q.282
In stroke play, a competitor touches his line of putt in repairing a ball mark on the putting green. What is the penalty?
Answer: There is no penalty. Rule 16-1a(vi).
Note: This is one of seven exceptions to the Rule that the line of putt must not be touched.

Q.283
Dominic and Shane are playing a match on a handicap basis. Shane has the honour at the 2nd tee. Both players score five at the 2nd hole but Dominic receives a handicap stroke and therefore has a net four. Does Dominic take the honour at the 3rd hole?
Answer: Yes. Rules 2-1 and 10-1a.
Note: Dominic won the 2nd hole with the lower net score and therefore takes the honour at the next teeing ground.

Q.284
In stroke play, Tom holds his ball at shoulder height and arm's length and purposely puts a spin on it when dropping it under the Rules. What is the ruling?
Answer: Unless he re-drops the ball correctly before playing his next stroke Tom incurs a penalty of one stroke. Decision 20-2a/2.
Note: Tom dropped his ball in an improper manner by putting spin on it.

Q.285
What is the name given to a player in a stroke play competition?
Answer: A competitor. Definition of Competitor.
Note: A fellow competitor is any person with whom the competitor plays.

Q.286
Linda and Sandy are playing in a stroke play competition. While they are waiting for the green to clear, Linda lifts Sandy's ball off the fairway to inspect it. Has a penalty been incurred?
Answer: No. Rule 18-4.
Note: There is no penalty for a fellow competitor moving another competitor's ball. Sandy should replace her ball where it lay before Linda picked it up.

Multiple Choice

Q.287
Which is not a loose impediment on the apron of a green?
A) A plug of earth removed during hollow-tining.
B) An unattached divot.
C) Loose soil.
D) A worm.
Answer: C) Loose soil. Definition of Loose Impediments.
Note: Sand and loose soil are loose impediments on the putting green, but not elsewhere.

Q.288
In stroke play, Cherie picks up her ball that is overhanging the hole without holing out but adds one to her score. After she returns her score card, a spectator brings this to the attention of the Committee. What is the ruling?
A) The Committee should admonish Cherie but waive the penalty of disqualification.
B) The Committee should modify the disqualification penalty to a penalty of one stroke.
C) The Committee should modify the disqualification to a penalty of two strokes.
D) The Committee should not waive the penalty of disqualification.
Answer: D) The Committee should not waive the penalty of disqualification. Decision 33-7/2.
Note: In stroke play, the player must hole out or they have not played the course.

Q.289
In a match, Avril uses a long, plastic tee to mark her ball on the putting green. Nicola, her opponent, putts from several feet away and her ball hits Avril's tee and is diverted away from the hole. What is the ruling?
A) There is no penalty and Nicola may take her putt again.
B) Nicola incurs a penalty of one stroke and must play her ball from where it comes to rest.
C) There is no penalty and Nicola must play her ball from where it comes to rest.
D) Avril incurs a one stroke penalty and Nicola may take her putt again.
Answer: C) There is no penalty and Nicola must play her ball from where it comes to rest. Decision 20-1/17.
Note: Nicola should have requested Avril to move her tee one or more clubhead-lengths to the side or to re-mark the position of her ball with a ball-marker, a small coin or other similar object.

Q.290
In stroke play, Scottie suggests to his fellow competitor Paddy, whose ball lies in a very difficult spot in a gorse bush, that he declare his ball unplayable. What is the ruling?
A) There is no penalty.
B) There is no penalty, providing that Paddy does not take the advice and proceeds under a different option.
C) Scottie incurs a penalty of one stroke.
D) Scottie incurs a penalty of two strokes.
Answer: D) Scottie incurs a penalty of two strokes. Decision 8-1/16.
Note: As Scottie's suggestion could have influenced Paddy in determining his play it constituted advice (Definition of Advice). Had Scottie merely told Paddy what his options were for a ball unplayable then no penalty would have been incurred.

Q.291
Where on the course is a caddie or a player's partner, permitted to stand immediately behind the player's line of play during their stroke?
A) On the tee.
B) Through the green.

C) On the putting green.
D) Nowhere on the course.
Answer: D) Nowhere on the course. Rule 14-2b.
Note: A player must not make any stroke with his caddie, his partner or his partner's caddie positioned on or close to an extension of the line of play or line of putt behind the ball.

Q.292
In stroke play, Mary moves her ball, which lies in a bunker, when she removes a large leaf lying next to it. What is the ruling?
A) Mary incurs a penalty of one stroke and the ball must be replaced.
B) Mary incurs a penalty of two strokes and the ball must be replaced.
C) Mary incurs total penalties of three strokes and the ball must be replaced.
D) Mary incurs total penalties of four strokes and the ball must be replaced.
Answer: B) Mary incurs a penalty of two strokes and the ball must be replaced. Decision 13-4/15.
Note: As a single act by Mary resulted in two Rules being breached (moving her ball and removing a loose impediment from a bunker), in equity (Rule 1-4), only one penalty, the more severe penalty of two strokes, is applied (Decision 1-4/15).

Q.293
Ronnie's young son has been playing with his clubs and after he has commenced his round he realises that he has only three woods and nine irons in his bag. How many clubs is he permitted to add during the round?
A) One club.
B) Two clubs.
C) Three clubs.
D) No clubs may be added after the start of a round.
Answer: B) Two clubs. Rule 4-4a.
Note: A player may add clubs to a maximum of 14 providing he does not unduly delay play and the clubs have not been used by any other player on the course.

Q.294
In singles match play, may Charles putt out after Maurice has conceded his next putt?
A) No, if Charles putts he incurs a one stroke penalty.
B) No, if Charles putts he loses the hole.
C) Yes.
D) Yes, but if he misses, the concession is considered to have been refused and he will have to putt out.
Answer: C) Yes. Decision 2-4/6.
Note: A concession may not be withdrawn. However, if the act would be of assistance to a partner in a four-ball or best-ball match, the partner is, in equity (Rule 1-4), disqualified for the hole.

Q.295
Martin and William are playing a match and after 15 holes Martin is three up. Which statement is correct?
A) Martin and William are dormie.
B) William is dormie.
C) Martin is dormie.
D) Neither Martin nor William is dormie.
Answer: C) Martin is dormie. Rule 2-1.
Note: A side is dormie when it is as many holes up as there are holes remaining to be played.

Q.296
In which two of the following is a ball unfit for play?
A) It is out of shape.
B) Its markings have been scratched and scraped to the point that they are illegible.
C) It is covered in mud.
D) It is cut.
Answer: A) and D). Rule 5-3.
Note: A ball is unfit for play if it is visibly cut, cracked or out of shape. A ball is not unfit for play solely because mud or other materials adhere to it, its surface is scratched or scraped or its paint is damaged or discoloured.

Q.297
When may a player add a strip of lead tape to a driver?
A) Before a round.
B) During a round.
C) At any time.
D) Never.
Answer: A) Before a round. Decision 4-2/0.5.
Note: The playing characteristics of a club must not be purposely changed by adjustment or by any other means during a round.

Q.298
Vanessa's ball lies against a course boundary wall. She lifts her ball to take relief from the wall, which she says is an immovable obstruction. Her fellow competitor, Emer, says that she has incurred a penalty of one stroke for lifting her ball in play. What is the ruling?
A) Vanessa may drop her ball, without penalty within one club-length of the nearest point of relief.
B) There is no penalty if Vanessa replaces her ball against the boundary wall.
C) Vanessa incurs a penalty of one stroke for touching her ball in play and must replace it.
D) Vanessa incurs a penalty of two strokes for lifting her ball in play and must replace it.
Answer: C) Vanessa incurs a penalty of one stroke for touching her ball in play and must replace it. Decision 18-2a/3 and Definition of Obstructions.
Note: Objects defining out of bounds such as walls, fences, stakes and railings, are not obstructions and are deemed to be fixed. Vanessa must replace her ball before playing her next stroke or she will incur a total penalty of two strokes.

Q.299
Which of the following statements is correct under the Rules?
A) A player may not take free relief from wooden steps leading into a bunker.
B) A player may not take free relief from a metal fence erected at the side of a tee box.
C) A player may not take free relief from a tree stump.
D) A player may not take free relief from a direction sign to the next tee box.
Answer: C) A player may not take free relief from a tree stump. Decision 25/8.
Note: A tree stump still in the ground is a natural object and there is no relief without penalty from it, unless it has been marked as ground under repair. The other artificial objects are immovable obstructions from which relief without penalty is available.

Q.300
In which of the following circumstances does a player incur a penalty for moving her ball?
A) In measuring which ball is farther away from the hole.
B) In marking her ball on the putting green.
C) In removing a leaf lying close to her ball on a putting green.
D) In searching for her ball in deep rough.
Answer: D) In searching for her ball in deep rough. Rule 18-2.

Note: When a player causes her ball in play to move, except as permitted by a Rule, there is a penalty of one stroke.

Q.301
In stroke play, Helena makes a stroke at and misses a ball that is not hers. What is the ruling?
A) There is no penalty as Helena did not move the wrong ball.
B) Helena must add the missed stroke to her score but incurs no penalty.
C) Helena incurs a penalty of two strokes for making a stroke at a wrong ball.
D) Helena incurs a penalty of two strokes for making a stroke at a wrong ball and a further stroke for the miss.
Answer: C) Helena incurs a penalty of two strokes for making a stroke at a wrong ball. Decision 15/1.
Note: The penalty is the same as if Helena had struck a wrong ball.

Q.302
Which action may a player take when his ball lies in a water hazard, but is not in the water?
A) Remove a rock lying in front of his ball.
B) Place a spare club that he brought into the hazard on the ground in the hazard while he plays his stroke.
C) Ground his club behind the ball when taking his stance.
D) Clean his club in the water before making his stroke.
Answer: B) Place a spare club that he brought into the hazard on the ground in the hazard while he plays his stroke. Exception 1b to Rule 13-4.
Note: Providing he does not test the condition of the hazard or improve his lie, there is no penalty if the player places his clubs in a hazard.

Q.303
Which of the following statements is correct concerning the teeing ground?
A) It is the whole of the area prepared by the greenkeeper for commencing the play of holes from variably placed tee-markers.
B) It is a rectangular area one club-length in depth, the front and the sides of which are defined by the outside limits of two tee-markers.
C) It is a rectangular area two club-lengths in depth, the front and the sides of which are defined by the outside limits of two tee-markers.
D) It is a rectangular area the front and the sides of which are defined by the outside limits of two tee-markers, with no limit as to how far behind the markers the player may tee his ball.
Answer: C) It is a rectangular area two club-lengths in depth, the front and the sides of which are defined by the outside limits of two tee-markers. Definition of Teeing Ground.

Q.304
During a match Philip marks the position of his ball on the putting green and moves the ball to the side, leaving it on the green. By mistake, he later putts the ball from the spot at which he set it aside. What is the ruling?
A) Philip incurs a penalty of one stroke and must correct his mistake by replacing the ball at the correct spot before playing from the next tee.
B) Philip incurs a penalty of two strokes and must correct his mistake by replacing the ball at the correct spot before playing from the next tee.
C) Philip loses the hole.
D) Philip must add one penalty stroke to his score but his putt from the wrong place stands.
Answer: C) Philip loses the hole. Decision 15/4.
Note: When Philip marked and lifted his ball he took it out of play. By playing a ball that was out of play he played a wrong ball and lost the hole. If it had been a stroke play competition he would incur a penalty of two strokes and must correct his mistake by replacing the ball at the correct spot and playing out the hole before playing from the next tee.

Q.305
In stroke play, Mark leaves his trolley close to where his ball lies, which is under a tree. In playing his next, awkward shot his club hits his bag as he follows through on his stroke. What is the penalty?
A) Mark incurs no penalty.
B) Mark incurs no penalty and may play his stroke again.
C) Mark incurs a penalty of one stroke.
D) Mark incurs a penalty of two strokes.
Answer: A) Mark incurs no penalty.
Note: No Rule penalises a player for hitting his equipment with his club (which is also his equipment).

Q.306
In match play, Cara absent-mindedly marks and then lifts her ball from the apron of a putting green. She cleans the ball before replacing it. What is the ruling?
A) Cara incurs no penalty.
B) Cara incurs a penalty of one stroke.
C) Cara incurs total penalties of two strokes.
D) Cara incurs total penalties of three strokes.
Answer: B) Cara incurs a penalty of one stroke. Decision 18-2a/13.
Note: Cara incurs a penalty of one stroke for lifting her ball in play and cleaning it. Rule 21 permits a ball to be cleaned when lifted, except when it has been lifted in accordance with Rules 5-3, 12-2 or 22.

Q.307
In a Stableford competition, a direction sign interferes with Mary's area of swing. She easily removes the sign and then plays her stroke. What is the ruling?
A) There is no penalty.
B) Mary incurs a penalty of one stroke.
C) Mary incurs a penalty of two strokes.
D) Mary is disqualified.
Answer: A) There is no penalty. Rule 24-1.
Note: As the sign may be moved without unreasonable effort it is a movable obstruction and may be moved within the Rules. However, it should be replaced afterwards for the benefit of other players.

Q.308
In match play, Art's ball is lying four inches from the hole. He casually walks up to his ball holding his putter in one hand and pushes the ball into the hole. What is the ruling?
A) There is no penalty and the ball is holed.
B) Art is penalised one stroke and the putt stands.
C) Art is penalised one stroke and he has to replace the ball where it was and putt again.
D) Art loses the hole.
Answer: D) Art loses the hole. Rule 14-1a.
Note: The ball must be fairly struck at with the head of the club and must not be pushed, scraped or spooned. In stroke play, the penalty is two strokes.

Q.309
In the final of a match play competition, John accidentally walks down Christie's line of putt leaving deep footprints in the green. What is the ruling?
A) John incurs a penalty of one stroke.
B) John incurs a penalty of two strokes.
C) John loses the hole.
D) There is no penalty.
Answer: D) There is no penalty. Decision 16-1a/13.

Note: However, Christie is entitled to the lie and line of putt he had when his ball came to rest, so his line of putt may be restored to its original condition. A penalty would have been incurred if John had intentionally walked on Christie's line of putt so as to affect the playing of the hole.

Q.310
Which one of the following statements is incorrect?
A) When searching for his ball a player may touch or bend brambles and long grass, but only enough to find and identify his ball and providing that he does not improve the lie of the ball, area of intended swing or line of play.
B) When he thinks his ball is in a bunker covered in leaves the player may rake and probe the leaves with his club until he is able to see a ball. He may then mark the position of the ball, and invite an opponent or fellow competitor to witness him lifting the ball so he may properly identify it as his.
C) A player is entitled to see his ball when he is making a stroke.
D) There is no penalty if a player accidentally moves his ball lying in water in a water hazard during search.
Answer: C) A player is entitled to see his ball when he is making a stroke. Rule 12-1.
Note: A player is not necessarily entitled to see his ball when he is making a stroke.

Q.311
In which of the following circumstances does Sammie incur a penalty?
A) Sammie moves her ball in removing a bottle lying next to it.
B) Sammie moves her ball while searching for it under leaves in a bunker.
C) In preparing to putt Sammie's visor falls off and moves her ball.
D) Sammie moves her ball in measuring whose ball is farthest from the hole.
Answer: C) In preparing to putt Sammie's visor falls off and moves her ball. Rule 18-2.
Note: If a player's equipment causes the ball to move, the player incurs a penalty of one stroke.

Q.312
In stroke play, Pat's ball lies on a path that is covered with wood chips. She removes some of the chips around her ball before playing from off the path. What is the ruling in stroke play?
A) There is no penalty.
B) Pat incurs a penalty of one stroke for removing the wood chips.
C) Pat incurs a penalty of two strokes for removing the wood chips.
D) Pat incurs a penalty of two strokes for playing off the path.
Answer: A) There is no penalty. Decision 23/14.
Note: Wood chips are loose impediments and a player may remove loose impediments under Rule 23-1. Pat could also have taken relief from the path, which is an obstruction, unless there was a Local Rule making it an integral part of the course.

Q.313
Which of the following may not be used to mark a ball under the Rules?
A) A tee peg.
B) A clubhead.
C) A loose divot.
D) A pitch-mark located immediately to the left side of the ball.
Answer: D) A pitch-mark located immediately to the left side of the ball. Decision 20-1/16.
Note: The position of the ball has to be physically marked. Reference to an existing mark on the ground is not acceptable.

Q.314
In stroke play, Margarita leaves her bag between the 4th and 5th fairways, as she knows that she will be playing back to the same area from the next tee. As luck has it, her tee shot from the 5th hits her bag. What is the ruling?
A) Margarita incurs no penalty and she plays her ball from where it lies.
B) Margarita incurs no penalty but she has to replay her tee shot.
C) Margarita incurs a penalty of one stroke.
D) Margarita incurs a penalty of two strokes.
Answer: C) Margarita incurs a penalty of one stroke. Rule 19-2.
Note: If a player's ball is accidentally deflected or stopped by herself, her partner either of their caddies or their equipment, she incurs a penalty of one stroke.

Q.315
Adam's ball is at rest partly on the putting green and partly on the apron of the green and there is sand lying on his line of putt. He sweeps the sand away with the back of his hand before playing his stroke. What is the ruling?
A) Adam incurs a penalty of one stroke for removing sand from his line of putt.
B) Adam incurs a penalty of two strokes for removing sand from his line of putt.
C) Adam incurs a penalty of two strokes for the method by which he removed the sand.
D) There is no penalty for removing sand from the putting green by whatever means.
Answer: D) There is no penalty for removing sand from the putting green by whatever means. Decision 23-1/1.
Note: Loose impediments may be moved by any means, except that, the player must not press anything down on his line of putt.

Q.316
In match play, Jodi marks his ball on the green and puts it inside his wet suit pocket to keep it dry. When it is his turn to putt he removes a ball from his pocket, replaces it at his marker and putts it into the hole. He then realises that he has taken a different ball from his pocket. What is the ruling?
A) There is no penalty but Jodi must take his putt again, playing the original ball from the spot where his marker was.
B) There is a penalty of one stroke but the putt stands.
C) There is a penalty of one stroke and Jodi must take his putt again, playing the original ball from the spot where his marker was.
D) Jodi loses the hole.
Answer: D) Jodi loses the hole. Rule 15-2.
Note: If a player substitutes a ball when not permitted to do so under the Rules, and then makes a stroke at that ball, they lose the hole in match play and incur a penalty of two strokes in stroke play.

Q.317
In match play, while waiting to play his ball that lies in a bunker, Ruben casually leans on his sand wedge, without testing the condition of the hazard. What is the ruling?
A) There is no penalty.
B) There is a penalty of one stroke.
C) There is a penalty of two strokes.
D) There is a penalty of loss of hole.
Answer: D) There is a penalty of loss of hole. Decision 13-4/2.
Note: As Ruben was not using his club to prevent himself from falling he is penalised for touching the ground in the bunker with his club before making a stroke. In stroke play, the penalty would have been two strokes.

Q.318
Which of the following is an outside agency?
A) Wind.
B) A four-ball partner's ball.
C) A player's own golf bag.
D) A squirrel.
Answer: D) A squirrel. Definition of Outside Agency.
Note: An outside agency is any agency other than the player's side (and the opponent's side in match play), any caddie of either side, any ball played by either side at the hole being played or any equipment of either side.

Q.319
Caz's ball lies in casual water through the green. How may she take relief?
A) By dropping a ball within two club-lengths of where it last crossed the margin of the casual water, not nearer the hole.
B) By dropping a ball within two club-lengths of the nearest point of relief, not nearer the hole.
C) By dropping a ball within one club-length of the nearest point of relief, not nearer the hole.
D) By dropping a ball at the nearest point of relief, not nearer the hole.
Answer: C) By dropping a ball within one club-length of the nearest point of relief, not nearer the hole. Rule 25-1b.
Note: When taking relief from an abnormal ground condition Caz must lift her ball and drop it, without penalty, within one club-length of the nearest point of relief, not nearer the hole.

Q.320
Frank's ball is on the putting green and he notices a small area of bird droppings on his line of putt. He may remove these loose impediments with which of the following?
A) A tee peg.
B) A towel.
C) His putter.
D) All of the above.
Answer: D) All of the above. Rule 16-1a(i).
Note: Frank is permitted to remove the droppings (loose impediment) with any object, and touch his line of putt in the process, providing he does not press anything down.

Q.321
The honour of who plays first is determined by gross scores (i.e. without taking handicaps into account) when playing ...
A) In a match play event on a handicap basis.
B) In a strokes competition on a handicap basis.
C) In Stableford competitions.
D) In any format competition.
Answer: B) In a strokes competition on a handicap basis. Decision 10-2a/1.
Note: In stroke play competitions on a handicap basis, the handicap is deducted at the end of the round and not at individual holes.

Q.322
A stroke play foursome is ...
A) When a group of four players play together.
B) When the better-ball of two players, playing as partners, is taken as their score for that hole.
C) When two players, playing as partners, play alternate strokes with one ball.
D) When one player plays against the best ball of three other players.
Answer: C) When two players, playing as partners, play alternate strokes with one ball. Definition of Forms of Stroke Play.

Q.323
Which of the following statements is incorrect?
A) A player must re-drop a ball without penalty if it rolls onto a putting green.
B) A player must re-drop a ball without penalty if it rolls into a hazard.
C) A player must re-drop a ball without penalty if it rolls more than one club-length away from where it first hit the course.
D) A player must re-drop a ball without penalty if it rolls nearer the hole than its original position.
Answer: C) A player must re-drop a ball without penalty if it rolls more than one club-length away from where it first hit the course. Rule 20-2c.
Note: The drop is valid if it comes to rest less than two club-lengths from where it first struck a part of the course and not nearer the hole.

Q.324
Which of the following statements is incorrect?
A) A player may touch her line of putt to repair an old hole plug on the green.
B) A player may touch her line of putt to flatten spike marks made by the previous playing group on the green.
C) A player may touch her line of putt to repair damage made by the impact of a ball.
D) A player may touch her line of putt to remove loose impediments.
Answer: B) A player may touch her line of putt to flatten spike marks made by the previous playing group on the green. Rule 16-1a.
Note: The only damage to a putting green that a player may repair is an old hole plug or damage caused by the impact of a ball.

Q.325
Which of the following is defined as an obstruction in the Rules of Golf?
A) Tree leaves piled for removal.
B) An out of bounds stake.
C) A water hazard stake.
D) The player's golf trolley.
Answer: C) A water hazard stake. Definition of Obstructions.
Note: Leaves piled for removal are ground under repair, an out of bounds stake is deemed to be fixed from which no relief is available, the player's trolley is equipment, the water hazard stake is artificial and is a movable obstruction.

Q.326
In the Rules of Golf a partner is ...
A) A fellow competitor in a stroke play competition grouping.
B) A player associated with another player on the same side.
C) An opponent in match play.
D) Someone who accompanies a player in order to carry his clubs and give advice.
Answer: B) A player associated with another player on the same side. Definition of Partner.

Q.327
Which of the following is not an obstruction?
A) A wooden pencil.
B) Pieces of coconut shell.
C) A recycled paper bag.
D) A cube of ice.
Answer: B) Pieces of coconut shell. Definition of Obstructions.
Note: An obstruction is anything artificial. Coconut shell is natural and is therefore a loose impediment.

Q.328
Mae finds her ball in thick rough after a two minute search, leaves the area to get a club, which takes another minute, and then is unable to find the ball again. How much time is there left for her to resume the search for her ball?
A) Five minutes.
B) Three minutes.
C) Two minutes.
D) Zero minutes.
Answer: B) Three minutes. Decision 27-3.
Note: The time taken for a player to get the club is not included in the search time allowed of five minutes.

Q.329
Stacey plays her tee shot over a water hazard into a bunker behind the putting green. She thins her bunker shot and it rolls across the green into the water and disappears from sight. Which of the following options is correct under penalty of one stroke?
A) Stacey may drop her ball within two club-lengths of the place where her ball crossed the margin of the water hazard at the side of the putting green.
B) Stacey may cross back over the water hazard to the teeing side and drop a ball, keeping the point at which the original ball last crossed the hazard margin (i.e. on the putting green side) between the hole and the spot on which the ball is dropped.
C) Stacey may place a ball in the bunker at the spot where her tee shot came to rest and replay her shot to the green.
D) Stacey may return to the teeing ground to play her fourth stroke.
Answer: B) Stacey may cross back over the water hazard to the teeing side and drop a ball, keeping the point at which the original ball last crossed the hazard margin (i.e. on the putting green side) between the hole and the spot on which the ball is dropped. Decision 26-1/6.
Note: Although Stacey's ball last crossed the margin on the putting green side, it is unlikely that there is a spot to drop her ball that complies with the option in Rule 26-1b. In these circumstances it is usually necessary for the player to return to the tee side of the hazard and play over the hazard again. If Stacey opts to play a ball at the spot where her ball came to rest in the bunker, she must drop a ball, not place it.

Q.330
Seb's ball lies just off the putting green and there are lumps of sand, on both the apron of the green and the putting green itself, between his ball and the hole. What is the ruling?
A) Seb must not remove any of the sand.
B) Seb may remove the sand wherever it lies, as sand is a loose impediment.
C) Seb may only remove the sand that is on the putting green.
D) Seb may only remove the sand that is on the apron of the green.
Answer: C) Seb may only remove the sand that is on the putting green. Definition of Loose Impediments.
Note: Sand and loose soil are loose impediments on the putting green, but not elsewhere.

Q.331
In a singles match play competition Jan and June's balls are side by side in a bunker. Jan plays first, but as she climbs out she sees her ball still in the bunker and realises that she has played the wrong ball. What is her penalty?
A) Jan incurs no penalty as you cannot play a wrong ball out of a bunker.
B) Jan incurs a penalty of one stroke.
C) Jan incurs a penalty of two strokes.
D) Jan loses the hole.
Answer: D) Jan loses the hole. Rule 15-3.
Note: In match play, if a player makes a stroke at a wrong ball, she loses the hole. In stroke play, the penalty is two strokes.

Q.332
Which of the following statements is incorrect?
A) Players may suspend play if there is an electrical storm in the vicinity.
B) In stroke play, competitors may take shelter for up to 10 minutes during a heavy rain shower.
C) Players may leave the course to take a quick bathroom break between holes.
D) A player may return to a previous teeing ground to retrieve his club, providing he does not unduly delay play.
Answer: B) In stroke play, competitors may take shelter for up to 10 minutes during a heavy rain shower. Rule 6-8a.
Note: Bad weather is not of itself a good reason for players to discontinue play.

Q.333
In stroke play, Kiely has holed out on the 14th hole when she approaches her fellow competitor, Debbie, and demonstrates how she should play her next chip shot over the bunker. What is the ruling?
A) There is no penalty for Kiely or Debbie.
B) There is no penalty for Debbie but Kiely incurs a penalty of two strokes.
C) There is no penalty for Kiely but Debbie incurs a penalty of two strokes.
D) Both Kiely and Debbie incur a penalty of two strokes.
Answer: B) There is no penalty for Debbie but Kiely incurs a penalty of two strokes. Decision 8-1/14.
Note: Kiely incurred a penalty of two strokes for giving advice to Debbie. Debbie was not penalised as she did not seek advice. As Debbie had not completed the 14th hole, the penalty would be applied at that hole.

Section 2: 333 more difficult questions relevant to both casual golfers and Golf Club members

True or False?

Q.334
In stroke play, a player always incurs a one stroke penalty when taking relief from a water hazard. True or False?
Answer: True. Rule 26-1.
Note: The player may choose to play the ball as it lies within the water hazard, without penalty or take one of the two options for relief under penalty of one stroke.

Q.335
A player may always advise a player on what his options are under the Rules. True or False?
Answer: True. Definition of Advice.
Note: Information on the Rules is not advice.

Q.336
A ball overhanging the edge of a bunker but not touching the sand is in the bunker. True or False?
Answer: False. Definition of Bunker.
Note: A ball is only in a bunker when any part of it touches the bunker. The margin of a bunker extends vertically downwards, but not upwards.

Q.337
As a player reaches the top of his backswing on a tee shot the ball falls off the tee. He completes his stroke topping the ball just five yards forward. There is no penalty and he must play the ball as it lies. True or False?
Answer: True. Rule 11-3.
Note: If a stroke is made at a ball that is not yet in play, whether the ball is moving or not, the stroke counts, but there is no penalty.

Q.338
A ball is in a water hazard when it touches the outside edge of a stake defining the water hazard. True or False?
Answer: True. Definition of Water Hazard.
Note: The margin of the hazard is defined by the nearest outside points of the stakes at ground level.

Q.339
In stroke play, the maximum penalty a player may incur from playing a wrong ball is two strokes, no matter how many times he plays it. True or False?
Answer: True. Rule 15-3b.
Note: The competitor must correct his mistake by playing the correct ball into the hole or he will be disqualified.

Q.340
Sand and loose soil are loose impediments that may be removed on the putting green and through the green. True or False?
Answer: False. Definition of Loose Impediments.
Note: Sand and loose soil are loose impediments only on the putting green.

Q.341
Billy's shot bounced off the back of a pot bunker and came to rest inside the bunker next to a piece of chocolate that had been dropped by a player in a previous group. Under the Rules Billy may not remove the chocolate until after his next stroke. True or False?
Answer: False. Definition of Obstructions.
Note: Chocolate is artificial and is therefore an obstruction, which may be removed from anywhere on the course without penalty. If the ball moves during the removal of the chocolate it must be replaced and there is no penalty.

Q.342
In a handicap Stableford competition, Brian inadvertently returns his score card to the Committee with a score of six at the 11th hole when his score for the hole was actually seven. The 11th hole is a par 4 at which the competitor receives no handicap strokes. The player is disqualified. True or False?
Answer: False. Decision 32-2a/4.
Note: Brian gets away with his mistake as the lower score did not affect the result of the hole. He scored no Stableford points with a six or a seven.

Q.343
A caddie may be shared between two players and may give advice to them both. True or False?
Answer: True. Definition of Caddie.

Q.344
In match play, a player loses the hole if they play their tee shot from outside the teeing ground. True or False?
Answer: False. Rule 11-4a.
Note: There is no penalty, but the opponent has the choice of letting the tee shot stand or immediately requiring the player to cancel the stroke and play again from within the teeing ground.

Q.345
The status of manufactured ice on the golf course is an obstruction. True or False?
Answer: True. Definition of Obstructions.
Note: An obstruction is anything artificial, including manufactured ice.

Q.346
A player must always record their full handicap on their score card even if they are playing in a competition where players will not receive their full handicap (e.g. on a shortened course). True or False?
Answer: True. Decision 6-2b/0.5.
Note: It is the Committee's responsibility to adjust the handicap according to the conditions of competition.

Q.347
Bogey, Par and Stableford competitions are all forms of stroke play. True or False?
Answer: True. Rule 32-1.
Note: They are forms of stroke play in which play is against a fixed score at each hole.

Q.348
A player is entitled to discontinue play if she hears thunder. True or False?
Answer: True. Rule 6-8a(ii).
Note: A player is entitled to discontinue play if she believes there is danger from lightning. The sound of thunder signifies that there could be lightning in the area.

Q.349
There is no penalty if a ball lying in ground under repair moves during search. True or False?
Answer: True. Rule 12-1d.
Note: Ground under repair (GUR) is an abnormal ground condition. If the player opts to play the ball from the abnormal ground condition, rather than taking relief, the ball that was moved during search must be replaced.

Q.350
If a player makes any strokes in a hazard with a wrong ball there is no penalty. True or False?
Answer: False. Rule 15-3a and 15-3b.
Note: If a competitor makes a stroke at a wrong ball anywhere on the course he incurs a penalty of loss of hole in match play or two strokes in stroke play.

Q.351
A player drops his glove onto his ball causing it to move. He incurs a penalty of one stroke and the ball must be replaced. True or False?
Answer: True. Decision 18-2a/17.
Note: A glove is equipment of the player. There is a penalty of one stroke if equipment of the player causes his ball to move.

Q.352
A player drops his ball fairly under the Rules but it hits his own equipment lying within two club-lengths of where the ball first touches the ground. He incurs a penalty of one stroke. True or False?
Answer: False. Rule 20-2a.
Note: If a dropped ball touches the equipment of the player before or after it strikes the course, the ball must be re-dropped, without penalty.

Q.353
A player may not practice on the competition course prior to a match play round due to be played on the same day. True or False?
Answer: False. Rule 7-1a.
Note: A player may practice on the competition course on the same day as his match but not on the same day as a stroke play competition that he is playing in.

Q.354
A competitor that signs her card showing a handicap lower than she is entitled to is disqualified. True or False?
Answer: False. Rule 6-2.
Note: If she records a handicap higher than that to which she is entitled she is disqualified. In signing for a lower handicap her score stands but the Committee has to calculate her net score based on the handicap that she signs for.

Q.355
In both match and stroke play, if players accidentally touch their ball in play, they always incur a penalty stroke. True or False?
Answer: False. Rule 18-2.
Note: There is no penalty if the ball is touched accidentally and does not move.

Q.356
The position of a ball must be marked with a ball-marker, a small coin or other similar object. True or False?
Answer: False. Note to Rule 20-1.

Note: The Rule states that a ball should be marked by such an object, but it is not mandatory.

Q.357
In taking relief from casual water you may not drop the ball on the fairway if your ball is lying in the rough, even if this is the nearest point of relief. True or False?
Answer: False. Definition of Nearest Point of Relief.
Note: If the nearest point of relief, as defined, is on the fairway then the ball must be dropped within one club-length of that point, not nearer the hole.

Q.358
A player may not rake footprints and other irregularities in a bunker that is on his line of play even if his ball does not lie in that bunker. True or False?
Answer: True. Decision 13-2/0.5.
Note: Such an action would improve his line of play contrary to Rule 13-2.

Q.359
Information on matters such as the location of the hole on the putting green, during play of the hole, is not advice. True or False?
Answer: True. Definition of Advice.
Note: Information on the Rules, distance or matters of public information, such as the position of hazards or the location of the hole, is not advice.

Q.360
A player may use his putter as a plumb-line to assist him in determining the slope on a putting green. True or False?
Answer: True. Decision 14-3/12.
Note: Use of a club in this manner is traditionally accepted, but any artificial device used for this purpose, such as a weight suspended on a piece of string, would breach the Rule.

Q.361
Ground under repair includes material piled for removal whether it is marked or not. True or False?
Answer: True. Definition of Ground Under Repair.
Note: The material does not have to be marked and relief may be taken providing it has definitely been piled for removal.

Q.362
A player may ask for the flagstick to be attended when he is making a stroke from anywhere on the course. True or False?
Answer: True. Rule 17-1.
Note: The person attending the flagstick must not let the ball hit it otherwise the player who made the stroke will incur a penalty of two strokes in stroke play or loss of hole in match play.

Q.363
A player may not repair a divot hole that is on the line of play between his ball and the hole. True or False?
Answer: False. Decision 13-2/0.5.
Note: There is no penalty unless by repairing the divot hole the player gains a potential advantage with respect to the position or lie of his ball, the area of his intended stance or swing, his line of play or a reasonable extension of that line beyond the hole, or the area in which he is to drop or place a ball.

Q.364
Through the green a player has addressed the ball when he has taken his stance. True or False?
Answer: False. Definition of Addressing the Ball.
Note: A player has addressed their ball when they have grounded their club immediately in front of or immediately behind the ball, whether or not they have taken their stance.

Q.365
A player may touch his line of putt on the putting green to remove loose soil. True or False?
Answer: True. Rule 16-1a(i).
Note: Loose impediments may be removed, providing nothing is pressed down, and loose soil is defined as a loose impediment on the putting green (but not elsewhere on the course).

Q.366
A ball lands on a banana skin through the green. The player must either play the ball as it lies or deem it unplayable for a penalty of one stroke. True or False?
Answer: True. Decision 23-4.
Note: A banana skin is a natural object and is therefore a loose impediment. Through the green a loose impediment may only be removed if the player can remove it without touching or moving his ball.

Q.367
In handicap Bogey, Par and Stableford competitions, the competitor who has the lowest score at a hole takes the honour at the next teeing ground. True or False?
Answer: False. Rule 32-1.
Note: In these competitions it is the player with the lowest net score at a hole that takes the honour.

Q.368
A referee authorises a player to take a drop away from a crack in the ground even though it is not marked as ground under repair. The player is absolved from penalty in such a case. True or False?
Answer: True. Decision 34-2/2.
Note: The referee's decision is final, even when he is wrong!

Q.369
Two players competing in the same competition at different times on the same day may act as caddie for each other. True or False?
Answer: True. Decision 6-4/8.
Note: There is no Rule that prevents a caddie from practising on the course before the round that he is caddy in, on the same day as the competition.

Q.370
The out of bounds line extends vertically upwards and downwards. True or False?
Answer: True. Definition of Out of Bounds.

Q.371
On a links course a player wants to putt his ball, which lies 12 feet off the putting green. However, there is a divot hole just in front of his ball on his line of play. The player may not replace the divot before playing his next stroke. True or False?
Answer: True. Decision 13-2/6.
Note: A player may not improve their line of play by eliminating an irregularity of surface.

Q.372
A player is not permitted to draw a circle around their golf ball to assist them in putting through a straight line. True or False?
Answer: False. Rule 6-5.
Note: Each player should put an identification mark on their ball. There is no restriction as to how this is done.

Q.373
In match play, Bill incurs a penalty stroke for lifting his ball to identify it without marking it. However, neither Bill nor his opponent realise that a penalty has been incurred. The Committee would be justified in disqualifying both players for waiving a Rule. True or False?
Answer: False. Decision 1-3/5.
Note: Since the players were not aware a penalty had been incurred, there could have been no agreement between them to waive the penalty.

Q.374
A player's ball lies just inches from the putting green, on the apron, and only nine feet from the hole. He wants to putt his ball but casual water on the green intervenes between his ball and the hole. He is entitled to relief. True or False?
Answer: False. Decision 25-1a/2.
Note: Relief for casual water on a line of putt is only available if the player's ball lies on the putting green. Also, the player is prohibited from removing the casual water from his line of play.

Q.375
A player may declare his ball unplayable at any place on the course except when the ball is in a water hazard. True or False?
Answer: True. Rule 28.
Note: The player is the sole judge as to whether his ball is unplayable. There are then three options as to where to play the next stroke from, all of which incur a penalty of one stroke.

Q.376
Changes are made to the Rules of Golf every two years. True or False?
Answer: False. The Rules of Golf are revised every four years.
Note: The Decisions on the Rules of Golf are revised every two years.

Q.377
In a singles match play, Alex and his opponent, Jon, share a golf cart that is stationary with Jon sitting in it. Alex plays a stroke and his ball is deflected by Jon's golf bag strapped to the cart. Alex is not penalised as it was Jon's equipment that was hit. True or False?
Answer: False. Alex incurs a penalty of one stroke. Definition of Equipment & Rule 19-2.
Note: The cart and everything in it are deemed to be the equipment of the player sharing the cart whose ball is involved.

Q.378
The only hazards in golf are bunkers and water hazards. True or False?
Answer: True. Definition of Hazards.
Note: Water hazards include lateral water hazards.

Q.379
If his ball lies in a lateral water hazard a player is not permitted to lift his ball under the Rules to see if it is unfit for play. True or False?
Answer: False. Rule 5-3.
Note: A player may lift his ball under the Rules anywhere on the course in order to ascertain

whether it is unfit for play but he must follow the correct procedure to avoid incurring a penalty.

Q.380
The Committee may rule that an asphalt road is an integral part of the course from which relief from an immovable obstruction may not be obtained. True or False?
Answer: True. Definition of Obstructions.
Note: A Committee may declare any construction to be an integral part of the course. The famous Road Hole, the 17th at the Old Course, St Andrews, is a good example.

Q.381
A player may treat snow and natural ice as casual water and take relief accordingly. True or False?
Answer: True. Definition of Casual Water.
Note: Snow and natural ice may also be treated as loose impediments.

Q.382
In match play, Stuart concedes a hole to Callum, his opponent, and then learns that Callum has played a wrong ball from a bunker. There is no penalty and Stuart's concession stands. True or False?
Answer: False. Decision 2-4/9.
Note: Callum lost the hole before Stuart conceded it to him (Rule 15-3a).

Q.383
On Captain's Day Denis is due to tee off at 10.00am. He arrives at the 1st tee at 10.06am but because of slow play earlier in the morning the groupings are starting about 15 minutes late. Denis is still disqualified for arriving on the 1st tee after his start time. True or False?
Answer: False. Decision 6-3a/4.
Note: As the group is unable to start at the time originally established by the Committee and the player arrives before it can do so, the player is not in breach of Rule 6-3a.

Q.384
A player putting from off the putting green wishes to leave the flagstick in the hole. However, he notices that the flagstick is leaning towards his line of putt, which he considers to be a disadvantage. He may centre the flagstick in the hole. True or False?
Answer: True. Decision 17-4.
Note: The flagstick may be left as it is or centred in the hole, but it may not be intentionally adjusted to a more favourable position than centred.

Q.385
A player who plays off scratch (zero) did not record this handicap on his score card. The Committee may allow his score to stand. True or False?
Answer: False. Rule 6-2b.
Note: If a player does not record his handicap on his score card before it is returned he is disqualified.

Q.386
A ball lands on the wooden steps of a raised par 3 putting green. The player must play the ball as it lies. True or False?
Answer: False. Decision 24-12.
Note: Wooden steps are constructions and are therefore immovable obstructions.

Q.387
When signing his stroke play score card a player must initial any alterations before returning it to the Committee. True or False?

Answer: False. Decision 6-6a/6.
Note: Nothing is laid down in the Rules of Golf as to how alterations should be made on a score card.

Q.388
The penalty for failing to sign a score card in match play is disqualification. True or False?
Answer: False. Rule 2-3.
Note: In match play, the game is played by holes. A match is won when one side leads by a number of holes greater than the number remaining to be played. There is no requirement to keep a score card.

Q.389
There is no penalty for any breach of etiquette on the golf course. True or False?
Answer: False. Rule 33-7.
Note: The Committee may disqualify a player who they consider is guilty of a serious breach of etiquette.

Q.390
In all forms of play, providing the competition is not delayed, the players may agree to start at a time other than that established by the Committee. True or False?
Answer: False. Rule 6-3a.
Note: Players must start at the time established by the Committee.

Q.391
In match play, there is a loss of hole penalty if, after a putt on the green, the player's ball hits any other ball at rest that is also on the green. True or False?
Answer: False. Rule 19-5a.
Note: There is no penalty in match play if a player's ball in motion after a stroke is deflected or stopped by a ball in play and at rest. The player must play his ball as it lies, whereas the other ball must be replaced where it was.

Q.392
A ladybird is sitting on a player's ball in a bunker. He may not touch the insect without incurring a penalty. True or False?
Answer: True. Rule 13-4c.
Note: The insect is a loose impediment and may not be touched or physically removed when the player's ball is in a hazard. However, the player may, without penalty, take such action as waving his hand or a towel, to encourage the insect to move.

Q.393
Through the green is the whole area of the course except all hazards and the putting green of the hole being played. True or False?
Answer: False. Definition of Through the Green.
Note: The teeing ground of the hole being played is also an exception to the definition of through the green.

Q.394
Snow lying on a player's line of putt may be brushed away with his hand or putter. True or False?
Answer: True. Definition of Loose Impediments.
Note: The player may treat snow as either casual water or a loose impediment.

Q.395
If play is suspended after a player has played a stroke from the teeing ground of a hole, the other players in the group must discontinue play immediately. True or False?

Answer: False. Decision 6-8b/2.
Note: When play is suspended players may choose to discontinue play immediately or continue play of the hole, providing they do so without delay.

Q.396
On the 18th putting green Roger has a long, curving putt to tie his match. He sees a small twig lying on the green and moves it one inch to the left to give himself a guide as to the line he should take. He loses the match. True or False?
Answer: True. Rule 8-2b.
Note: A mark must not be placed anywhere to indicate a line for putting. The penalty in match play is loss of hole.

Q.397
If during a round, a player's clubs are transported in a motorised cart that is driven by a friend who performs no other function, he is not a caddie. True or False?
Answer: False. Decision 6-4/2.5.
Note: By driving the cart or pulling the trolley, the friend is deemed to be carrying the player's clubs and is therefore a caddie.

Q.398
Stakes defining out of bounds are not obstructions. True or False?
Answer: True. Definition of Out of Bounds.
Note: Objects defining out of bounds are not obstructions and are deemed to be fixed.

Q.399
In stroke play, a player may practice putting on the 1st teeing ground before starting a round. True or False?
Answer: True. Rule 7-1b.
Note: Practice putting or chipping on or near the 1st teeing ground before starting a round is permitted.

Q.400
Chad was in the middle of his downswing when a spectator coughed loudly behind him. He could not completely stop his follow-through but was able to change direction enough to miss his ball by some inches. His stroke does not count. True or False?
Answer: True. Definition of Stroke.
Note: If a player checks his downswing voluntarily before the clubhead reaches the ball he has not made a stroke.

Q.401
While Giorgio is preparing to make his tee shot, he uses his driver to tap down an uneven surface behind where his ball is teed, which could mentally interfere with his backswing. In stroke play he incurs a penalty of two holes. True or False?
Answer: False. Rule 13-2.
Note: There is no penalty for creating or eliminating irregularities of surface within the teeing ground.

Q.402
The Committee selects the location of the teeing ground, including its width and depth. True or False?
Answer: False. Definition of Teeing Ground.
Note: The teeing ground has to be a rectangular area two club-lengths in depth, the front and the sides of which are defined by the outside limits of two tee-markers.

Q.403
A player's ball lies behind a rock that is only partially embedded in the surrounding earth. He incurs a penalty stroke if he removes the rock. True or False?
Answer: False. Definition of Loose Impediments.
Note: However, if a rock is solidly embedded the player may not remove it.

Q.404
Tim lifts a fellow competitor's ball on the putting green without his authority. He incurs a penalty of one stroke. True or False?
Answer: False. Decision 20-1/4.
Note: Tim incurs no penalty and the ball must be replaced. In match play there is a penalty of one stroke for touching an opponent's ball in play. Rule 18-3b.

Q.405
If a player thinks that a ball may be assisting another player he may lift the ball if it is his ball or ask for any other ball to be lifted. True or False?
Answer: True. Rule 22-1.
Note: However, the ball may not be lifted once another ball is in motion.

Q.406
Even if it is obvious that, when it is dropped, a ball will roll into a hazard, the player may not place the ball instead of dropping it. True or False?
Answer: True. Decision 20-2c/3.
Note: The ball must be dropped and then re-dropped in order to see whether it will definitely roll into the hazard, and to establish where the ball must be placed, if necessary.

Q.407
Tomas hits his first ball out of bounds from the teeing ground and then tees up another ball. While addressing this ball, he accidentally knocks it off the tee. Tomas incurs a penalty of one stroke and must replace his ball. True or False?
Answer: False. Decision 11-3/3.
Note: Tomas incurs no penalty, because a teed ball is not in play until a stroke has been made at it. The ball may be re-teed.

Q.408
In stroke play, no alteration may be made to a card by a competitor after he has returned it to the Committee. True or False?
Answer: True. Rule 6-6c.
Note: Once the card has been returned it is too late to alter it.

Q.409
A player cannot physically determine the nearest point of relief from an immovable obstruction because that point is within the trunk of a large tree. He may take relief from the obstruction from the nearest point where no such physical interference exists. True or False?
Answer: False. Decision 24-2b/3.5.
Note: In this circumstance the nearest point of relief must be estimated and the player must drop the ball within one club-length of the estimated point, not nearer the hole.

Q.410
A player is entitled to hold his ball, to stop it moving, while moving aside a movable obstruction under the Rules. True or False?
Answer: False. Decision 24-1/4.
Note: Even though there is no penalty if a ball moves during removal of a movable obstruction, providing the movement of the ball is directly attributable to the removal of the obstruction, a player would be in breach of Rule 18-2 if he purposely touched his ball.

Q.411
When a player's ball lies in a water hazard he may remove pine cones lying in the hazard which are more than one club-length from his ball. True or False?
Answer: False. Rule 23-1.
Note: A pine cone is a loose impediment. When a ball and the loose impediment lie in the same hazard the loose impediment may not be removed.

Q.412
In taking relief from an obstruction in a strokes competition, a player drops a ball within one club-length of the nearest point of relief and it rolls a few inches nearer the hole than where his original ball was at rest. He then plays his ball from this wrong place. He should be disqualified. True or False?
Answer: False. He incurs a penalty of two strokes. Rule 20-7c.
Note: However, if the Committee decide that he has gained a significant advantage by playing from the wrong place, he is disqualified.

Q.413
A player may back into a tree, bending back low hanging branches as he does so, in order to fairly take his stance to play his ball, which lies close to the trunk of the tree. True or False?
Answer: True. Decision 13-2/1.
Note: The player is limited to do what is reasonably necessary to take a stance for the selected stroke without unduly improving the lie of his ball, area of intended stance or swing or line of play.

Q.414
A player may only remove loose impediments on his line of putt by picking them up or by brushing them aside with his hand or a club. True or False?
Answer: False. Decision 23-1/1.
Note: Loose impediments may be moved by any means, except that, in removing loose impediments on the line of putt, the player must not press anything down (Rule 16-1a).

Q.415
A player's tee shot may be out of bounds or it may be in a water hazard. He may not play a provisional ball. True or False?
Answer: False. Decision 27-2a/2.2.
Note: A player is entitled to play a provisional ball if his original ball might be lost outside the water hazard or out of bounds. But if the original ball is found in the water hazard, the provisional ball must be abandoned.

Q.416
In match play, if a player is in doubt as to the procedure he may complete the hole with two balls, choosing which ball he wants to count if it is within the Rules. True or False?
Answer: False. Rule 2-5.
Note: In a match, a player may not play a second ball. Where there is disagreement between the players the opponent must make a claim following the procedures set out in Rule 2-5.

Q.417
A player removes the flagstick from the hole and places it on the ground. When his fellow competitor putts too hard he sees that the ball might strike the flagstick. He is penalised one stroke if he moves the flagstick while the ball is in motion. True or False?
Answer: False. Neither player incurs a penalty. Rule 24-1.
Note: Rule 24-1 provides that anyone may move the equipment of any player or a removed flagstick, to prevent it being struck by a ball in motion.

Q.418
The wall or lip of a bunker not covered with grass, is part of the bunker. True or False?
Answer: True. Definition of Bunker.

Q.419
There is no penalty for looking into a fellow competitor's bag to determine which club they used for their last stroke. True or False?
Answer: True. Decision 8-1/10.
Note: Information obtained by observation is not advice. However, a player is prohibited from obtaining such information through a physical act such as moving a towel covering the clubs.

Q.420
In stroke play, Mae and Rita agree to play out of turn on their 14th hole in order to save time. They did not do so in order to give one of them an advantage. They should be disqualified for agreeing to waive a Rule concerning order of play. True or False?
Answer: False. Decision 10-2c/2.
Note: In stroke play, if a competitor plays out of turn, there is no penalty and the ball is played as it lies, providing that competitors have not agreed to play out of turn to give one of them an advantage.

Q.421
There is no restriction on the length of a tee peg. True or False?
Answer: False. Appendix IV – 1.
Note: A tee must not be longer than four inches (101.66 millimetres).

Q.422
A player may not putt with one hand while holding the flagstick with the other. True or False?
Answer: False. Decision 17-1/5.
Note: The player may hold the flagstick while putting providing a) he does not use the flagstick for assistance, and b) the ball does not strike it. If the ball were to strike the flagstick, a breach of Rule 17-3a would occur and there would be a penalty of two strokes in stroke play or loss of hole in match play.

Q.423
A player may remove or replace a divot that is still attached when it interferes with her backswing. True or False?
Answer: False. Decision 13-2/5.
Note: A player may not improve her lie or area of intended swing by moving, bending or breaking anything growing or fixed.

Q.424
In stroke play, a player removes a piece of paper lying alongside his ball in a water hazard before playing from the hazard. He incurs two penalty strokes. True or False?
Answer: False. Rule 24-1.
Note: The status of anything artificial is an obstruction that may be removed from a hazard or anywhere on the course, providing that the ball is at rest.

Q.425
As a player approaches his ball on a putting green, with a ball-marker in his hand, he drops his putter from under his arm and it falls onto his ball, moving it several inches. He is not penalised because he was in the act of marking his ball. True or False?
Answer: False. Decision 20-1/14.
Note: A penalty of one stroke is incurred because the movement of the ball was not directly attributable to the specific act of marking the position or lifting the ball.

Q.426
If a player does not enter a score for a hole in a par competition he is disqualified. True or False?
Answer: False. Rule 32-1.
Note: The scoring for bogey and par competitions is made as in match play. Any hole for which a competitor makes no return is regarded as a loss.

Q.427
In a stroke play competition a player did not have a playing partner to mark her card so she played with two players who were not in the competition and asked one of them to be her marker. The Committee should accept her card. True or False?
Answer: True. Decision 6-6a/1.
Note: Since the Committee failed to provide a marker they should give retrospective authority to the player who acted as the competitor's marker.

Q.428
If a player's ball is on a putting green he may mop up casual water lying on his line of putt with a towel. True or False?
Answer: False. Decision 16-1a/1.
Note: This is not one of the exceptions to the Rule that a player may not touch his line of putt.

Q.429
In a foursome match the composition of either side may not be changed once any of the four players has teed off at the 1st hole. True or False?
Answer: True. Decision 29-1.

Q.430
Anne Marie holes out for a four and Shirley has a putt to halve the hole. Anne Marie tells Shirley that her putt is just inside the right edge of the hole. Shirley does not need to take her putt as the hole is halved. True or False?
Answer: True. Rule 2-2.
Note: When a player has holed out and her opponent has been left with a stroke for the half, if the player subsequently incurs a penalty, the hole is halved.

Q.431
In stroke play, if a competitor's ball in motion after a stroke strikes his equipment, the competitor shall incur a penalty of two strokes. True or False?
Answer: False. Rule 19-2.
Note: The player incurs a penalty of one stroke.

Q.432
Dick's ball is overhanging the hole. He walks up to the hole and jumps twice in the hope that this action may cause his ball to fall into the hole. It doesn't, so there is no penalty. True or False?
Answer: True. Decision 1-2/4.
Note: There is no penalty where the action does not result in a change in the position of the ball at rest.

Q.433
A player whose ball lies within a ditch designated as a lateral water hazard may drop a ball within the Rules on either side of the ditch. True or False?
Answer: True. Rule 26-1.
Note: The ball may be dropped within two club-lengths of and not nearer the hole than the

point where the original ball last crossed the margin of the water hazard or a point on the opposite margin of the water hazard equidistant from the hole.

Q.434
In addressing his ball on the putting green, Cyril inadvertently touches his ball with his club. The ball was in an aeration hole and although it moved it settled back to its original position. Cyril incurs a penalty of one stroke for moving his ball while in play. True or False?
Answer: False. Definition of Moved.
Note: A ball is only deemed to have moved if it leaves its position and comes to rest in any other place.

Q.435
A player whose ball lies in a hazard is entitled to swat away a fly hovering close to his ball, even though under the Rules an insect is a loose impediment. True or False?
Answer: True. Decision 13-4/16.5.
Note: In equity, even though the margin of a hazard extends vertically upwards, and therefore the insect is in the hazard, the player may swat it away.

Q.436
A player may not ask a fellow competitor the distance between his ball and the flagstick. True or False?
Answer: False. Decision 8-1/2.
Note: Information regarding the distance between two objects is public information and not advice.

Q.437
Craig putts from on the putting green with the flagstick removed. He misjudges the slope and the ball rolls past the hole and off the green on the other side. He cannot replace the flagstick. True or False?
Answer: False. Rule 17-1.
Note: Craig may choose to replace the flagstick in the hole unattended, have it attended or leave it removed from the hole.

Q.438
In stroke play, a ball that has been played from outside a teeing ground by a player starting play of a hole is not in play. True or False?
Answer: True. Definition of Ball in Play.
Note: Rule 11-4 applies. The player incurs a penalty of two strokes and must play a ball from within the teeing ground to avoid disqualification.

Q.439
A player is entitled to free relief if his ball lies close to a wire fence that may be reasonably claimed to provide mental interference to his next shot. True or False?
Answer: False. Rule 24-2a.
Note: Interference by an immovable obstruction only occurs when a ball lies in or on the obstruction or when the obstruction interferes with the player's stance or area of intended swing.

Q.440
Wind is an outside agency when it blows a ball at rest on the putting green away from the hole. True or False?
Answer: False. Definition of Outside Agency.
Note: Neither wind nor water is an outside agency.

Q.441
An aeration hole on a putting green is a hole made by a greenkeeper and so the player may take relief from it. True or False?
Answer: False. Decision 25/15.
Note: An aeration hole is not a hole made by a greenkeeper within the meaning of that term in the definition of ground under repair. However, a Committee may adopt a temporary Local Rule permitting relief from aeration holes.

Q.442
A player may return a score card different from the one issued by the Committee at the start of the round. True or False?
Answer: True. Decision 6-6a/7.
Note: The Committee should accept the new score card providing it contains the competitor's name, handicap and scores and was signed by both him and his marker.

Q.443
The ball may not be pushed into the hole with the head of the club (e.g. on a short putt). True or False?
Answer: True. Rule 14-1a.
Note: The ball must be fairly struck at with the head of the club and must not be pushed, scraped or spooned.

Q.444
During a stroke play competition players are not allowed to discontinue play and take shelter for 10 minutes while a rainstorm blows over. True or False?
Answer: True. Rule 6-8.
Note: Unless the Committee suspends play, players may not discontinue play for bad weather, unless they believe that there is danger from lightning. Players are subject to a penalty of two strokes for unduly delaying play.

Q.445
In match play, a player may only practice on or near the 1st teeing ground before starting a round. True or False?
Answer: False. Rule 7-1a.
Note: In match play, a player may practice anywhere on the course on the match day, but in stroke play the player may only practice on or near the 1st teeing ground before the start of the competition.

Q.446
On the final hole of a match a player asks a spectator to run up to the hole and see how far his opponent's ball is from the hole and what kind of putt he has. The player loses the hole. True or False?
Answer: False. Decision 8-1/5.
Note: The player has not breached a Rule by asking about matters of public information.

Q.447
In a four-ball stroke play both partners must sign their score card. True or False?
Answer: False. Rule 31-3.
Note: Only one of the partners need sign and return the score card.

Q.448
Loose soil may be removed anywhere on the course other than in a hazard. True or False?
Answer: False. Definition of Loose Impediments.
Note: Sand and loose soil are loose impediments on the putting green but not elsewhere.

Q.449
During a stipulated round a player is not permitted to make a practice swing using any device that has been designed as a training or swing aid, and does not conform to the requirements for a club. True or False?
Answer: True. Decision 14-3/10.
Note: The player may not use an artificial device to assist him in his play.

Q.450
Stakes defining a water hazard or lateral water hazard that interfere with a player's stance or swing may be moved by the player. True or False?
Answer: True. Definition of Obstructions.
Note: In accordance with Rule 24-1 a player may remove a movable obstruction anywhere on the course, irrespective of whether his ball lies in a water hazard or not.

Q.451
A player's ball is in a bunker, lying in one of a series of footprints that have obviously been made by a fox, which are often seen on the course. This is an abnormal ground condition from which he may take free relief. True or False?
Answer: False. Decision 25/19.5.
Note: A footprint is an irregularity of surface from which there is no free relief.

Q.452
On the 14th hole Katelyn's tee shot ricocheted off several trees and came to rest behind a tee-marker on the teeing ground of the 16th hole. Katelyn is not permitted to move the tee-marker before making her next stroke. True or False?
Answer: False. Decision 11-2/1.
Note: Tee-markers are deemed to be fixed when playing the first stroke with any ball from the teeing ground, but are movable obstructions thereafter.

Q.453
A player may not play a provisional ball if it is virtually certain that his ball is in a water or lateral water hazard. True or False?
Answer: True. Rule 27-2.
Note: If a player does play a provisional ball for a ball that is virtually certain to be in a water hazard the second ball is the one in play since it cannot be a provisional ball under the Rules.

Q.454
In a four-ball competition a player's partner may not stand directly behind him when he is making a stroke from anywhere on the course. True or False?
Answer: True. Rule 14-2b.
Note: When making a stroke, a player must not allow his caddie, playing partner or his partner's caddie to position themselves on or close to, an extension of the line of play or the line of putt behind the ball.

Q.455
A player does not have to mark where her ball lies before taking relief from casual water or other abnormal ground condition. True or False?
Answer: True. Rule 25-1b.
Note: The position of a ball need only be marked when it is lifted under a Rule that requires it to be replaced (e.g. Rule 16-1b or 20-1). A ball to be dropped or placed in any other position, such as when taking relief from an immovable obstruction, an abnormal ground condition or an unplayable lie, does not have to be marked. But it is good practice to do so!

Q.456
If a ball at rest is moved by a spectator the player shall incur no penalty and the ball shall be played from its new position. True or False?
Answer: False. There is no penalty but the ball must be replaced. Rule 18-1.
Note: If a ball at rest is moved by an outside agency, there is no penalty and the ball must be replaced.

Q.457
If leaves are knocked down during a practice swing on the area of the intended swing there is always a two strokes penalty. True or False?
Answer: False. Decision 13-2/0.5 (New).
Note: There is only a penalty if the area of the intended swing is improved so that it creates a potential advantage for the player in their play. When several leaves are knocked down from a tree with a practice swing, but there are still so many leaves or branches remaining that the area of intended swing has not been materially affected, it is unlikely that the player has received any potential advantage. However, it is feasible that a player may accidentally knock down a single leaf from a tree with a practice swing and because it was one of very few leaves that might either interfere with their swing, or fall and thereby distract them, the area of intended swing has been materially affected.

Q.458
The player is responsible for entering his points score in a Stableford competition. True or False?
Answer: False. Rule 33-5.
Note: In Stableford competitions, the Committee is responsible for applying the handicap recorded on the score card to determine the points scored for each hole and the total score.

Q.459
In stroke play, Al's tee shot strikes a tree and rebounds back onto the same tee box, but outside of the teeing ground. With his foot Al presses down some raised turf behind his ball before he plays. There is no penalty. True or False?
Answer: False. There is a penalty of two strokes. Rule 13-2.
Note: A player must not improve the position or lie of his ball. The exception that allows the elimination of irregularities of surface within the teeing ground does not apply to anywhere else on the tee box.

Q.460
A player is permitted to place a stick or a stone against her ball to prevent it from moving as she moves other loose impediments close to the ball. True or False?
Answer: False. Decision 18-2a/32.
Note: The player would incur a penalty of one stroke for purposely touching her ball in play even though she had not physically touched her ball.

Q.461
A player may have one person carrying his clubs and another person giving him advice on his play at the same time. True or False?
Answer: False. Rule 6-4.
Note: A player is limited to only one caddie at any one time.

Q.462
In stroke play, a player may not move aside a large weed growing next to his ball. True or False?
Answer: True. Rule 13-2.
Note: A player must not improve his lie, area of intended stance or swing or line of play by moving, bending or breaking anything growing or fixed.

Q.463
Wesley is playing a match in monsoon conditions and the worn grips of his clubs become so slippery that he cannot hold them during his swing. He is entitled to replace a club as it is obviously unfit for play, providing he does not unduly delay play. True or False?
Answer: False. Decision 4-3/5.
Note: A club is unfit for play if it is substantially damaged, but not just because the grip becomes slippery.

Q.464
The player with the lowest handicap always has the honour on the 1st tee. True or False?
Answer: False. Rule 10-1a and 10-2a.
Note: The honour at the 1st teeing ground is determined by the order of the draw. In the absence of a draw, the honour should be decided by lot.

Q.465
In match play, a player must require his opponent to cancel a stroke if he plays when it was not his turn to play. True or False?
Answer: False. Rule 10-1c.
Note: The player has the option to require his opponent's stroke to be cancelled or to let his stroke stand.

Q.466
In a four-ball or foursome competition a player may ask advice from his partner's caddie. True or False?
Answer: True. Rule 8-1b.
Note: A player may ask for advice from his partner, his caddie or his partner's caddie.

Q.467
A player may remove a dead crab from a bunker, but not a live one. True or False?
Answer: False. Decision 23-6.
Note: A dead crab is a loose impediment and cannot therefore be removed from a hazard. A live crab is an outside agency and the player can encourage it to crawl out of the hazard.

Q.468
Earth piles made by a burrowing animal are loose impediments. True or False?
Answer: False. Definition of Abnormal Ground Conditions.
Note: A hole, cast or runway on the course made by a burrowing animal is an abnormal ground condition.

Q.469
A player may test the condition of a bunker located 10 yards away from the bunker that his ball is lying in. True or False?
Answer: False. Rule 13-4a.
Note: A player may not test the condition of the hazard his ball lies in or any similar hazard.

Q.470
On any day of a match play competition, a player may practice on the competition course before her round. True or False?
Answer: True. Rule 7-1a.
Note: However, in stroke play the competitors must not practice on the competition course before their round on the day of the competition, although practice putting or chipping on or near the 1st teeing ground before starting a round or play-off, is permitted.

Q.471
In stroke play, if a player is doubtful of his rights or the correct procedure to follow during play of a hole, he should agree the facts of the situation with his fellow competitors, continue to play his ball as they think best and report to the Committee before signing his card. True or False?
Answer: False. Rule 3-3a.
Note: In stroke play competitions the procedure is that the player must announce to his fellow competitors that he is going to complete the hole with two balls and specify which ball he wishes to count if the Rules permit. When he has finished his round he must report the facts of the situation to the Committee before returning his score card, otherwise he is disqualified.

Q.472
There is a dandelion growing on the teeing ground, immediately behind where a player wishes to tee her ball. She is permitted to pull it out without penalty. True or False?
Answer: True. Decision 13-2/3.
Note: A player is permitted to create or eliminate irregularities of surface within the teeing ground.

Q.473
Rub of the green is when a player has a bad break, such as his ball settling in another player's divot or hitting course furniture and deflecting away from the hole. True or False?
Answer: False. Definition of Rub of the Green.
Note: A rub of the green occurs when a ball in motion is accidentally deflected or stopped by any outside agency.

Q.474
The line of putt is the line which the player wishes his ball to take after a stroke with his putter. True or False?
Answer: False. Definition of Line of Putt.
Note: The line of putt includes a reasonable distance on either side of the intended line.

Q.475
A ball is outside the teeing ground when any part of it lies outside the teeing ground. True or False?
Answer: False. Definition of Teeing Ground.
Note: A ball is outside the teeing ground when all of it lies outside the teeing ground.

Q.476
Frost is a loose impediment, which may be removed without penalty. True or False?
Answer: False. Definition of Loose Impediments.
Note: Dew and frost are not loose impediments.

Q.477
If a ball is lodged in a tree overhanging a water hazard the ball is in the water hazard. True or False?
Answer: True. Definition of Water Hazard.
Note: The margin of a water hazard extends vertically upwards and downwards.

Q.478
In match play, if a player is entitled to five strokes over his opponent, the opponent always receives them on stroke indexes 1-5. True or False?
Answer: False. Rule 33-4.
Note: The Committee must publish a table indicating the order of holes at which handicap

strokes are to be given or received. In many cases this will be different from the stroke indexes on the score card so that the strokes are more evenly spread over the 18 holes.

Q.479
In the Rules, the teeing ground is the whole area or areas, prepared by the greenkeeper for commencing the play of holes and is commonly referred to as the tee box. True or False?
Answer: False. Definition of Teeing Ground.
Note: The teeing ground is a rectangular area two club-lengths in depth, the front and the sides of which are defined by the outside limits of two tee-markers.

Q.480
If his caddie breaks a Rule at any time during a round the player incurs the applicable penalty. True or False?
Answer: True. Rule 6-1.
Note: Like the player, the caddie is responsible for knowing the Rules.

Q.481
A player may play a ball lying through the green with his stance on a putting green other than that of the hole being played. True or False?
Answer: True. Rule 25-3a.
Note: Interference to a player's stance or the area of his intended swing is not, of itself, interference under this Rule.

Open Answer

Q.482
When is a player's ball deemed to have moved?
Answer: When the ball leaves its position and comes to rest in any other place. Definition of Move or Moved.
Note: If a ball moves from its spot but returns to the same spot it is not deemed to have moved under the Rules.

Q.483
Sophie's ball lies on grass on the lip of a bunker, but she has to take her stance in the bunker. Without thinking she grounds her club lightly in the sand as she addresses her ball. What is the ruling?
Answer: Sophie has not incurred any penalty. Decision 13-4/1.
Note: You are permitted to ground your club in a hazard if your ball lies outside the hazard.

Q.484
In stroke play, Silu marks and lifts his ball from the putting green and puts it in his pocket. He then takes a different ball from his pocket, putts out and plays from the next teeing ground. What is the ruling?
Answer: Silu is penalised two strokes. Decision 15-2/3.
Note: Silu substituted a ball when not entitled to do so.

Q.485
During match play, Terry fails to get his ball out of a pot bunker and swings his club into the sand in anger. As his ball had landed several yards away he does not affect his new lie in the bunker with this action. What is the ruling?
Answer: Terry incurs the penalty of loss of hole. Decision 13-4/35.
Note: A player is not permitted to touch the ground in the bunker with his hand or club when he has to make his next stroke out of the same bunker.

Q.486
At the completion of a competitive round, Noel reviews, signs and gives his score card to a member of the Committee. As he enters the locker room he realises that his marker had entered a five on the long, par 4 16th when, in fact, he had a par. May he retrieve his card and make the correction?
Answer: No. Rule 6-6c.
Note: This one has caused a lot of heartache over the years. Noel may not retrieve the card and make the correction. No alteration to the score card may be made after it has been returned to the scoring area designated by the Committee. This may be in a tent, a trailer, the golf shop, by the scoreboard, a box in the locker room, etc.

Q.487
A player's ball last crosses the margin of a lateral water hazard at the side of a putting green, but it is impossible to drop a ball within two club-lengths of the point where the ball last crossed the hazard margin without dropping it nearer to the hole. What is the procedure in such a case?
Answer: The player must take one of the other options provided in Rule 26-1. Decision 26-1/18.
Note: If the player cannot play the ball from within the water hazard his only options are to play a ball as nearly as possible at the spot from which the original ball was last played or drop a ball behind the water hazard, keeping the point at which the original ball last crossed the margin of the water hazard directly between the hole and the spot on which the ball is dropped, with no limit to how far behind the water hazard the ball may be dropped.

Q.488
A ball played by a player in the following group just misses Michael. Without thinking he angrily hits the ball back towards the group. Has Michael played a practice stroke or a wrong ball?
Answer: No. Decision 1-4/4.
Note: However, in equity, Michael should incur the general penalty of loss of hole in match play or two strokes in stroke play.

Q.489
Stuart hits his ball onto a road that is covered with gravel. He chooses to play his ball off the road, rather than take relief from it as an obstruction. Is Stuart permitted within the Rules to remove gravel that otherwise might interfere with his stroke?
Answer: Yes. Gravel is a loose impediment and may be removed. Decision 23/14.
Note: The same principle applies to roads or paths constructed with stone, crushed shell, wood chips or the like.

Q.490
In stroke play, a player attaches a device to his golf cart for the purpose of measuring the distance of shots. What is the penalty?
Answer: Disqualification. Rule 14-3b.
Note: However, the Committee may make a Local Rule allowing players to use devices that measure or gauge distance only.

Q.491
Andy and Robert are playing a match on a windy day. As they approach the elevated green, where Andy's ball is at rest, a gust of wind blows it away down a slope and into the rough. Andy says that his ball was moved by an outside agency and wants to replace it at the spot where it was at rest on the green. Is he correct?
Answer: No. Andy must play the ball from where the wind blew it to. Definition of Outside Agency.
Note: Neither wind nor water is an outside agency.

Q.492
While waiting for the green to clear on the 4th hole, Simon fills some divots on the teeing ground with sand provided for that purpose. He then takes his stance on the area that he has just repaired. What is the ruling?
Answer: There is no penalty. Rule 13-2.
Note: A player is specifically permitted to create or eliminate irregularities of surface within the teeing ground of the hole being played.

Q.493
Avril forgets to bring a small ball-marker onto the 1st putting green. She marks the position of her ball with a daisy that she picks from an area of rough at the side of the green. Does Avril incur a penalty?
Answer: No. Decision 20-1/16.
Note: The Note to Rule 20-1 recommends that the position of a ball to be lifted should be marked by placing a ball-marker, a small coin or other similar object immediately behind the ball. However, there is no penalty for failing to act in accordance with this note, providing the position of the ball is physically marked and not with reference to something like a blemish on the putting green.

Q.494
On a par 3, Mike hits his tee shot into thick heather. Believing that his ball may be lost, he announces that he is going to play a provisional ball and plays a great shot to within inches of the hole. He says that he wants his provisional ball to count but his opponent, Viv,

searches in the heather and quickly finds the original ball. How must Mike proceed?
Answer: Since Viv has found Mike's original ball, it is neither lost nor out of bounds and so the provisional ball is no longer in play and Mike must play his original ball from under the heather. Rule 27-2.
Note: If Mike had been able to get to his provisional ball and putt it before Viv found the original ball, the provisional ball would then have been in play. Because they are competing in a match, Viv can still require Mike to replace the provisional ball where it has come to rest from the tee shot, as he had played out of turn, but by taking the putt Mike had put that provisional ball in play.

Q.495
A player's ball is lodged behind a tree. He declares it unplayable and exchanges it for a different ball, which he then drops according to the Rules. What is the penalty?
Answer: There is a penalty of one stroke. Rule 28.
Note: Under this Rule there is no additional penalty for not playing the original ball as the three options under penalty of one stroke permit continuing the hole with a ball (and not the ball).

Q.496
In match play, a player accidentally touches his ball with his putter as he prepares to putt and the ball moves a fraction sideways. What is the penalty?
Answer: There is a penalty of one stroke. Rule 18-2.
Note: If the ball leaves its position and comes to rest in any other place then the player is penalised one stroke and the ball must be replaced.

Q.497
Steve's ball strikes a rock and bounces farther away from the hole than the spot from where he played his shot. He finds his ball at rest in a large bush. May Steve declare it unplayable and invoke the stroke and distance option under Rule 28, thereby dropping his ball nearer to the hole than where he found it?
Answer: Yes. Decision 28/8.
Note: In this case the option of playing a ball as nearly as possible at the spot from which the original ball was last played means that it will be dropped nearer the hole.

Q.498
Is there a Rule of Golf that permits taking line of play relief from a sprinkler at the side of the green?
Answer: No, but there is a specimen Local Rule should the Committee wish to introduce it. Appendix I, Part B, 6.

Q.499
After taking proper relief under the Rules from an artificial road the player finds that a bench cemented into the ground interferes with his swing. What is the procedure?
Answer: The player is entitled to take the appropriate relief from the second obstruction. Decision 24-2b/9.
Note: There is no limit as to how many times a player can take appropriate relief under the Rules.

Q.500
Tiger begins his downswing with the intention of striking the ball but is distracted by a noise behind him. He is unable to stop his club before it reaches the ball, but he is able to swing intentionally over the top of the ball. Does he incur a penalty?
Answer: No. Decision 14/1.5.
Note: As Tiger checked his downswing voluntarily during the downswing, thereby missing

the ball, there was no intent to strike the ball and he is not considered to have made a stroke.

Q.501
May a player request his caddie to stand in a position that shields his ball from bright sunlight while he makes his stroke?
Answer: No. Rule 14-2a.
Note: A player must not make a stroke while accepting physical assistance or protection from the elements.

Q.502
As she approaches her ball on the apron of the putting green, Ella sees that there are blades of grass stuck to her ball. She carefully peels them off one-by-one, without touching or moving her ball. Do the Rules permit Ella to remove grass from her ball in play?
Answer: No. Decision 21/2 and Definition of Loose Impediments.
Note: Anything adhering to a ball is not a loose impediment. Ella incurs a penalty of one stroke in either match play or stroke play.

Q.503
Pino plays a blind shot over trees towards the putting green. He is then disappointed to find his ball in a greenside bunker and plays out the hole from there. During play of the next hole players on an adjoining hole say that they had seen a young boy run onto the green, pick up Pino's ball and throw it into the bunker. What penalty has Pino incurred?
Answer: Pino has not incurred any penalty. Decision 18-1/3.
Note: It would be inequitable to penalise Pino for playing from the wrong place when he was not aware that his ball had been moved by an outside agency. The score with the moved ball stands.

Q.504
Garvin's ball lands some way off the fairway in a pile of grass cuttings that had been there for some time. May he take relief from the pile by claiming that it is ground under repair?
Answer: No. Definition of Ground Under Repair.
Note: Grass cuttings on the course that have been piled and abandoned are not ground under repair unless so marked.

Q.505
Tatiana's ball is lying on the downslope of a bunker. As she starts her backswing her club lightly brushes the sand. What is the ruling?
Answer: Tatiana incurs a penalty of loss of hole in match play or two strokes in stroke play. Decision 13-4/31.
Note: Tatiana is in breach of Rule 13-4b when she grounds her club in the bunker before making her stroke. A stroke commences on the forward movement of the club after the backswing.

Q.506
Mia witnesses a Rules breach by Lauren, her opponent in match play, but says nothing. Mia loses that hole and subsequently the match by one hole. Mia then informs the Committee of the Rules breach that she has witnessed and claims the match. How should the Committee decide?
Answer: The Committee must reject Mia's claim. Rule 2-5.
Note: In match play, if a doubt or dispute arises between the players, a player may make a claim. The claim must be made before any player in the match plays from the next teeing ground. Once the result of the match has been officially announced, a later claim may not be considered by the Committee, unless it is satisfied that the opponent knew that she was

giving wrong information. Also, note that only in match play may a player disregard a breach of Rules by her opponent and then only if there is no agreement between the players.

Q.507
In which form of play must a player not test the surface of any putting green on the course before a round on the day of the competition?
Answer: Stroke play. Rule 7-1b.
Note: However, testing the surface of any putting green on the course before a round on the day of the competition is permitted in match play.

Q.508
Joy takes her stance for a short putt but decides not to ground her putter as there is a strong breeze. The ball begins to roll away from the hole without her touching it. Has she incurred a penalty?
Answer: Joy has not incurred a penalty as she has not addressed her ball. Definition of Address.
Note: Outside of a hazard a player has addressed the ball when she has grounded her club immediately in front of or immediately behind her ball, whether or not she has taken her stance.

Q.509
May a player change balls between holes so that he is playing a soft ball on short holes and a hard ball on long holes?
Answer: Yes, providing the player only plays balls that conform to the requirements specified in Appendix III. Rule 5-1.
Note: However, there may be a Rule of Competition requiring the player to play a ball that is named on the current List of Conforming Golf Balls issued by the USGA and R&A.

Q.510
In stroke play, a player's ball lies in a bunker. While entering the bunker, he accidentally kicks a large stone into it. Before taking his stance he removes the stone, which does not affect the position of the ball or his line of play. Does the player incur a penalty?
Answer: Yes. The player incurs a penalty of two strokes. Decision 13-4/14.
Note: A stone is a loose impediment and may not be removed when both the ball and the loose impediment lie in the same bunker.

Q.511
After a wayward stroke a ball hits a boundary wall and breaks into pieces, one of which lands over the wall. How should the player proceed?
Answer: The stroke is cancelled and the player must play a ball, without penalty, as nearly as possible at the spot from which the original ball was played. Rule 5-3.
Note: As the ball broke into pieces as a result of a stroke it may be replaced without penalty.

Q.512
Amanda's ball comes to rest against a rake that prevents it from entering a bunker. She lifts the ball, removes the rake, and replaces the ball where it had come to rest. Has Amanda breached any Rules?
Answer: Yes. Amanda is penalised one stroke for moving her ball in play. Rule 18-2.
Note: Amanda should have carefully removed the rake and if her ball moved while doing so she could then have replaced it, without penalty (Rule 24-1a). There is no additional penalty for her lifting her ball without marking it.

Q.513
Marissa's ball lies deep in the rough. She announces to her marker that she is going to identify her ball, and then touches her ball and rotates it, without moving it from its spot. By

so doing she is able to confirm that the ball is indeed her ball. What is the ruling?
Answer: Marissa incurs a penalty of one stroke for not marking her ball before touching it. Decision 12-2/2.
Note: Before touching her ball in play, Marissa must announce her intention to her opponent or fellow competitor and then mark the position of her ball.

Q.514
Sami's approach shot hooks towards an area of trees. As the ball might be lost outside a water hazard, he announces to his fellow competitors that he intends to play a provisional ball. What is the order of play for Sami's provisional ball?
Answer: Except when playing a provisional ball from the teeing ground, the order of play for a provisional ball is for the player playing the provisional ball to do so immediately, before his fellow competitors make their next strokes. Decision 10-4.

Q.515
In match play, Sheba's ball lies in long grass in a water hazard. As she takes a practice swing in the water hazard, without grounding her club, she bends long grass growing behind her ball in the process. What is the penalty?
Answer: There is no penalty. Decision 13-4/4.
Note: However, Sheba has to be careful that in moving grass with her club during her practice swing she is not improving her area of intended swing by flattening or breaking the grass.

Q.516
What is the penalty for a player who, during a stipulated round, gives advice to a fellow competitor on how to grip her club?
Answer: A penalty of two strokes. Decision 8-1/13.
Note: Advice is any suggestion that could influence a player in determining her play, the choice of club or the method of making a stroke.

Q.517
Just as Cormac is starting the forward movement of his stroke on the teeing ground his fellow competitor, Kent, accidentally drops a ball, which rolls within a few inches of Cormac's teed ball. The distraction of seeing the moving ball causes Cormac to top his tee shot. In equity should Cormac be allowed to replay his stroke?
Answer: No. Decision 1-4/1.
Note: Players have to accept that there may be distractions during a round of golf.

Q.518
Gerard's ball lies behind a tree. Rather than taking relief under penalty of one stroke he attempts to play the ball, missing it completely. In his frustration he hits his club against the tree, bending the shaft to a 30° angle. Do the Rules allow him to repair it himself or have it repaired during the round?
Answer: No. Rule 4-3b.
Note: If, during a stipulated round, a player's club is damaged other than in the normal course of play, rendering it non-conforming or changing its playing characteristics, the club must not subsequently be used or replaced during the round.

Q.519
In making a short putt Eddie stands across an extension of his line of putt behind the ball so as to avoid standing on his playing partner's line of putt. Has Eddie incurred a penalty?
Answer: No. Exception to Rule 16-1e.
Note: There is no penalty if the stance is inadvertently taken on or astride the line of putt or is taken to avoid standing on another player's line of putt.

Q.520
When Chandler's ball comes to rest on a path, neither he nor his fellow competitors are sure whether he may take relief from it. Chandler says that he will play two balls for the remainder of the hole, dropping one ball at the nearest point of relief and playing the original ball as it lies. Is he permitted to play two balls out on the same hole?
Answer: Chandler may and should play two balls in this situation. Rule 3-3a.
Note: In stroke play, if a competitor is doubtful of his rights or the correct procedure to follow during the play of a hole, he may, without penalty, complete the hole with two balls. He must announce this intention to his marker or a fellow competitor and decide which ball he wishes to count if the Rules permit. He must also report the facts of the situation to the Committee before returning his score card or he will be disqualified.

Q.521
In stroke play, Sean's approach shot strikes an overhead power cable and drops onto the green within three feet of the hole. There is a Local Rule at the course he is playing stating that if a ball strikes an overhead power line, the player must replay the shot without penalty. However, Sean putts his ball from where it came to rest. What is the ruling?
Answer: By putting his ball Sean incurs the general penalty of two strokes for breaking a Local Rule. Rule 33-8.
Note: If Sean does not replay his stroke from where he played prior to his ball hitting the power cable before teeing off at the next hole, the Committee would be justified in disqualifying him for playing from the wrong place. There is a specimen Local Rule relating to temporary power lines in Appendix I, Part B, 7b 3.

Q.522
In taking relief from an immovable obstruction, Dion drops his ball in such a position that a second immovable obstruction is 10 feet in front of him directly in his intended line of flight. May he take relief again?
Answer: No. Dion must play his ball as it lies. Rule 24-2a.
Note: There is no relief from intervention by an immovable obstruction on the line of play, except on the putting green.

Q.523
How far may a ball roll, not nearer the hole, after it has been dropped according to the Rules, without a re-drop being necessary?
Answer: Up to two club-lengths from where it first struck the course. Rule 20-2c(vi).
Note: It is not two club-lengths from where the limit of the drop may have been marked, but from where the ball first hits the course.

Q.524
Meg has taken two clubs from her bag and walks over to her ball. She decides to play the 6-iron and carefully puts the other club down in front of her and the ball. Her fellow competitor, Jade, notices that the club on the ground is pointing in the exact line of play that Meg is setting herself up for. What action should Jade take?
Answer: Jade should inform Meg that if she leaves her club where it is it could be construed that she has left it there to indicate her line of play, which is against the Rules. Rule 8-2a.
Note: Jade has a duty to all the other players in the stroke play competition to ensure that her fellow competitors comply with the Rules. Giving information on the Rules is not advice.

Q.525
On a wet, winter's day four players are on the 1st tee preparing themselves for a strokes competition. Perry says that because of the poor course conditions they should all place their balls within six inches when they are at rest on the fairways, Benjy says nothing, Elliot agrees with Perry and Roland says he will play the ball as it lies. Are any players guilty of a breach of a Rule?

Answer: By agreeing to waive a Rule of Golf Perry and Elliot face disqualification. Rule 1-3.
Note: Players must not agree to exclude the operation of any Rule or to waive any penalty incurred.

Q.526
In stroke play, Elton breaks the dead branch of a tree that is interfering with his intended area of swing. What is the penalty?
Answer: Elton incurs a penalty of two strokes. Rule 13-2.
Note: A player must not improve or allow to be improved, the area of his intended stance or swing.

Q.527
Siggy is marking Basil's card in a stroke play competition. He agrees the score on each hole with Basil, gives the card back to him, and then leaves in a hurry as he is late for another engagement. Basil realises that whilst Siggy has entered each gross score on his card he has not signed it. Basil writes Siggy's name in the marker's signature box and returns his card to the Committee. What is the ruling?
Answer: Basil is disqualified. Rule 6-6a.
Note: On completion of the round, the marker must sign the score card.

Q.528
In a Stableford competition, Nancy putts to about three feet from the hole and walks up to her ball with the intent of putting again. Helga, who has a putt from 15 feet on a similar line, objects, saying that it is her turn to putt. Nancy says that she is entitled to finish out the hole in these circumstances. Is she?
Answer: Yes, providing she has not lifted her ball and it is at rest in a place where Helga would require her to lift her ball before putting. Decision 10-2b/1.
Note: There is no penalty for putting out of turn in stroke play. Nancy's action is not in conflict with the intent of Rule 10-2b, and it may help to speed up play.

Q.529
In stroke play, Brook marks and lifts his ball from the putting green. He tosses the ball to his caddie for cleaning. The caddie is distracted and the ball rolls into a water hazard, where it cannot be retrieved. Brook takes another ball from his bag and plays out the hole. What is the ruling?
Answer: Brook incurs a penalty of two strokes. Decision 15-2/1.
Note: A ball that is lifted from the putting green may not be substituted unless it is agreed that it is unfit for play.

Q.530
On the morning of a semi-final match with their local rivals Hedge Row G C, three members of Trees Green G C play nine holes on the stipulated course. Should they be disqualified from playing for their team in the afternoon matches?
Answer: No. Rule 7-1a.
Note: On any day of a match play competition, players may practice on the competition course before a round. However, if it had been a stroke play competition they would be disqualified.

Q.531
Arleen plays a provisional ball from the teeing ground because she thinks that her original ball may be lost deep in a wood. A spectator helps her find her first ball, which is wedged in the roots of a large tree with no stroke possible. If Arleen declares her ball unplayable may she play her provisional ball?
Answer: No. Rule 27-2c.

Note: Having found her original ball, Arleen must pick up her provisional ball and choose one of the three options available for an unplayable ball. Rule 28.

Q.532
In a match between Arthur and King, Arthur putts out of turn. King claims that Arthur loses the hole for putting out of turn. Arthur protests but concedes the hole. Later, Arthur, having checked the Rule book, lodges a protest with the Committee. How should the Committee rule?
Answer: Arthur lost the hole when he conceded it. Decision 2-4/12.
Note: A concession may not be refused or withdrawn.

Q.533
Mark's short putt lips around the circumference of the hole and rolls away. Annoyed with himself Mark taps the ball into the hole while it is still moving. What is the ruling?
Answer: Mark incurs a penalty of two strokes but the putt stands. Rule 14-5.
Note: A player must not make a stroke at his ball while it is moving.

Q.534
In match play, to identify that a ball is his, a player rotates his ball on the fairway without moving it off its spot and without first marking its position. What is the penalty?
Answer: There is a penalty of one stroke.
Note: Before touching the ball to identify it the player must announce his intention to his opponent or fellow competitor and mark the position of the ball. The penalty is the same in both match play and stroke play.

Q.535
Keith searches for his ball in dense trees for a minute or two and then walks forward, intending to play his provisional ball, which is lying just short of the green. Just as he is addressing his provisional ball, and well within the five minutes allowed for search, a fellow competitor finds his original ball. What is the ruling?
Answer: Keith must proceed with his original ball. Decision 27-2b/6.
Note: The original ball is still in play as it was found within five minutes after search for it had begun and Keith had not played a stroke with his provisional ball from nearer the hole than where he believed his original ball to be lost.

Q.536
Cameron is assessing his pitch to the putting green when he notices a pitch-mark made by a fellow competitor's ball on the apron of the green in the vicinity of where he intends to land his pitch. May Cameron repair this damage made by a ball?
Answer: Cameron may only repair the ball damage off the putting green if it was made by another player's ball after his own ball had come to rest. In equity (Rule 1-4) if this is the case he may repair the pitch-mark without penalty. Decision 13-2/8.
Note: A player is entitled to the lie he had when his ball came to rest.

Q.537
After missing a short putt Mark throws his club in the air in frustration. Unfortunately, he doesn't catch it cleanly on the way down and it falls onto his ball, moving it away from the hole. What is the ruling?
Answer: Mark is penalised one stroke for moving his ball in play and must replace his ball. Rule 18-2.
Note: If equipment of the player or his partner, causes the ball to move, the player incurs a penalty of one stroke and the ball must be replaced.

Q.538
An amateur player wins a voucher as a prize for winning a competition. Is he permitted to exchange the voucher for cash?
Answer: No. Rules of Amateur Status 3-2c.

Q.539
On a blustery day, Mal addresses his ball on the putting green and as he prepares to make his stroke it is moved by the wind. What is the procedure?
Answer: Mal does not incur any penalty, as he did not cause his ball to move. He must play the ball from where it comes to rest, as wind is not an outside agency. Definition of Outside Agency and Rule 18-2.
Note: There is no penalty under Rule 18-2 as it was known or virtually certain that Mal did not cause his ball to move. (Revised January 2016).

Q.540
The stipulated round in a stroke play competition started at the 10th hole. Ashley returns a card with scores for the first nine holes recorded in the boxes for the second nine holes, and vice versa. Should Ashley be disqualified?
Answer: Yes. Decision 6-6d/3.
Note: Unless the scores on each of the nine holes were exactly the same as the other nine holes then some holes would have been marked with scores lower than were actually taken.

Q.541
Raoul's ball lies at rest against a bird's nest through the green. How should he continue?
Answer: Without penalty, Raoul may drop a ball within one club-length of and not nearer the hole than the nearest spot, not nearer the hole, that will allow him to make his stroke without damaging the nest. Decision 1-4/9.
Note: It is unreasonable to expect a player to play from such a situation and unfair to impose a penalty stroke.

Q.542
In match play, a player whose ball lies in a bunker touches grass which is growing in that bunker as he prepares to make a stroke at his ball. What is the penalty?
Answer: There is no penalty. Note to Rule 13-4.
Note: In a hazard, the player may touch, with a club or otherwise, any grass, bush, tree or other growing thing, but must not touch the ground of the hazard.

Q.543
In match play, how do players determine the order of play after their tee shots if their balls are equidistant from the hole?
Answer: By lot. Rule 10-1b.
Note: For example, players may agree to toss a coin to see who plays first.

Q.544
Without realising, Paco and a fellow competitor, Morris, play from the wrong tee-markers on the 5th hole. Paco plays his tee shot on the 6th and then a member of the following group catches up with them and informs them of their mistake. How do they proceed under the Rules?
Answer: As Paco has already started play of the 6th hole, it is too late for him to rectify his error and he is disqualified from the competition. Morris must return to the 5th teeing ground and play the hole again, incurring a penalty of two strokes for originally playing from outside the teeing ground. Rule 11-5.
Note: If the competitor makes a stroke from the next teeing ground without first correcting his mistake or, in the case of the last hole of the round, leaves the putting green without first declaring his intention to correct his mistake, he is disqualified.

Q.545
By agreement, Roy and Glynn discontinue their match after four holes due to worsening weather conditions. There is still over a week in which they may continue their match without delaying the competition. Should they be disqualified?
Answer: No. Exception to Rule 6-8a.
Note: Players discontinuing a match by agreement are not subject to disqualification, unless by so doing the competition is delayed.

Q.546
Prior to putting, a player discovers that in windy conditions the flagstick has made a slight indentation to the rim of the hole. May the player repair the hole without penalty before taking his putt?
Answer: No. The player must take his putt without repairing the hole. Decision 16-1a/6.
Note: If the player touches the hole in such circumstances he incurs a penalty of loss of hole in match play or two strokes in stroke play, for touching his line of putt. The only damage that a player is permitted to repair on the putting green is a ball mark or an old hole plug.

Q.547
Helen and Hilary are partners in a four-ball stroke play competition. Their balls lie very close together in a bunker. Hilary walks into the bunker and removes a large twig lying in the way of both their balls. Hilary incurs a penalty of two strokes but does Helen incur a penalty?
Answer: As Hilary's infringement, of removing a loose impediment from the bunker assists her partner Helen's play, Helen also incurs a penalty of two strokes. Decision 31-8/1.

Q.548
As Jeremy enters a bunker he slips and uses his sand wedge to stop himself falling. His club makes a deep score in the sand. Does Jeremy incur a penalty for grounding his club in the bunker?
Answer: No. Rule 13-4 Exception 1(a).
Note: Jeremy may ground his club to prevent himself from falling, providing that nothing is done that constitutes testing the condition of the hazard or improves the lie of his ball.

Q.549
Are steps which have been cut into the earth of a steep bank, but which have not been covered with any artificial material such as wooden planks or gravel, obstructions?
Answer: No. Decision 24-12.
Note: However, wooden steps, which have been constructed on a steep bank, are immovable obstructions.

Q.550
In stroke play, a player's ball lies between two creepers. In taking his stance he purposely treads on one of them so as to give himself a clearer path for his stroke. What is the ruling?
Answer: There is a penalty of two strokes. Rule 13-2.
Note: Treading on a creeper affecting the lie of a ball does not constitute fairly taking a stance.

Q.551
Cindy is preparing for her tee shot on the 1st hole of her match, early on a cold winter's morning. She bends down and with her gloved hand clears an area of frost around the area where she is going to tee her ball. Does this action incur a penalty?
Answer: No. Rule 13-2.
Note: A player does not incur a penalty in removing dew, frost or water from the teeing ground.

Q.552

There is casual water across the line of putt of a player whose ball is on the putting green. The nearest position affording complete relief, which is not nearer the hole or in a hazard, is off the green and in the rough. May the player find another point of relief on the putting green, not nearer the hole or must he place his ball in the rough?
Answer: He must place his ball at the nearest point of relief in the rough or play through the casual water from where his ball lies. Decision 25-1b/10.
Note: Because the player lifted his ball from the putting green he must place his ball in the rough, not drop it.

Q.553
What portion of a ball has to lie out of bounds for it to be considered out of bounds?
Answer: All of it. Definition of Out of Bounds.

Q.554
May a Committee make a Local Rule declaring a movable obstruction to be an immovable obstruction?
Answer: Yes. Definition of Obstructions.

Q.555
In a match, Duane, mistakenly thinking that he has won the hole, picks up the coin that he was using to mark his ball. What is the penalty?
Answer: Duane incurs a penalty of one stroke and must replace his ball. Decision 20-1/8.
Note: A ball that is in play must be marked before being lifted from the putting green. The player has to replace the ball at the spot where the marker was before it was lifted.

Q.556
Malik decides to take relief from a fixed ball washer. He finds the nearest point of relief, not nearer to the hole, and drops his ball according to the Rules. On hitting the ground the ball rolls down a slope to about 20 feet from where it first struck the course when dropped, but away from the hole. Does Malik have to drop the ball again?
Answer: Yes. Rule 20-2c.
Note: A ball that has been dropped must be re-dropped if it rolls and comes to rest more than two club-lengths from where it first struck a part of the course.

Q.557
When taking relief from an artificial path running laterally to the fairway is the nearest point of relief always in a different place for a left-handed player than it is for a right-handed player?
Answer: Yes, with the very occasional exception where they may be equidistant. Definition of Nearest Point of Relief.
Note: Decision 25-1b/2 includes useful diagrams to illustrate this point.

Q.558
How is casual water defined for the purpose of taking relief?
Answer: Casual water is any temporary accumulation of water on the course that is visible before or after the player takes his stance that is not in a water hazard.

Q.559
After a poor tee shot Sacha's ball comes to rest several yards from a storm shelter that is located between fairways. There is no way that she can play her next stroke towards the green as the shelter, an immovable obstruction, is immediately in her line of play. What are her options?
Answer: Sacha may either play her ball as it lies or declare her ball unplayable and take one of the three options for relief under penalty of one stroke. Rule 24-2a.
Note: Intervention on a line of play by an immovable obstruction is not interference within the Rules.

Q.560
As weather conditions become untenable the tournament Committee sounds a claxon horn, signifying the suspension of play, just after one of four players in a four-ball has struck her tee shot. All players in the group finish out the hole before heeding the suspension of play warning. Do the players incur any penalty?
Answer: No. Rule 6-8(b).
Note: If players have commenced play of a hole when play is suspended, they may either continue to play out that hole or discontinue play immediately, unless the Committee has established a Rule that calls for immediate cessation of play in potentially dangerous situations.

Q.561
In match play, what is the penalty for a player having two caddies at the same time, e.g. one carrying his clubs and another one giving him line of putt advice, for four holes?
Answer: A maximum deduction of two holes. Rule 6-4.
Note: At the conclusion of the hole at which the breach is discovered, the state of the match is adjusted by deducting one hole for each hole at which a breach occurred, with a maximum deduction of two holes.

Q.562
In stroke play, what is the penalty for practice putting on or near the 1st teeing ground before starting a round?
Answer: There is no penalty. Exception to Rule 7-1b.
Note: Practice putting or chipping on or near the 1st teeing ground before starting a round is permitted.

Q.563
In match play, after completing play of the 8th hole, Sarah incorrectly tells Jane, her opponent, that she has scored a six, whereas in fact, she has scored a seven. This results in the hole being halved. Several holes later Sarah realises her mistake. What is the ruling?
Answer: Sarah lost the 8th hole when she gave wrong information and the state of the match must be adjusted accordingly. Decision 9-2/9.
Note: Sarah loses the 8th hole notwithstanding the original outcome – won, lost or halved.

Q.564
Who is responsible for the addition of scores and the application of handicaps recorded on players' score cards?
Answer: The Committee. Rule 33-5.
Note: The Committee is responsible for the addition of scores and the application of handicaps recorded on stroke play score cards.

Q.565
Do the Rules permit a player to ground their club in front of the ball, on their line of putt, while they are going through their putting routine?
Answer: Yes. Rule 16-1a(ii). Definition of Address.
Note: The player may place their putter in front of the ball when addressing it, providing they do not press anything down. Once the player has grounded their club in front of the ball they have completed address.

Q.566
What is the penalty for slow play in a strokes competition?
Answer: The player incurs a penalty of two strokes for the first offence and disqualification for a subsequent offence. Rule 6-7.
Note: The player must play without undue delay and in accordance with any pace of play

guidelines that the Committee may establish. Between completion of a hole and playing from the next teeing ground, the player must not unduly delay play.

Q.567
Michelle's backswing was impeded by the overhanging branches of a tree that was rooted inside an area marked as ground under repair (GUR). Michelle informed her opponent, Mavis that she was going to take free relief away from the branches. Mavis objected saying that no relief was available as Michelle's ball was at rest outside of the white line that defined GUR. Who was right?
Answer: Michelle was right. Decision 25-1a/1 and Definition of Ground Under Repair.
Note: All ground and any grass, bush, tree or other growing thing within the ground under repair are part of the ground under repair.

Q.568
Mel's drive has probably come to rest in a water hazard as it cannot be found in the long grass in the area where he thought it landed. Mel wants to drop his ball behind the hazard and incur a penalty of one stroke. What is the ruling?
Answer: Because it is not known or virtually certain, that Mel's ball is in the water hazard it must be treated as a lost ball and the options for a ball lost in a water hazard do not apply. Rule 27-1c.
Note: Mel has to return to the teeing ground and play his drive again under penalty of stroke and distance. It will be his third stroke.

Q.569
During a match a player's ball is on the downslope of a bunker and he touches the sand with his club in preparation for his stroke. What is the penalty?
Answer: The player loses the hole. Rule 13-4b.
Note: There would have been a penalty of two strokes had this breach of Rule occurred during stroke play.

Q.570
In match play, Junior plays a ball that had rolled more than two club-lengths from where it first hit the course when he dropped it under the Rules. What is the penalty?
Answer: Junior loses the hole. Rule 20-7b.
Note: In match play, loss of hole is always the penalty for playing from the wrong place, whereas playing from the wrong place in stroke play incurs a minimum penalty of two strokes and may incur disqualification if the Committee decide that the player has gained a significant advantage by playing from the wrong place.

Q.571
In a stroke play competition Hank notices that his fellow competitor, Boris, has failed to rake the bunkers after he has played from them, doesn't repair his ball marks on the green, scuffs up the surface of the green with his metal spikes, plays his ball when the group in front are still in range and keeps talking when others are preparing for and playing their shots. Can Hank impose any penalty on Boris?
Answer: No. Only the Committee may decide whether Hank's behaviour warrants disqualification for serious breaches of etiquette. Rule 33.7.
Note: However, Hank should bring Boris's awful course behaviour to the attention of the Committee who should consider taking appropriate disciplinary action against him.

Q.572
Ant is marking Jos's score card. Initially, he puts Jos down for a six on the 5th hole but then realises he had a five. He scratches out the original score and puts the actual score taken in the column alongside and does not initial the change. At the end of the round both Jos and Ant sign the score card and return it to the Committee. What is the ruling?

Answer: The score card has been completed correctly. Decision 6-6a/6.
Note: There is nothing in the Rules specifying how alterations should be made on a score card.

Q.573
In match play, if the equipment of a player causes the player's ball to move, what is the penalty?
Answer: The player incurs a penalty of one stroke. Rule 18-2.
Note: The ball must be replaced at the spot that it was at rest when moved by the player's equipment.

Q.574
In a Stableford competition, Rom had scored only one point on each of the first three holes when it is pointed out to him that he has 15 clubs in his bag. He incurs a penalty of four strokes (Rule 4-4). How is this penalty applied to his score?
Answer: The Committee will deduct four points from the total points scored by Rom for his round. Note 1 to Rule 32-1b.
Note: Rom must report the facts to the Committee before returning his score card or he is disqualified.

Q.575
On a par 3, Murray plays a really bad tee shot, landing in a wooded area close to a boundary ditch. His opponent, Duke, is already safely on the green. In frustration Murray says, "Your hole Duke" as they leave the tee box. As they approach the green Murray sees his ball on the fringe of the green and realises that it must have taken a favourable bounce off a tree. Naturally, he would like to play out the hole. What are Duke's options?
Answer: Duke has no option. He won the hole when Murray made the concession. He may not decline the concession or he would be in violation of the Rules. Rule 2-4.
Note: A concession may not be declined or withdrawn.

Q.576
Marcia is pleased with her shot over the trees but as she approaches the putting green she cannot see her ball. After searching in the area around the green for five minutes she returns to where she last played her ball and puts another ball into play under stroke and distance penalty. A fellow competitor then discovers Marcia's original ball in the hole. What is the ruling?
Answer: Marcia's score with her original ball counts. Decision 1-1/2.
Note: The play of the hole had already been completed before Marcia put another ball in play.

Q.577
On the putting green Bjorn drops his ball, which he had just marked and lifted, and it strikes and moves his opponent's ball, which was at rest on the putting green. Does Bjorn incur a penalty?
Answer: Yes. Bjorn incurs a penalty of one stroke and his opponent must replace his ball. Decision 18/7.5.
Note: A ball that has been lifted and not put back into play is equipment. However, if Bjorn had been taking part in a stroke play competition there would have been no penalty.

Q.578
Cheryl's ball lies just in bounds but a movable white stake is in her area of intended swing. May she remove the stake?
Answer: No. Definition of Out of Bounds.
Note: White stakes identifying out of bounds are not obstructions and are deemed to be fixed. There is no relief from them.

Q.579
A ball lands on a paper bag in a bunker. Does the player have to play it as it lies as the ball is not touching the sand?
Answer: No. When a ball lies in or on an obstruction, the ball may be lifted and the obstruction removed. Rule 24-1b.
Note: In a hazard or through the green, the ball must be dropped as near as possible to the spot directly under the place where the ball lay, but not nearer the hole.

Q.580
Maureen's caddie is attending the flagstick while she takes a long putt from off the green. As Maureen putts her caddie is distracted and her ball strikes the flagstick before he can remove it. What is the ruling in a match play competition?
Answer: Maureen loses the hole. Rule 17-3.
Note: The player's ball must not strike the flagstick when it is attended, removed or held up.

Q.581
Before he starts his round Dusty asks another competitor, who has just finished his round, about the speed of the greens, the consistency of the sand in the bunkers, the direction of the wind and what clubs he used on the par 3s. Should Dusty be penalised?
Answer: No. Decision 8-1/18.
Note: The Rule on advice applies only during the play of a round.

Q.582
Mac hits his drive to the bottom of a steep incline. In playing his next, difficult stroke he hits his ball twice. He counts the stroke and adds a penalty stroke, so he was lying three. His fellow competitor, Baz, thinks that since the ball was hit twice, two strokes should be counted and a penalty stroke added, so Mac should be lying four. Who is right?
Answer: Mac is right. He must count the stroke and add one penalty stroke, making two strokes in all. Rule 14-4.

Q.583
Merv is playing with two fellow competitors who are unknown to him. He is putting out on the 2nd green when he sees his friend, Dai, teeing off with one other player on the 1st. Having obtained the permission of his two fellow competitors he finishes out the 2nd hole and waits to join Dai and his fellow competitor on the 3rd tee box. Has Merv incurred a penalty?
Answer: Yes. Merv should be disqualified. Rule 6-3b.
Note: In stroke play, the competitor must remain throughout the round in the group arranged by the Committee.

Q.584
After knocking down his tee shot, in frustration Tam swings his driver at a tee-marker and it comes out of the ground breaking in two pieces. What is the penalty?
Answer: There is no penalty. Decision 11-2/2d.
Note: This is obviously very poor etiquette, which is discouraged, but there is no penalty. The tee-marker should be replaced.

Q.585
Wayne was playing in an open strokes competition while on holiday in Australia. On the 16th hole his ball stopped just short of a lake. As he was approaching, a small crocodile emerged from the water and rested close to where his ball lay, inside the margin of the hazard. Is Wayne permitted to take relief without penalty with another ball?
Answer: Yes. Decision 1-4/10.
Note: When a ball comes to rest in a situation dangerous to the player he may take the option, without penalty, of dropping a ball within one club-length of and not nearer the hole

than the nearest spot that is not dangerous. In Wayne's case, where his ball was in a water hazard, it should be dropped, if possible, in the same hazard and, if not, in a similar nearby hazard.

Q.586
Mica is concentrating hard on the line of his putt as he seeks advice from a fellow competitor's caddie, whom he was mistaking for his own caddie. He realises his error and tells the caddie not to answer. What is the ruling?
Answer: No penalty is incurred. Decision 8-1/17.

Q.587
On a particularly rainy day Jaime's tee shot lands just outside of a bunker. However, he would have to stand in a puddle in the bunker in order to play his next shot. He opts to take relief from the casual water claiming that he is permitted to drop his ball within one club-length of the nearest point of relief that is not in the bunker. Fergus, a fellow competitor, says that the nearest point of relief is in the bunker so Jaime has to drop the ball within one club-length of that point. Who is right?
Answer: Jaime is right. Rule 25-1b.
Note: If the ball lies through the green the nearest point of relief for taking relief must not be in a hazard or on a putting green.

Q.588
François decides to take relief under the Rules from course furniture that is bolted down. If his ball is lying in the rough is he entitled to drop his ball on the fairway, providing he correctly drops it within one club-length of the nearest point of relief, not nearer the hole and it does not roll more than two club-lengths from where it first touches the ground?
Answer: Yes. There is no distinction in the Rules between fairway and rough. Decision 24-2b/8.
Note: Both fairway and rough are covered by the definition of Through the Green.

Multiple Choice

Q.589
Which of the following is not a loose impediment?
A) A spider.
B) Dew.
C) A small stone.
D) Animal dung.
Answer: B) Dew. Definition of Loose Impediments.
Note: Dew and frost are not loose impediments.

Q.590
In a match, Ralph holes out for a five. He then concedes his opponent, Bruce's two foot putt for a five, and a half on the hole. However, Bruce refuses Ralph's concession and then misses his short putt. What is the result of the hole?
A) Ralph wins the hole because Bruce was not permitted to putt after the hole had been conceded.
B) Ralph wins the hole because Bruce had not holed out after five strokes.
C) The hole is halved.
D) Bruce loses the next hole for taking a practice putt between holes.
Answer: C) The hole is halved. Rule 2-4.
Note: A concession may not be declined or withdrawn.

Q.591
In stroke play, Brynn marks his ball two putter head lengths from where it comes to rest on the putting green because it is on the line of putt of his fellow competitor, Seve. However, he forgets that he has done this when he comes to take his own putt and holes out from the wrong place. He is then reminded of how he had marked his ball to the side and he replaces his ball in the right place and holes out. What is the ruling?
A) The score with the ball played from the right place counts and Brynn must add a penalty of two strokes to his score.
B) The score with the ball played from the wrong place counts and Brynn must add a penalty of two strokes to his score.
C) The score with the ball played from the right place counts and there is no penalty.
D) The score with the ball played from the right place counts and Brynn must add a penalty of one stroke to his score.
Answer: B) The score with the ball played from the wrong place counts and Brynn must add a penalty of two strokes to his score. Decision 20-7c/1.
Note: Brynn incurs no penalty for having putted from the right place after holing out from a wrong place.

Q.592
In match play, Rachel's chip from off the green stops three inches short of the hole. She removes the flagstick, holding it in her left hand, while she putts the ball one-handed with her right. Joan, her playing partner, claims the hole saying that Rachel is not permitted to hold the flagstick while putting. What is the ruling?
A) There is no penalty.
B) Rachel incurs a penalty of one stroke.
C) Rachel incurs a penalty of two strokes.
D) Rachel loses the hole.
Answer: A) There is no penalty. Decision 17-1/5.
Note: Rachel may putt the ball while holding the flagstick, providing the ball does not strike the flagstick and she does not lean on it for assistance.

Q.593
Mary's ball lies in ground under repair through the green. She elects to take relief and drops her ball within one club-length of the nearest point of relief, not nearer the hole. The ball remains outside the ground under repair area but it rolls to a position where Mary would have to stand in the ground under repair to play her next stroke. Should Mary re-drop the ball?
A) No, Mary may play her ball as it lies even though she is standing in the GUR.
B) No, Mary must play her ball as it lies but take a stance whereby she is not standing in the GUR.
C) No, Mary must place the ball in a position whereby she is not standing in the GUR.
D) Yes, Mary must re-drop the ball.
Answer: D) Yes, Mary must re-drop the ball. Decision 20-2c/0.5.
Note: The ball has rolled and come to rest in a position where there is still interference by the condition from which relief is being taken, so the drop must be made again.

Q.594
Under what circumstances is a player prohibited from cleaning their ball when they lift it in play?
A) To determine if it is unfit for play.
B) Beyond what is necessary for identification.
C) Because it is assisting or interfering with play.
D) All of the above.
Answer: D) All of the above. Rule 21.
Note: It is not permitted to clean a ball that has been lifted without penalty under the above circumstances. Rules 5-3, 12-2 and 22.

Q.595
In stroke play, Terry plays a good approach shot to an elevated putting green. On arriving at the green, he holes a ball he thinks is his but as he bends down to pick this ball out of the hole he finds his original ball already there. What is the ruling?
A) Terry has played a wrong ball and is penalised two strokes on the hole being played.
B) Terry has played a wrong ball and is penalised two strokes on the next hole.
C) Terry had completed play of the hole when the original ball was holed out and there is no penalty for subsequently playing a wrong ball.
D) Terry must add a penalty of one stroke to his score with the original ball.
Answer: C) Terry had completed play of the hole when the original ball was holed out and there is no penalty for subsequently playing a wrong ball. Decision 1-1/4.
Note: Since the play of the hole was completed when the original ball was holed, the player was not in breach of Rule 15-3 for subsequently playing a wrong ball.

Q.596
While playing a match Hilary drops her ball under a Rule. In determining whether it has rolled more than two club-lengths, she accidentally moves her ball with the club that she is using for the measuring process. What is the ruling?
A) There is no penalty and Hilary must replace her ball.
B) Hilary incurs a penalty of one stroke and must play the ball from where it comes to rest.
C) Hilary incurs a penalty of one stroke and must replace her ball.
D) Hilary loses the hole.
Answer: A) There is no penalty and Hilary must replace her ball. Rule 18-6.
Note: If a ball or ball-marker is moved during measuring, the ball or ball-marker must be replaced.

Q.597
Mark, who is putting from off the putting green, asks his fellow competitor, Adam, not to lift his ball as it could assist him when he takes his putt. Adam acknowledges the request and

leaves the ball. What is the ruling?
A) There is no penalty.
B) Mark is penalised two strokes.
C) Mark and Adam are both penalised two strokes.
D) Mark and Adam are both disqualified.
Answer: D) Mark and Adam are both disqualified. Decision 22/6.
Note: In stroke play, if the Committee determines that competitors have agreed not to lift a ball that might assist any competitor, they are disqualified.

Q.598
In a stroke play competition, Kate and Carol both hit their tee shots into a shallow water hazard. Kate asks her caddie to retrieve both balls and, in error, the balls are exchanged. Kate and Carol both take relief from the water hazard under penalty of one stroke and continue to play out the hole with balls exchanged. What is the ruling?
A) There is no penalty.
B) Kate incurs a penalty of two strokes as it was her caddie who caused the incorrect substitution.
C) Both Kate and Carol incur a penalty of two strokes for playing a wrong ball.
D) Both Kate and Carol are disqualified.
Answer: A) There is no penalty. Decision 15-1/4.
Note: Rule 26-1b authorises the player to drop a ball (not the ball). Accordingly, the substitution of another ball is permissible and so neither player has incurred a penalty.

Q.599
In four-ball stroke play, Jack picks up while his partner, Oliver, completes the hole for a five. The marker attributes the five to Jack and records no score for Oliver. The better-ball score is correct. The score card is signed and returned to the Committee. What is the ruling?
A) The Committee should accept without penalty their score card, since the better-ball score of the side was correct.
B) The Committee should correct the error by entering the correct score into the proper box on the score card.
C) The Committee may accept the score card if Jack, Oliver and the marker are available to re-sign the card before the competition closes.
D) The Committee should disqualify Jack and Oliver, since the wrong score was recorded for Jack who did not finish the hole.
Answer: D) The Committee should disqualify Jack and Oliver, since the wrong score was recorded for Jack who did not finish the hole. Rules 31-7a and 6-6d.
Note: Jack and Oliver are responsible for the correctness of their scores recorded for each hole on the score card. As they returned a wrong score for Jack, who did not finish the hole, they are disqualified. A side is disqualified from the competition if either partner incurs a penalty of disqualification.

Q.600
In stroke play, Alice breaks a young tree, situated out of bounds, which interferes with her swing. What is the ruling?
A) There is no penalty.
B) Alice incurs a penalty of one stroke.
C) Alice incurs a penalty of two strokes.
D) Alice is disqualified.
Answer: C) Alice incurs a penalty of two strokes. Decision 13-2/19.
Note: A player must not improve the area of her intended stance or swing, by moving, bending or breaking anything growing or fixed. It does not matter that the tree was situated out of bounds.

Q.601
Which is correct regarding a player testing the surface of the putting green?
A) He may not test the putting green for wetness of the grass by placing the palm of his hand on the putting green behind his line of putt.
B) He does not incur a penalty if his caddie tests the surface of the putting green by roughening the grass.
C) He may clean his ball by rubbing it on the putting green, providing the act is not for the purpose of testing the surface of the putting green.
D) After marking his ball he may not roll it across the putting green by hitting it with the back of his putter.
Answer: C) He may clean his ball by rubbing it on the putting green, providing the act is not for the purpose of testing the surface of the putting green. Decision 16-1d/5.
Note: Although a player does not incur a penalty for cleaning their ball by rubbing it on the putting green, providing they do not do so to test the surface, it is a bad practice, which should be avoided.

Q.602
On the fairway, Gary carefully tries to remove a twig that is touching his ball but his hand is shaky and the ball does move off its spot. What is the ruling?
A) The ball must be played as it lies without penalty.
B) The ball must be played as it lies and Gary incurs a penalty of one stroke.
C) The ball must be replaced without penalty.
D) The ball must be replaced and Gary incurs a penalty of one stroke.
Answer: D) The ball must be replaced and Gary incurs a penalty of one stroke. Rule 18-2.
Note: If a player, his partner or either of their caddies causes a ball in play to move, except as permitted by a Rule, they incur a penalty of one stroke and the ball must be replaced.

Q.603
In match play, Bing decides to leave his bag and trolley behind the green that he has just played as he walks back to the next tee. He soon regrets this decision as his sliced tee shot bounces off the wheels of his trolley and into the rough. What is the ruling?
A) There is no penalty.
B) Bing incurs a penalty of one stroke.
C) Bing incurs a two strokes penalty.
D) Bing loses the hole.
Answer: B) Bing incurs a penalty of one stroke. Rule 19-2.
Note: If a player's ball is accidentally deflected or stopped by himself, his partner or either of their caddies or equipment, he incurs a penalty of one stroke.

Q.604
Christian is about to chip his ball from some way off the green when he notices two large indentations on the putting green on his line of play. On inspection, he sees that they are obviously pitch-marks caused by balls. He carefully repairs them both and then chips his ball up to the hole. His opponent, Pierrot, claims the hole saying that Christian may not repair anything on the putting green before playing his ball from off the putting green. What is the ruling?
A) There is no penalty.
B) Christian incurs a penalty of one stroke.
C) Christian loses the hole.
D) Pierrot loses the hole for making an incorrect claim.
Answer: A) There is no penalty. Rule 16-1c.
Note: A player may repair ball marks on the putting green before playing from anywhere on the course.

Q.605
Which of the following is not the equipment of a player?
A) A club cover.
B) A coin used to mark the ball on the putting green.
C) A motorised golf cart.
D) An open umbrella.
Answer: B) A coin used to mark the ball on the putting green. Definition of Equipment.
Note: The definition of equipment excludes any small object, such as a coin or a tee, when used to mark the position of a ball or the extent of an area in which a ball is to be dropped.

Q.606
In a handicap foursome stroke play competition, partners Eve and Eleanor correctly calculate their combined handicap allowance and record it on their score card, rather than their individual handicaps. What is the ruling?
A) There is no penalty.
B) Eve and Eleanor are disqualified.
C) Eve and Eleanor incur a penalty of one stroke.
D) Eve and Eleanor incur a penalty of two strokes.
Answer: B) Eve and Eleanor are disqualified. Decision 6-2b/4.
Note: In all stroke play competitions, it is the responsibility of the competitors to ensure that their individual handicaps are recorded on their score card before returning it to the Committee.

Q.607
In stroke play, Tyler's ball lies next to a large boulder. He asks Phil, his fellow competitor, to help him remove it and between them they move it sufficiently to give Tyler a clear shot to the green. What is the ruling?
A) There is no penalty.
B) Tyler incurs a penalty of two strokes and Phil incurs no penalty.
C) Both Tyler and Phil incur a penalty of two strokes.
D) Both Tyler and Phil are disqualified.
Answer: A) There is no penalty. Decision 23-1/3.
Note: The competitor may ask anyone to assist him in removing a loose impediment providing there is no undue delay in doing so.

Q.608
On a left-handed, dog-leg hole JP tees his ball as far right of the teeing ground as he is permitted. With his ball in this position an overhanging branch interferes with his area of swing. He breaks off the branch maintaining that as his ball is not yet in play there is no penalty for doing so. Which is correct in a match play situation?
A) There is no penalty.
B) There is no penalty providing JP tees up at a different position on the teeing ground, which would not have been affected by the branch he removed.
C) JP incurs a one stroke penalty for improving the area of his intended swing.
D) JP incurs a loss of hole penalty for improving the area of his intended swing.
Answer: D) JP incurs a loss of hole penalty for improving the area of his intended swing. Decision 13-2/14.
Note: Although players may eliminate irregularities of surface on the teeing ground, they are not permitted to do anything to improve their area of intended swing.

Q.609
While waiting to putt in a stroke play competition, Mikey puts down another ball and takes two practice putts on the apron of the green as his two fellow competitors are chipping in. What is the ruling?
A) There is no penalty.

B) Mikey incurs a penalty of one stroke.
C) Mikey incurs a penalty of two strokes.
D) Mikey is disqualified.
Answer: C) Mikey incurs a penalty of two strokes. Rule 7-2.
Note: A player must not make a practice stroke during play of a hole.

Q.610
In match play, Lorraine putts her ball from the putting green. Her ball strikes her opponent, Sinead's, ball which is also on the putting green. What is the ruling?
A) Lorraine incurs a penalty of one stroke.
B) Lorraine loses the hole.
C) Lorraine incurs no penalty.
D) Both Lorraine and Sinead incur a penalty of one stroke.
Answer: C) Lorraine incurs no penalty. Rule 19-5a.
Note: Lorraine must play her next putt from where her ball comes to rest. Sinead must replace her ball where it was before it was moved. In the same circumstances in a stroke play competition Lorraine would incur a penalty of two strokes.

Q.611
On a very hot summer's day Eamon is playing a match with Chris. After nine holes Eamon insists on walking back to the pro shop to get a cold drink. There is quite a queue in the shop and he takes 15 minutes to return to the 10th tee, where the following pair is also waiting. What is the ruling?
A) Unfortunately, there is no penalty for delaying play.
B) Eamon loses the 9th hole.
C) Eamon loses the 10th hole.
D) Eamon is disqualified.
Answer: C) Eamon loses the 10th hole. Note 1 to Rule 6-7.
Note: If a player unduly delays play between holes, he is delaying the play of the next hole and the penalty applies to that hole. The difficult playing conditions are not an excuse for undue delay of play, it is up to the player to prepare himself adequately.

Q.612
Which is correct regarding a player addressing her ball?
A) She has not completed her address until she has taken her stance
B) If, as part of her putting routine, she places her putter on the ground in front of her ball, she has addressed the ball.
C) If she grounds her putter immediately behind her ball on the putting green and then moves away from the ball, she is not deemed to have addressed her ball.
D) In a bunker she has addressed her ball when she has completed her stance.
Answer: B) If, as part of her putting routine, she places her putter on the ground in front of her ball, she has addressed the ball. Definition of Addressing the Ball.
Note: a player has addressed the ball simply by grounding her club immediately in front of or behind the ball, regardless of whether or not she has taken her stance. Therefore, a ball cannot now be addressed in a hazard.

Q.613
Which of the following statements is incorrect?
A) A ball that is touching the stake of a water hazard is in the water hazard.
B) A ball that is touching the line of an area marked as ground under repair is in ground under repair.
C) A ball that is touching the course side of a line defining out of bounds is out of bounds.
D) A ball that is touching a putting green is on the putting green.
Answer: C) A ball that is touching the course side of a line defining out of bounds is out of

bounds. Definition of Out of Bounds.
Note: A ball is only out of bounds when all of it lies out of bounds.

Q.614
While in a hazard Zak accidentally touches his ball with his club without it moving. What is the penalty in stroke play?
A) There is no penalty.
B) Zak incurs a penalty of one stroke.
C) Zak incurs a penalty of two strokes.
D) Zak loses the hole.
Answer: A) There is no penalty. Decision 13-4/12.
Note: Touching a ball without moving it does not constitute touching the ground of the hazard.

Q.615
When a ball is embedded in its own pitch-mark on a closely-mown area through the green, what option does the player have other than playing it as it lies?
A) Lift, clean and place the ball, without penalty, within one club-length of where it was embedded, but not nearer the hole.
B) Lift, clean and drop the ball, without penalty, within one club-length of where it was embedded, but not nearer the hole.
C) Lift, clean and place the ball, without penalty, as near as possible to where it was embedded, but not nearer the hole.
D) Lift, clean and drop the ball, without penalty, as near as possible to where it was embedded, but not nearer the hole.
Answer: D) Lift, clean and drop the ball, without penalty, as near as possible to where it was embedded, but not nearer the hole. Rule 25-2.
Note: If the ball embeds again when it is dropped or if it falls in the same ball pitch-mark as before, the player may re-drop the ball.

Q.616
Joyce's marker, Jennifer, signs her score card with an incorrect score for a hole and gives it back to Joyce. Before returning the card to the Committee, Joyce notices the mistake and corrects it without consulting with Jennifer or informing the Committee. Then, she returns the corrected card. What is the ruling?
A) There is no penalty.
B) Joyce incurs a penalty of one stroke.
C) Joyce incurs a penalty of two strokes.
D) Joyce is disqualified.
Answer: D) Joyce is disqualified. Decision 6-6b/7.
Note: By making an alteration on the score card after the marker had signed it Joyce effectively returned a score card which had not been properly signed by her marker.

Q.617
In a strokes competition, Deirdre plays a stroke at her ball that has come to rest out of bounds. She has to return to where she played her last stroke and play a ball under penalty of stroke and distance. Has she incurred any other penalty?
A) There is no other penalty for playing her ball that was out of bounds.
B) Deirdre incurs a penalty of two strokes for playing a practice stroke.
C) Deirdre incurs a penalty of two strokes for playing a wrong ball.
D) There is no other penalty providing her fellow competitors do not challenge her.
Answer: C) Deirdre incurs a penalty of two strokes for playing a wrong ball. Decision 15/6.
Note: A ball lying out of bounds is no longer in play and thus is a wrong ball. Also, Deirdre must return to where she played her last stroke and play a ball under penalty of stroke and distance.

Q.618
In a stroke play competition played in heavy rain Matthew takes out a small mat on the 2nd tee and stands on it when playing from the teeing ground. What is the ruling?
A) There is no penalty.
B) Matthew is disqualified.
C) Matthew incurs a penalty of one stroke.
D) Matthew incurs a penalty of two strokes.
Answer: D) Matthew incurs a penalty of two strokes. Decision 13-3/1.
Note: Matthew would be building a stance contrary to the Rules.

Q.619
In match play, Mick's ball lies in a large fairway bunker. He makes a stroke at the ball and it comes to rest in the same bunker, several yards away from its previous spot. He rakes the area where he played his previous stroke. What is the ruling?
A) There is no penalty.
B) There is no penalty but Mick must recreate the surface of the bunker sand as it was after he made his stroke.
C) Mick incurs a penalty of two strokes.
D) Mick loses the hole.
Answer: A) There is no penalty. Rule 13-4 Exception 2.
Note: Mick or his caddie may smooth sand or soil in the hazard, provided this is for the sole purpose of caring for the course and nothing is done to improve the position or lie of his ball, the area of intended stance or swing, or his line of play, with respect to his next stroke.

Q.620
Which of the following statements is correct relating to whether a player is permitted to use a distance-measuring device during a competition?
A) The Rules of Golf do not allow distance-measuring devices to be used under any circumstances.
B) Distance-measuring devices may be used in match play providing both sides agree.
C) The Committee may establish a Local Rule allowing the use of devices that measure distance.
D) Distance-measuring devices can now be used in all competitions.
Answer: C) The Committee may establish a Local Rule allowing the use of devices that measure distance. Decision 14-3/0.5.
Note: Even when the Local Rule is in effect, the device must not be used for any purposes that are prohibited by Rule 14-3 (e.g. measuring slope, wind speed or direction, or recommendation of club selection or type of shot).

Q.621
Jerome's ball is unplayable behind a bush and so he drops the ball, under penalty of one stroke, within two club-lengths of where it lay not nearer the hole. The ball rolls back into the same unplayable lie as where it originally lay. What is the ruling?
A) Jerome may place the ball where it first hit the course when he dropped it, without penalty.
B) Jerome may re-drop the ball without penalty.
C) Jerome must play the ball as it lies.
D) Jerome may play the ball as it lies or take another penalty drop for an unplayable ball.
Answer: D) Jerome may play the ball as it lies or take another penalty drop for an unplayable ball. Decision 28/3.
Note: Unfortunately for Jerome, the ball is in play once he has dropped it within the Rules. So, if his ball comes to rest in the same position, his only options are to play it as it lies or take another penalty drop.

Q.622

What is a player not permitted to do when his ball lies in a hazard?
A) Ground his club outside of a bunker when preparing to make a stroke at his ball that lies in the bunker.
B) Ground his club on a bridge extending over a water hazard.
C) Lightly brush the sand in the bunker with the club on his backswing.
D) Remove a piece of rubbish from the hazard.
Answer: C) Lightly brush the sand in the bunker with the club on his backswing. Rule 13-4b.
Note: Before commencing the downswing of a stroke at a ball that is in a bunker the player may not touch the ground in the bunker with his hand or club.

Q.623
On checking his score card Ian finds that there is no Local Rule relating to staked trees. His ball was close to such a stake, which was deeply embedded in the ground and not easily removable. Which is correct in stroke play?
A) As there is no Local Rule allowing relief from staked trees Ian must play the ball as it lies or take relief under penalty.
B) Ian may play his ball as it lies but, if he does and his ball touches any part of the tree, he incurs a penalty of two strokes.
C) Ian may take relief, without penalty, from the stake as it is an immovable obstruction.
D) Ian may take relief without penalty as there is always relief from staked trees.
Answer: C) Ian may take relief, without penalty, from the stake as it is an immovable obstruction. Decision 13-2/16.
Note: The Rules of Golf do not automatically provide relief from staked trees. Committees have to establish a Local Rule if they wish to protect young trees. In this situation, Ian may take relief from the stake, if it is interfering with his area of intended stance or swing (Rule 24-2b) but not from any part of the tree.

Q.624
Ron hits his ball against a nearby tree and it rebounds, hitting his caddie on the shin. What is the penalty?
A) There is no penalty because Ron's caddie is an outside agency.
B) Ron incurs a penalty of one stroke and the ball must be played as it lies.
C) Ron incurs a penalty of one stroke and the stroke must be replayed.
D) Ron incurs a penalty of two strokes.
Answer: B) Ron incurs a penalty of one stroke and the ball must be played as it lies. Rule 19-2.
Note: If a player's ball is accidentally deflected or stopped by himself, his partner or either of their caddies or equipment, the player incurs a penalty of one stroke.

Q.625
A husband and wife are playing partners in a four-ball match. He plays her ball by mistake. What is the ruling?
A) He incurs a penalty of one stroke.
B) He is disqualified from the hole but she incurs no penalty.
C) They lose the hole.
D) His only penalty is that she will probably not speak to him.
Answer: B) He is disqualified from the hole but she incurs no penalty. Decision 30-3c/1.
Note: If the wrong ball belongs to another player, its owner must place a ball on the spot from which the wrong ball was first played.

Q.626
Which statement is correct concerning mental interference?
A) A player may have another ball lifted if it interferes mentally with his play.
B) A player may take relief from a fixed obstruction if it interferes mentally with his play.
C) Before playing from a teeing ground a player may move a tee-marker if it interferes

mentally with his play.
D) All of the above.
Answer: A) A player may have another ball lifted if it interferes mentally with his play.
Decision 22/1.
Note: The ball does not have to be on the player's line of play to constitute mental interference, it may just be in a position where it catches his eye.

Q.627
In a Stableford competition, in which of the following circumstances should a player be disqualified?
A) A player signs his card in the place reserved for the marker and the marker signs the card in the place reserved for the player.
B) A player initials his card instead of using his full signature.
C) A marker records some scores in the wrong order. He alters the numbers of the holes on the card to correct his error.
D) A player does not record his handicap on his card but correctly calculates his Stableford points score before signing his card.
Answer: D) A player does not record his handicap on his card but correctly calculates his Stableford points score before signing his card. Rule 6-2b.
Note: A player is disqualified if no handicap is recorded on his score card before it is returned or if the recorded handicap is higher than that to which he is entitled and this affects the number of strokes received.

Q.628
In match play, Richard observes a breach of the Rules by his opponent, Leo, but decides to disregard it. What is the ruling?
A) Both Richard and Leo are disqualified.
B) Richard is disqualified for waiving a penalty.
C) Leo is disqualified for not declaring that he incurred a penalty.
D) There is no penalty as a player may overlook an opponent's breach of the Rules.
Answer: D) There is no penalty as a player may overlook an opponent's breach of the Rules. Note 1 to Rule 2-5.
Note: A player may disregard a breach of the Rules by his opponent providing there is no agreement between the players. There is a difference between overlooking an opponent's breach and agreement with the opponent to waive a penalty, which would result in both players being disqualified.

Q.629
Rocco has teed his ball on the 15th hole and is taking several practice swings to keep loose on a cold day when he accidentally strikes his ball with the toe end of his driver moving it forward 60 yards. What is the ruling?
A) Rocco must play a ball from the teeing ground, his first stroke on the hole.
B) Rocco is penalised one stroke and must play a ball from the teeing ground, his second stroke on the hole.
C) Rocco must play his second stroke from where his ball came to rest.
D) Rocco is penalised one stroke and must play his third stroke from where his ball came to rest.
Answer: A) Rocco must play a ball from the teeing ground, his first stroke on the hole.
Decision 18-2a/19
Note: As Rocco did not intend to hit his ball he did not make a stroke at it and so it is not yet in play. He must play a ball from the teeing ground, without penalty.

Q.630
Flash hits his tee shot into a stream running alongside the putting green and defined as a hazard by red stakes and lines. If Flash decides not to play another ball from the tee where

is the correct place for him to drop a ball under penalty of one stroke?
A) Flash may drop a ball behind the water hazard, keeping the point at which the original ball last crossed the margin of the water hazard directly between the hole and spot on which the ball is dropped.
B) Flash may drop a ball outside the water hazard within two club-lengths of and not nearer the hole than the point where the ball last crossed the margin of the hazard.
C) Flash may drop a ball within two club-lengths of a point on the opposite side of the water hazard that is equidistant from the hole from where the ball last crossed the margin of the hazard.
D) All of the above.
Answer: D) All of the above. Rule 26-1.
Note: The optional dropping points must be determined by reference to where the ball last crossed the margin of the hazard.

Q.631
Which of the following statements is incorrect?
A) A player may use a device to warm their ball before the start of a round.
B) A player may use a device to warm their hands during a round.
C) A player is disqualified for using a device to warm their ball during a round.
D) A player is disqualified for using a device to warm their hands during a round.
Answer: D) A player is disqualified for using a device to warm their hands during a round.
Note: A player may use a device to warm their hands, but not their ball during a round. Decision 14-3/13.5.

Q.632
Which of the following is not an outside agency?
A) A spectator.
B) A player's own caddie.
C) A greenkeeper.
D) A bird.
Answer: B) A player's own caddie. Definition of Outside Agency.

Q.633
In stroke play, on every putting green, a player marks the position of his ball, lifts the ball and places it nearer the hole than the spot from which it was lifted and then plays the ball. What is the ruling?
A) There is no penalty.
B) There is a penalty of one stroke for each occasion of improper replacing.
C) There is a penalty of two strokes for each occasion of improper replacing.
D) The player should be disqualified.
Answer: D) The player should be disqualified. Decision 33-7/6.
Note: The Committee may disqualify a player if it considers that a player is guilty of a serious breach of etiquette.

Q.634
As he was playing a stroke from beside a power pylon, Dan's club touched a stay wire on his backswing. He continued with the stroke moving the ball forward several yards. There was no Local Rule permitting relief from the pylon. What is the ruling?
A) There is no penalty for touching an obstruction during a stroke, Dan must play his ball as it lies.
B) Dan should have taken relief from the pylon and is penalised two strokes for touching part of the obstruction.
C) Dan must recover his ball and drop it within one club-length of the nearest point of relief from the obstruction and then replay his stroke.

D) Dan can choose whether to play his ball as it lies or return to where he last played from, without penalty.
Answer: A) There is no penalty for touching an obstruction during a stroke, Dan must play his ball as it lies. Rule 24-2b.
Note: Dan may choose to take relief, without penalty, from the stay wire, which is an immovable obstruction, but he does not have to.

Q.635
In stroke play, a marker signs the competitor's score card in the space provided for the competitor's signature and the competitor then signs in the spaces provided for the marker's signature. What is the ruling?
A) There is no penalty.
B) There is no penalty providing the player and marker are able to sign the card in the correct places before the competition closes.
C) The competitor is disqualified.
D) Both the competitor and the marker are disqualified.
Answer: A) There is no penalty. Decision 6-6b/1.
Note: As long as both the competitor and marker sign the score card it does not matter if they sign it in the wrong place.

Q.636
Dillon's ball lies close to a tree. He takes a practice swing just beside his ball and knocks down leaves in the area of his intended swing. Which of the following statements is incorrect?
A) If, during a practice swing, a player knocks down any leaves on his area of intended swing there is always a penalty.
B) Sometimes knocking down a number of leaves in a practice swing will not improve the area of intended swing as the player still has to swing through a number of remaining leaves when making his stroke.
C) Sometimes knocking down a single leaf might improve the area of the intended swing.
D) Players are permitted to take practice swings even when there are overhanging branches with leaves in their intended swing.
Answer: A) If, during a practice swing, a player knocks down any leaves on his area of intended swing there is always a penalty. Decision 13-2/0.5
Note: Dillon only incurs a penalty in this situation if the removal of the leaves results in him gaining a potential advantage by having improved the area of his intended swing.

Q.637
Marco practises with a weighted training club on the range. He then puts this club into his bag with 14 others and begins his match. On the 4th tee his opponent notices the training club and calls the referee to make a decision. What is the ruling?
A) There is no penalty as it is obvious that Marco is not going to use the training club during his round.
B) Marco loses the 4th hole.
C) The state of the match is adjusted by deducting two holes from Marco.
D) Marco is disqualified for carrying a non-conforming club.
Answer: C) The state of the match is adjusted by deducting two holes from Marco. Decision 4-4a/7.
Note: Marco started his round carrying more than 14 clubs in his bag. The penalty for carrying an excess club in match play is to deduct one hole for each hole at which a breach occurred with a maximum of two holes per round. If, after the penalty has been incurred, Marco uses the excess club during the remainder of the round he is disqualified.

Q.638

Without announcing her intention to her opponent Celia picks up her ball to see whether it is cut. She did not mark its position first and then cleaned the ball thoroughly before replacing it where it had come to rest. What penalties has Celia incurred?
A) Celia incurs a penalty of one stroke.
B) Celia incurs a penalty of two strokes.
C) Celia incurs three one stroke penalties.
D) Celia loses the hole.
Answer: A) Celia incurs a penalty of one stroke. Rule 5-3.
Note: Before lifting the ball, Celia must announce her intention to her opponent and mark its position. She must give her opponent or fellow competitor, the opportunity to observe the lifting and replacing and to examine the ball. She must not clean the ball. However, the penalty is just one stroke for failing to comply with any or all parts of this procedure.

Q.639
In stroke play, Eamon putts while his caddie stands on the fringe of the green, on an extension of the line of putt behind the ball. What is the ruling?
A) There is no penalty because the caddie is not standing on the putting green.
B) There is no penalty if the caddie inadvertently stands on an extension of the player's line of putt behind the ball, but is not doing so to assist or advise him.
C) There is a penalty of two strokes regardless of the circumstances.
D) There is no penalty but Eamon must replace his ball and putt again.
Answer: B) There is no penalty if the caddie inadvertently stands on an extension of the player's line of putt behind the ball, but is not doing so to assist or advise him. Exception to Rule 14-2b.
Note: If the caddie was standing on an extension of the line of putt in order to advise the player on alignment or otherwise assist him, then there would have been a penalty of two strokes.

Q.640
Theo's caddie, Moses, is attending the flagstick for him in a stroke play competition. He says to Theo, "Your line of putt is towards my left toe". He leaves his feet in place as Theo takes his putt. What is the ruling?
A) There is no penalty.
B) Theo incurs a penalty of two strokes for acting on advice from his caddie.
C) Theo incurs a penalty of two strokes because his caddie was acting as a mark.
D) Theo must retake the putt without penalty.
Answer: C) Theo incurs a penalty of two strokes because his caddie was acting as a mark. Decision 8-2b/2.
Note: The player must not position any person, or place any object, for the purpose of indicating a line of putt.

Q.641
Harry and Bill are playing a match. Harry plays his second shot onto the green from deep rough. Bill, having played five, concedes the hole to Harry. Harry then discovers that he has played a wrong ball to the green. What is the ruling?
A) Bill loses the hole.
B) Harry loses the hole.
C) The hole is halved.
D) Harry has to find his original ball and play out the hole.
Answer: B) Harry loses the hole. Decision 2-4/9.
Note: By playing a wrong ball before Bill conceded the hole, Harry had already lost the hole and so the concession was irrelevant.

Q.642

Roger has been searching for his ball for three minutes when play is suspended. How much time is he allowed for further search when play resumes?
A) Five minutes.
B) Two minutes, providing he does not continue searching during the suspension of play.
C) Two minutes, even if he continues searching during the suspension of play.
D) No additional time, as the player could have been searching for his ball during the suspension of play.
Answer: B) Two minutes, providing he does not continue searching during the suspension of play. Decision 27/1.5.
Note: The suspension of play has no effect on the five-minute search period. So, even if Roger continues searching for his ball during the suspension of play, he is still only permitted a total of five minutes.

Q.643
In a stroke play competition, Tommo, Taylor and Tam are drawn by the Committee to play together starting at 9.00am. Tommo and Taylor are present at the appointed time. Tam arrives at 9.02am, after Tommo and Taylor have teed off, but before they have left the 1st tee box. What is the ruling?
A) There is no penalty.
B) Tam is disqualified.
C) Tam incurs a penalty of one stroke.
D) Tam incurs a penalty of two strokes.
Answer: D) Tam incurs a penalty of two strokes. Decision 6-3 a/2.
Note: All competitors must be present and ready to play at the time laid down by the Committee. The order of play is not relevant. However, if a player arrives within five minutes of their starting time, the penalty under Rule 6-3a has been reduced from disqualification to two strokes, following the amendments to the Rules that became effective from 1st January 2012.

Q.644
Arnold's ball lies in a bunker against a rake. After marking the position of the ball, he lifts the rake and the ball rolls closer to the hole. He attempts to place the ball at rest as near as possible to where it lay within the bunker, but not nearer the hole. The ball still will not remain at rest. Which of the following options is correct?
A) Arnold may place the ball at the nearest spot, even if nearer the hole, where his ball will remain at rest.
B) Arnold may lightly press the ball into the sand so that it remains at rest at the nearest spot, not nearer the hole.
C) Arnold may place the ball in another bunker at a spot that is not nearer the hole.
D) Arnold may drop the ball outside the bunker and incur a penalty of one stroke.
Answer: D) Arnold may drop the ball outside the bunker and incur a penalty of one stroke. Decision 20-3d/2.
Note: Since Arnold could not place the ball in conformity with the Rules, he should proceed under the stroke and distance option of the unplayable ball Rule (Rule 28a) or, in equity (Rule 1-4), drop the ball, under penalty of one stroke, outside the bunker, keeping the point where the ball lay directly between the hole and the spot on which the ball is dropped.

Q.645
Which of the following aids is prohibited under the Rules?
A) Resin applied to the grip of a club.
B) A handkerchief wrapped around the grip of a club.
C) A golf ball warmer.
D) Standard binoculars.
Answer: C) A golf ball warmer. Rule 14-3.

Note: Use of a ball that has been purposely warmed during a stipulated round with an artificial device constitutes a breach of Rule 14-3.

Q.646
Nessa and Una are partners in a foursome. Nessa drives and as there is doubt as to whether the ball is out of bounds, Una plays a provisional ball. What is the ruling?
A) There is no penalty and if the original ball is found it is Una's turn to play.
B) Una's stroke is cancelled and Nessa must correct the error by playing the provisional ball under penalty of one stroke.
C) Una's stroke is cancelled and Nessa must correct the error by playing the provisional ball under penalty of two strokes.
D) The provisional ball becomes the ball in play irrespective of whether the original ball is found or not.
Answer: A) There is no penalty and if the original ball is found it is Una's turn to play. Decision 29-1/3.
Note: In a foursome partners must play alternately from the teeing grounds and alternately during the play of each hole. Penalty strokes do not affect the order of play.

Q.647
In which of the following circumstances may Max not clean his ball?
A) After lifting the ball from the putting green.
B) In taking relief from casual water.
C) In identifying his ball when there is mud on the top of it.
D) In taking relief from a fixed ball cleaner.
Answer: C) In identifying his ball when there is mud on the top of it. Rule 12-2.
Note: The ball must not be cleaned beyond the extent necessary for identification.

Q.648
Colm putts his ball from on the putting green and while the ball is still in motion, it is picked up and carried away in its beak by a magpie, which then drops it 10 yards from the hole on the other side of the green. What is the ruling?
A) The stroke counts and Colm must play the ball as it lies.
B) The stroke counts and Colm must place the ball at the point where it was when the magpie picked it up.
C) The stroke is cancelled and Colm must replace his ball.
D) The stroke counts and Colm must estimate where his ball would have come to rest and place it there.
Answer: C) The stroke is cancelled and Colm must replace his ball. Decision 19-1/7.
Note: The same procedure applies if the ball is deflected by any animate outside agency from a stroke made from on the putting green. However, if an animate outside agency picks up a ball at rest from a stroke made from off the putting green the ball is played from the spot where the ball was at rest when it was picked up.

Q.649
On a rainy day Wes carries an umbrella throughout his match. His ball on the 15th green is close to the hole and he walks up to it, removes the flagstick, places it on the putting green, holds his umbrella above him with one hand and putts the ball into the hole with the other. Does he incur a penalty?
A) Wes incurs no penalty.
B) Wes incurs a penalty of one stroke.
C) Wes loses the hole.
D) Wes is disqualified.
Answer: A) Wes incurs no penalty. Decision 14-2/2.
Note: While making a stroke, a player may not accept protection from the elements from anyone else. However, the Rules do not prohibit him from protecting himself.

Q.650
Which of the following statements is incorrect?
A) A dropped ball must be re-dropped without penalty if it rolls into a water hazard.
B) A dropped ball must be re-dropped without penalty if it rolls into the same pitch-mark that it was lifted from.
C) A dropped ball must be re-dropped without penalty if it rolls and comes to rest in an unplayable lie.
D) A dropped ball must be re-dropped without penalty if it is dropped in a bunker and rolls out of it.
Answer: C) A dropped ball must be re-dropped without penalty if it rolls and comes to rest in an unplayable lie. Rule 20-2c.
Note: Providing the ball was dropped properly under Rule 20-2 the fact that it came to rest in an unplayable lie is bad luck. The player must either play the ball as it lies or invoke Rule 28 Unplayable Ball, incurring a penalty stroke.

Q.651
In a strokes competition, Andy, who is not an expert on the Rules, makes several practice swings in a water hazard, touching the ground each time. What is the ruling?
A) Andy incurs a penalty of one stroke.
B) Andy incurs a penalty of two strokes.
C) Andy incurs a maximum penalty of four strokes.
D) As Andy does not know how many practice swings he has taken he cannot properly penalise himself and is disqualified.
Answer: B) Andy incurs a penalty of two strokes. Decision 13-4/3.
Note: A single penalty is incurred when related acts result in one Rule being breached more than once.

Q.652
In a strokes competition, Michel's ball is at rest within the margins of a water hazard. His knowledge of the Rules is poor and not only does he bend back some rushes so that he may see his ball better in making his stroke, he also grounds his club in the hazard. How many penalty strokes does Michel incur?
A) One stroke.
B) Two strokes.
C) Three strokes.
D) Four strokes.
Answer: D) Four strokes. Decision 1-4/12(5).
Note: Michel was not permitted to improve the area of his intended swing by bending something growing and he was not permitted to ground his club in a hazard. Multiple penalties are incurred when unrelated acts result in two Rules being breached.

Q.653
In which of the following situations does Jane not incur a penalty?
A) Jane's caddie accidentally moves her ball while searching for it.
B) Jane's ball moves after she has taken her stance and grounded her club.
C) Jane's ball moves while she is removing an acorn that is lying against her ball on the putting green.
D) Jane's ball moves while she is removing loose earth from behind her ball on the fringe of the green.
Answer: C) Jane's ball moves while she is removing an acorn that is lying against her ball on the putting green. Rule 18-2.
Note: There is no penalty if a player accidentally causes her ball to move in removing a loose impediment on the putting green.

Q.654
Which is correct regarding loose impediments?
A) Dung is not a loose impediment.
B) An unattached divot is a loose impediment.
C) A worm cast is not a loose impediment.
D) Loose soil is a loose impediment through the green.
Answer: B) An unattached divot is a loose impediment. Decision 23-13 and Definition of Loose Impediments.
Note: Loose soil is not a loose impediment, except on the putting green. However, a divot is not loose soil. Dung is a loose impediment.

Q.655
In stroke play, Farrell hooks her ball and it strikes her fellow competitor's trolley, rebounding to hit her own trolley. What is the ruling?
A) There is no penalty and Farrell can choose whether to replay her stroke or play her ball as it lies.
B) Farrell incurs a penalty of one stroke and must replay her stroke.
C) Farrell incurs a penalty of one stroke and must play her ball as it lies.
D) Farrell incurs a penalty of two strokes.
Answer: C) Farrell incurs a penalty of one stroke and must play her ball as it lies. Decision 19-3/3.
Note: If it were match play Farrell has the option of replaying her stroke without penalty, or playing the ball as it lies under penalty of one stroke, as her ball had struck her own trolley.

Q.656
Catherine elects to declare her ball unplayable and takes the option of dropping a ball within two club-lengths. Which is correct?
A) Catherine must mark her ball before lifting it and must measure the maximum of two club-lengths with a club from her bag.
B) Catherine may lift her ball without marking it but must measure the maximum of two club-lengths with a club.
C) Catherine must mark her ball before lifting it but may estimate the maximum of two club-lengths.
D) Catherine may lift her ball without marking it and may estimate the maximum of two club-lengths.
Answer: D) Catherine may lift her ball without marking it and may estimate the maximum of two club-lengths. Rule 28.
Note: While it is recommended that players mark the position of their ball and measure their relief after declaring it unplayable the Rules do not make it mandatory.

Q.657
In stroke play, Vinnie accidentally steps on and moves his ball-marker as it sticks to his shoe. What is the ruling?
A) There is no penalty.
B) Vinnie incurs a penalty of one stroke.
C) Vinnie incurs a penalty of two strokes.
D) Vinnie is disqualified.
Answer: B) Vinnie incurs a penalty of one stroke. Decision 20-1/5.5.
Note: Vinnie must replace the ball as near as possible to its original position. However, there is no penalty if a player's ball-marker is accidentally moved in the process of lifting the ball or marking its position.

Q.658
Which of the following statements is correct concerning an embedded ball?

A) A ball may be considered embedded if it rolls into someone else's pitch-mark on a closely-mown area through the green.
B) A ball may be considered embedded if it rolls into its own pitch-mark on a closely-mown area through the green.
C) A ball may be considered embedded if it rolls into its own pitch-mark through the green.
D) A ball may be considered embedded in all of the above circumstances.
Answer: B) A ball may be considered embedded if it rolls into its own pitch-mark on a closely-mown area through the green. Rule 25-2.
Note: Under the Rules a player may only obtain relief, without penalty, for an embedded ball if it comes to rest in its own pitch-mark in any closely-mown area through the green.

Q.659
On a resort course Simon hits his ball over a boundary wall into a garden. Several seconds later his fellow competitor, Patrick, sees a gardener pick up the ball and throw it back onto the course. He tells Simon what he has witnessed. Simon walks up to the ball, identifies it as his, and plays it onto the putting green claiming that it was the action of an outside agency and counts as rub of the green. What is the ruling?
A) Simon is correct and there is no penalty.
B) Simon incurs a penalty of two strokes but was correct in playing the ball from where it came to rest.
C) Simon incurs a penalty of two strokes for playing a wrong ball and also the stroke and distance penalty for his ball being out of bounds.
D) Simon is disqualified for playing from the wrong place.
Answer: C) Simon incurs a penalty of two strokes for playing a wrong ball and also the stroke and distance penalty for his ball being out of bounds. Decision 15/9.
Note: Simon's ball was no longer the ball in play when it came to rest out of bounds. When he subsequently made a stroke at it he played a wrong ball.

Q.660
Which of the following is not permitted by the Rules?
A) While waiting to play his shot to the putting green Stuart drops a ball on the fairway and practises his putting stroke.
B) Stuart practises putts on the 12th green while waiting for the group in front to finish the par 3 13th.
C) Stuart leaves the green on the 13th, drops a ball and plays two chip shots towards the 14th teeing ground.
D) Stuart practises putts on the 13th tee box while waiting for the 13th fairway to clear.
Answer: A) While waiting to play his shot to the putting green Stuart drops a ball on the fairway and practises his putting stroke. Rule 7-2.
Note: A player must not make a practice stroke during play of a hole.

Q.661
Brian has scored well in a stroke play competition. His score card has the correct scores for each hole but he has signed for a net score that is two lower than his actual score. What is the ruling?
A) Brian is disqualified for returning an incorrect score card.
B) Brian is not disqualified providing the Committee can find him to correct his mistake before the competition closes.
C) Brian is not penalised as it is the Committee that is responsible for calculating the net score.
D) Brian is penalised two strokes for signing for an incorrect score card.
Answer: C) Brian is not penalised as it is the Committee that is responsible for calculating the net score. Rule 33-5.
Note: In stroke play, the Committee is responsible for the addition of scores and the application of the handicap recorded on the score card.

Q.662
In stroke play, Shane bends back long grass lying across his ball so that he may see the ball when playing his stroke. What is the ruling?
A) No penalty is incurred.
B) Shane incurs a penalty of one stroke.
C) Shane incurs a penalty of two strokes.
D) Shane incurs a penalty of two strokes and must bend back the grass to where it was before he bent it.
Answer: C) Shane incurs a penalty of two strokes. Rule 12-1.
Note: A player is not necessarily entitled to see his ball when making a stroke. However, he may touch or bend long grass to the extent necessary to find and identify his ball.

Q.663
In stroke play, Stephen employs his young son, Sam, as a caddie for the first nine holes. For the second nine holes, he employs a friend, Ronan, who has just finished playing his round in the same event. What is the ruling?
A) There is no penalty.
B) Stephen incurs a penalty of two strokes.
C) Stephen incurs a maximum penalty of four strokes.
D) Stephen is disqualified.
Answer: A) There is no penalty. Decisions 6-4/7 & 6-4/8.
Note: A player may have more than one caddie during a round, providing he has only one at a time, and there is no Rule preventing someone who has played in the same competition from acting as caddie before or after their round.

Q.664
Which of the following incurs a penalty?
A) Roger looks into his opponent's bag to see which club he is using on a par 3.
B) Roger moves the waterproof hood covering his opponent's clubs so that he may see which club he is using.
C) Roger's caddie borrows a club from his opponent's bag and swings it to show Roger how to make his next stroke.
D) After they have both played their tee shots Roger asks his opponent what club he used.
Answer: B) Roger moves the waterproof hood covering his opponent's clubs so that he may see which club he is using. Decision 8-1/11.
Note: A player is prohibited from obtaining such information through a physical act.

Q.665
Which of the following statements is incorrect?
A) A player may declare his ball unplayable if it is in a bunker.
B) A player may exchange his ball with a different ball once he has declared it unplayable.
C) In match play, a player does not have to get the agreement of his opponent before declaring his ball unplayable.
D) A player may declare his ball unplayable if it is in a water hazard.
Answer: D) A player may declare his ball unplayable if it is in a water hazard. Rule 28.
Note: A player may deem his ball unplayable at any place on the course, except when his ball lies in a water hazard.

Q.666
In a foursome stroke play competition Anne lips out a putt out on the 12th green. Absent-mindedly she strolls up to the ball and taps it into the hole one-handed. What is the penalty?
A) There is no penalty but the ball has to be replaced and her partner has to take the putt.
B) The side incurs a penalty of one stroke and the ball has to be replaced.
C) The side incurs a penalty of two strokes and the ball has to be replaced.
D) The side incurs a penalty of two strokes and the ball is deemed holed.

Answer: C) The side incurs a penalty of two strokes and the ball has to be replaced. Rule 29-3.
Note: The side must correct the error by playing a ball in correct order as nearly as possible at the spot from which it first played in incorrect order, otherwise they are disqualified.

Section 3: 333 advanced questions for those seeking to expand their knowledge of the Rules

True or False?

Q.667
During a strokes competition if the Committee decide that a hole is waterlogged in its present position they may move it to another area on the same putting green. True or False?
Answer: False. Rule 33-2b.
Note: This Rule provides that all competitors in a single round play with each hole cut in the same position.

Q.668
A ball is visible in casual water but a player cannot retrieve it. Unless the player can positively identify the ball as his he must treat his ball as lost outside of the casual water. True or False?
Answer: False. Decision 25-1/1.
Note: The player is not obliged to use unreasonable effort to identify his ball. In either case, as the original ball is not immediately recoverable another ball may be substituted.

Q.669
Before commencing a round in a medal competition a competitor walks to the 18th putting green and tests the condition of a greenside bunker by simulating his stance, pushing a long tee into the sand and raking the area he has disturbed. Has he incurred any penalty?
Answer: No. Rules 7-1b and 13-4.
Note: Rule 13-4 only prohibits the competitor from testing the condition of the hazard or any similar hazard when his ball lies in the hazard. Rule 7-1b rules that a competitor must not practice on the competition course or test the surface of any putting green on the course by rolling a ball or roughening or scraping the surface. It does not prohibit a player from testing the condition of a hazard.

Q.670
Apart from when a ball is in motion, a player may always ask for another player's ball to be lifted if she considers that it interferes with her play. True or False?
Answer: True. Rule 22-2.
Note: A ball lifted under this Rule must be replaced and must not be cleaned unless it lies on the putting green.

Q.671
In match play, before starting a match, Manuel declares his handicap to be nine when in fact his handicap had changed to seven the week before. He remembers after five holes have been played. He is disqualified. True or False?
Answer: True. Rule 6-2a.
Note: Before starting a match in a handicap competition, the players should determine from one another their respective handicaps. If a player begins a match having declared a handicap higher than that to which he is entitled and this affects the number of strokes given or received, he is disqualified.

Q.672
If both finalists in a match play competition are disqualified for agreeing to waive the Rules, the Committee may decide to conclude the event without a winner. True or False?
Answer: True. Decision 33/3

Q.673
A player is allowed five minutes to search for his original ball and five minutes for his provisional ball even if they are lost in the same area. True or False?
Answer: False. Decision 27/4.
Note: If both balls are lost in the same area a total of five minutes to search for them is allowed. However, if the balls were lost in different areas of the course the player is allowed five minutes to search for each ball.

Q.674
The margin of a water hazard extends vertically downwards, but not upwards. True or False?
Answer: False. Definition of Water Hazard.
Note: The margin of a water hazard extends vertically upwards and downwards.

Q.675
If the flagstick is in the hole and anyone stands near it while a stroke is being made, they are deemed to be attending the flagstick. True or False?
Answer: True. Note 1 to Rule 17-1.
Note: If a person is standing close enough to the flagstick to touch it they are deemed to be attending it. Decision 17-1/1.

Q.676
A player is entitled to place his clubs in a bunker when his ball lies in the same bunker. True or False?
Answer: True. Rule 13-4 Exception 1(b).
Note: The player may place his club(s) in a hazard providing nothing is done that constitutes testing the condition of the hazard or improves the lie of his ball.

Q.677
The Committee may define a lateral water hazard as a water hazard. True or False?
Answer: True. Definition of Lateral Water Hazard.
Note: A water hazard is defined by yellow stakes and/or lines, and a lateral water hazard is defined by red stakes and/or lines.

Q.678
Patsy is attending the flagstick for her fellow competitor, Carol. Her attention is diverted by some noise coming from an adjacent green and she does not notice that Carol has taken her putt. Carol's ball hits Patsy's foot and comes to rest a few inches from the hole. Patsy is penalised two strokes. True or False?
Answer: False. It is Carol who is penalised two strokes. Rule 17-3.
Note: Because Carol had authorised Patsy to attend the flagstick the penalty is against her. The ball must be played as it lies.

Q.679
A player is allowed to use sand to raise his stance on the teeing ground. True or False?
Answer: True. Rule 13-2.
Note: A player may create or eliminate irregularities of surface within the teeing ground of the hole being played.

Q.680
A player's ball crosses over a yellow water hazard margin but comes to rest in a part of the water hazard that is marked with red stakes. The player may drop the ball anywhere within two club-lengths of where it crossed the margin of the water hazard, not nearer the hole. True or False?
Answer: False. Rule 26-1.
Note: The option of dropping the ball anywhere within two club-lengths of where it crossed the margin of the water hazard not nearer the hole is only available if the ball last crossed the margin of a lateral water hazard.

Q.681
Pierre putts from the edge of the putting green and his ball comes to rest touching the ball of his fellow competitor, Franz, which was also on the green. However, Franz's ball did not move at all, nor did it prevent Pierre's ball from rolling any farther. Pierre incurs a penalty of two strokes. True or False?
Answer: False. Because Pierre's ball was not deflected or stopped by Franz's ball he incurs no penalty. Decision 19-5/4.
Note: If there is any doubt as to whether Franz's ball moved or prevented Pierre's ball from rolling any farther, the decision should be resolved against Pierre.

Q.682
Benson's ball lodges in a tree. He is able to identify it from the ground and declares it unplayable. He then dislodges his ball by shaking the tree. He incurs no additional penalty for moving his ball in play. True or False?
Answer: True. Decision 18-2a/27.
Note: Because Benson has declared his ball unplayable, and will be playing his next stroke under penalty of one stroke, his original ball is out of play when he moves it.

Q.683
During their play of a 15-hole competition Alma and Tracey play two additional holes that were not included in the stipulated round. There is no penalty. True or False?
Answer: False. Decision 3/2.
Note: Players must play the holes of the course in the sequence prescribed by the Committee. In playing two additional holes Alma and Tracey incur the penalty of disqualification.

Q.684
A ball lands on a discarded chocolate wrapper through the green. The player is entitled to mark the spot, remove the wrapper and replace his ball at the marker without penalty. True or False?
Answer: False. Rule 24-1b.
Note: When a ball lies in or on an obstruction, the ball may be lifted and the obstruction removed. In a hazard or through the green, the ball must be dropped, not replaced, as near as possible to the spot directly under the place where the ball lay, but not nearer the hole.

Q.685
Except on the putting green, a caddie or playing partner may position themselves immediately behind the intended line of play of a player in order to closely watch the flight of the ball against a setting sun. True or False?
Answer: False. Rule 14-2b.
Note: In making a stroke anywhere on the course, a player must not allow his caddie, his partner or his partner's caddie to position themselves on or close to an extension of the line of play or the line of putt behind the ball.

Q.686
Based on information given by a spectator, a player was able to identify his ball. His ball should not be deemed lost in these circumstances. True or False?
Answer: True. Decision 27/12.
Note: Reliable information from a spectator, an outside agency, may be accepted as evidence of the identification of a player's ball.

Q.687
After conceding a hole to his opponent, Jo's caddie tells him that he was entitled to a handicap stroke on the hole and makes a claim. The Committee should revoke the concession. True or False?
Answer: False. Rule 2-4.
Note: A concession may not be declined or withdrawn. Jo must accept the consequences of forgetting about his handicap stroke.

Q.688
A Committee may waive the penalty of disqualification if a player arrives on the 1st tee more than 5 minutes after his start time because he encountered heavy traffic on his way to the course. True or False?
Answer: False. Decision 6-3a/1.5.
Note: It is the player's responsibility to ensure that he allows enough time to reach the course on time and he should make allowances for possible delays.

Q.689
Any temporary accumulation of water on the course that is visible before or after a player has taken his stance is casual water. True or False?
Answer: False. Definition of Casual Water.
Note: The definition states "...and is not in a water hazard", so any temporary accumulation of water inside the margins of a water hazard is not casual water.

Q.690
A player may not take relief from an abnormal ground condition if it is clearly impracticable for him to make a stroke because of interference by anything other than that abnormal ground condition. True or False?
Answer: True. Exception to Rule 25-1b.
Note: Similarly, a player may not take relief if interference by an abnormal ground condition would occur only through use of clearly unreasonable stroke or an unnecessarily abnormal stance, swing or direction of play.

Q.691
The Committee may make it a condition of the competition that competitors are responsible for the addition of their scores on their score card. True or False?
Answer: False. Decision 33-1/7.
Note: The Committee has no power to waive a Rule of Golf and such a condition would be a modification of Rule 33-5, which states that the Committee is responsible for the addition of scores.

Q.692
A caddie shared by players on opposite sides in a four-ball match accidentally moves a ball belonging to one of the players. There is no penalty. True or False?
Answer: False. Decision 30-1.
Note: The player whose ball it was that the caddie moved is penalised one stroke as the player incurs the applicable penalty for any breach of Rules by his caddie.

Q.693
If a player thinks his ball is in water in a water hazard he may probe with a club to try to find it. True or False?
Answer: True. Rule 12-1c.
Note: A player may probe for a ball in water with a club or otherwise. If the ball is moved during the probing there is no penalty. The ball must be replaced if the player intends to play it from the water without taking relief under Rule 26-1.

Q.694
Lesley holes out with her second shot on a par 4. After congratulating Lesley on her eagle, her opponent, Julie, who has already played two strokes, takes out her wedge and plays another stroke onto the green. Having lost the hole Julie also loses the next hole because she has played a practice pitch to the putting green between holes. True or False?
Answer: False. Decision 7-2/1.5.
Note: Strokes made in continuing the play of a hole, the result of which has been decided, are not practice strokes.

Q.695
A stile attached to a boundary fence is an obstruction. True or False?
Answer: True. Decision 24-1.
Note: However, the Committee could make a Local Rule declaring the stile to be an integral part of the course under Rule 33-2a(iv).

Q.696
A player's opponent's caddie is not an outside agent. True or False?
Answer: True. Definition of Outside Agency.
Note: In match play, an outside agency is any agency other than either the player's or opponent's side, any caddie of either side, any ball played by either side at the hole being played or any equipment of either side.

Q.697
If a player repairs a materially damaged hole when a Committee member is readily available, he will be penalised, unless the damage was created by the impact of a ball. True or False?
Answer: True. Decision 16-1a/6.
Note: Apart from damage by a ball a player may only repair material damage to a hole (i.e. where the proper dimensions of the hole have been changed materially) when a Committee member is not readily available.

Q.698
A boundary fence gate, when closed, is part of the boundary fence and may not be opened to play a stroke. True or False?
Answer: True. Decision 27/18.
Note: As part of the course boundary the gate is not an obstruction (Definition of Obstructions) and may not be moved.

Q.699
A player is permitted to test the condition of a bunker to see whether it is feasible for him to putt through it, if his ball does not lie in that bunker. True or False?
Answer: True. Decision 13-2/30.
Note: The Rules do not prohibit a player from testing the condition of a hazard except when his ball lies in or touches the hazard.

Q.700
A competitor does not have to sign his completed score card, he may initial it instead. True or False?

Answer: True. Decision 6-6b/2.
Note: Initialling the score card meets the requirements of Rule 6-6b, providing it is clear that the competitor and marker are doing so for the purpose of verifying the competitor's scores for all the holes.

Q.701
Chris's caddie reaches the putting green before him. As he is not sure which of two balls belongs to Chris he marks one of the balls and lifts it to check for the identification marks that Chris uses. It is not Chris's ball. He is penalised one stroke for touching an opponent's ball that is in play. True or False?
Answer: True. Rule 18-3b.
Note: If, other than during search for a player's ball, a caddie touches an opponent's ball, except as otherwise provided in the Rules, the player who they are caddying for is penalised one stroke.

Q.702
In a match, Yuri and Ivan play their second shots on a par 5 hole. However, neither ball is found within five minutes. Rather than proceeding under the lost ball Rule they agree to halve the hole. This is permitted. True or False?
Answer: True. Decision 2-1/1.5.
Note: An agreement to halve a hole during play of the hole does not of itself constitute an agreement to waive the Rules.

Q.703
Opponents in a match may not agree to discontinue play for bad weather. True or False?
Answer: False. Exception to Rule 6-8.
Note: Players discontinuing match play by agreement are not subject to disqualification, unless by so doing the competition is delayed.

Q.704
In match play, Johnnie makes a statement regarding his club selection which is purposely misleading and is obviously intended to be heard by his opponent. He loses the hole. True or False?
Answer: True. Decision 8-1/9.
Note: Johnnie's statement is considered to be a breach of Rule 8-1 because it could influence his opponent in making his choice of club.

Q.705
A runway made by a snake anywhere on the course is not considered to be an abnormal ground condition. True or False?
Answer: False. Definition of Abnormal Ground Conditions.
Note: An abnormal ground condition is any casual water, ground under repair or hole, cast or runway on the course made by a burrowing animal, a reptile or a bird.

Q.706
Everywhere in the world that golf is played the balls must be exactly the same size and weight. True or False?
Answer: False. Rule 5-1 & Appendix III.
Note: All golf balls must conform to the requirements specified in Appendix III. The weight must be not greater than 1.62 ounces avoirdupois and the diameter must be at least 1.68 inches. Naturally, nearly all golf balls conform to this specification but the Rules do not prevent a player playing with lighter or larger balls. See Appendix III in the Rules of Golf.

Q.707
A ball mark and a spike mark are close to each other on Rita's line of putt. After using her pitch-mark repairer to raise the ball mark she steps on the repaired area to flatten it. In doing so she also steps on the spike mark. Rita incurs a penalty of two strokes. True or False?
Answer: True. Decision 16-1a/16.
Note: Rita may not repair the spike mark unless it is so close to the ball mark that it is impractical to repair the ball mark without affecting the spike mark.

Q.708
If, in marking his ball on the putting green, a player treads down on his marker so that it is not raised above the level of the green, he is not penalised if the marker sticks to the sole of his shoe as he walks away. True or False?
Answer: True. Decision 20-1/6.
Note: As the movement of the ball-marker was directly attributable to the act of marking the ball there is no penalty (Rule 20-3c). The ball must be replaced as near as possible to the spot where the ball lay when the marker was moved.

Q.709
If a player finds it impossible to repair an old hole plug, he may discontinue play and request the Committee to raise or lower the plug. True or False?
Answer: True. Decision 16-1c/3.
Note: The player may discontinue play and request the Committee to raise or lower the plug. If the Committee cannot level the plug without unduly delaying play, the Committee should declare the plug to be ground under repair, in which case the player would be entitled to relief under Rule 25-1b(iii).

Q.710
A live snake is an outside agency and a dead snake is a loose impediment. True or False?
Answer: True. Decision 23/6.5.
Note: However, a dead snake is both an outside agency and a loose impediment. It is possible for an item or person to fall under more than one Definition.

Q.711
If a stone bridge within the margins of a water hazard interferes with a player's area of swing, and his ball lies outside the hazard, he is still entitled to free relief. True or False?
Answer: True. Rule 24-2b.
Note: A player may take relief from interference by an immovable obstruction except when his ball is in a water hazard or a lateral water hazard.

Q.712
When taking relief under the Rules from a rabbit hole the nearest point of relief may be within the trunk of a large tree. True or False?
Answer: True. Definition of Nearest Point of Relief and Decision 24-2b/3.7.
Note: The nearest point of relief is the point on the course nearest to where the ball lies that is not nearer the hole and avoids interference from the condition for which relief is sought. If the nearest point of relief is in the middle of a tree trunk the player must estimate the one club-length relief from that point, within which he must drop a ball.

Q.713
A condition of a stroke play competition is that ¾ of full handicaps apply. Trent records his handicap on his score card as 11 when it is in fact 10. He is disqualified. True or False?
Answer: False. Rule 6-2b.
Note: The player is disqualified only if his recorded handicap is higher than that to which he is entitled and this affects the number of strokes received for the competition. For the purpose of handicaps ¾ of 11 is the same as ¾ of 10, being 8.

Q.714
A ball used by a player during his play of a hole is equipment when it has been lifted and not put back into play at that hole. True or False?
Answer: True. Definition of Equipment.

Q.715
A competitor putts his ball from the putting green and his ball is deflected into the hole by a fellow competitor's caddie as he walks across the line of putt. The ball is holed out. True or False?
Answer: False. Rule 19-1b.
Note: The fellow competitor's caddie is an outside agency so the stroke is cancelled and the ball must be replaced and played again.

Q.716
A player should always play a provisional ball if they think that their original ball may be lost. True or False?
Answer: False. Definition of Provisional Ball.
Note: A provisional ball is a ball played under Rule 27-2 for a ball that may be lost outside a water hazard or may be out of bounds. So, if a player is not sure whether his ball is in a water hazard or not, but it is unlikely to be lost elsewhere, then he must not play a provisional ball.

Q.717
While waiting to start his match on the 1st tee, Mike, asks his friend John, a Club Professional, for tips that he may use during his round on his swing, putting and mental game. He has breached a Rule of Golf. True or False?
Answer: False. Rule 8-1.
Note: The Rule on giving or receiving advice only applies <u>during</u> a stipulated round. Definition of Advice.

Q.718
A wrong ball includes another player's ball, an abandoned ball, and the player's original ball when it is no longer in play. True or False?
Answer: True. Definition of Wrong Ball.

Q.719
A ball lying in long grass which is displaced vertically downwards after address is deemed to have moved. True or False?
Answer: True. Definition of Move or Moved.
Note: A ball is deemed to have moved if it leaves its position and comes to rest in any other place.

Q.720
The term Rule includes the specification on clubs and the ball in Appendices II and III. True or False?
Answer: True. Definition of Rule or Rules.
Note: The term Rule(s) includes, a) the Rules of Golf and their interpretations as contained in Decisions on the Rules of Golf, b) any Conditions of Competition established by the Committee under Rule 33-1 and Appendix I, c) any Local Rules established by the Committee under Rule 33-8a and Appendix I, d) the specifications on, (i) clubs and the ball in Appendices II and III and their interpretations as contained in A Guide to the Rules on Clubs and Balls, and (ii) devices and other equipment in Appendix IV.

Q.721
Tee-markers are deemed to be fixed and may not be moved under any circumstances. True or False?
Answer: False. Decision 11-2/1.
Note: Before a player makes their first stroke from the teeing ground the tee-markers are deemed to be fixed, but are movable obstructions thereafter.

Q.722
Rod's ball is lost in a lateral water hazard. He takes relief, using his best judgment to determine the point where the original ball last crossed the margin. After he has dropped a ball, but before he plays his next stroke, another player says that the original ball crossed the margin some distance from where the ball was dropped. Rod then finds the original ball where the other player said it would be. Rod must lift the dropped ball and proceed in accordance with any of the applicable options under Rule 26-1 with respect to the newly determined reference point. True or False?
Answer: True. Decision 26-1/16.
Note: Rod dropped his ball in a wrong place and must correct the error under Rule 20-6. As he had put a ball in play by dropping it (albeit in the wrong place) he is precluded from playing his original ball from the hazard, even if it was found within five minutes.

Q.723
In the Rules a player's line of play stops at the hole. True or False?
Answer: True. Definition of Line of Play.
Note: The line of play extends vertically upwards from the ground, but does not extend beyond the hole.

Q.724
A player marks his ball on the putting green and in the act of lifting it accidentally drops it and it rolls into a nearby lake. He is unable to retrieve it and substitutes another ball of the same form and make and holes out. In stroke play, he incurs a penalty of two strokes. True or False?
Answer: True. Decision 15-2/1.
Note: A player is not permitted to substitute another ball without penalty in these circumstances.

Q.725
If a player putts a ball from the putting green and it strikes the flag attached to a removed flagstick there is a penalty of two strokes. True or False?
Answer: True. Definition of Flagstick and Decision 17-3/5.
Note: The flag is part of the flagstick.

Q.726
Brendan's ball rolls into a stream traversing the 5th fairway. The flow of water in the stream carries his ball out of bounds. Brendan may choose one of the relief options under Rule 26 – Water Hazards. True or False?
Answer: False. Brendan's ball is out of bounds. Decision 26-1/7.
Note: Wind and water are not outside agencies, as per the definition, and so the ball has effectively been hit out of bounds by Brendan. In situations where a ball can be carried out of bounds by the flow of water, it is recommended that the Committee prevent such an occurrence by installing a screen.

Q.727
A player may stand out of bounds to play a ball lying in bounds. True or False?
Answer: True. Definition of Out of Bounds.

Q.728
In stroke play, if a competitor plays his ball from a wrong place that is significantly nearer to the hole than where he should have played from he is automatically disqualified, even if he realises his error. True or False?
Answer: False. Rule 20-7c.
Note: If a competitor becomes aware that he has played from a wrong place and believes that he may have committed a serious breach, he must, before making a stroke on the next teeing ground, play out the hole with a second ball played in accordance with the Rules. He must then report the facts to the Committee before returning his score card, otherwise he is disqualified.

Q.729
A player's ball comes to rest in such a position that it touches both a red line defining the margin of a lateral water hazard and the putting green. The player must not ground his club behind the ball when playing his next shot. True or False?
Answer: True. Decision 26/1.5.
Note: The player's ball is considered to lie in the lateral water hazard and he is not permitted to ground his club, nor may he mark his ball, even though part of it is touching the putting green.

Q.730
Jarleth is in a bunker about 70 yards from the putting green and asks his opponent, Benjamin, to attend the flagstick for him. Benjamin refuses, saying that it is unreasonable for Jarleth to ask for the flagstick to be attended in those circumstances. Benjamin loses the hole. True or False?
Answer: False. Decision 17-1/2.
Note: In both match play and stroke play a player has no redress if their opponent or fellow competitor declines to attend the flagstick.

Q.731
The Committee may get help from players to remove casual water from the putting green that they are still playing on. True or False?
Answer: True. Decision 33/1.
Note: However, a player would be in breach of Rule 13-2 if he were to mop up casual water on his line of play or line of putt without the Committee's permission.

Q.732
Simone is a playing captain in a team match play competition where the Committee has made a condition that each team may appoint one person who may give advice. This permits Simone to give advice to her team while playing in the competition. True or False?
Answer: False. Decision 8/2.
Note: While she is playing her match Simone may only give advice to her playing partner.

Q.733
A small part of an acorn is protruding from the green on a player's line of putt. As it is a natural object he may remove it without penalty. True or False?
Answer: False. Definition of Loose Impediments.
Note: Anything solidly embedded is not a loose impediment.

Q.734
Before starting his round, Geoff realises that he has 15 clubs in his golf bag. He declares his rescue club out of play, removes it from his bag, places it on the floor of his golf cart and begins his round. There is no penalty. True or False?
Answer: True. Decision 4-4c/1 (Revised).
Note: This Decision was revised at January 2016 to provide narrow circumstances where a

player declaring a club out of play before the start of the round, but keeping the club in his possession, will not be penalised under Rule 4-4a.

Q.735
A player is considered to have given wrong information to an opponent even if it is due to his failure to include a penalty that he is not aware he has incurred. True or False?
Answer: True. Rule 9-2b.
Note: It is the player's responsibility to know the Rules.

Q.736
A worm, which is half on top of the surface of the ground and half below is considered solidly embedded and is not a loose impediment. True or False?
Answer: False. Decision 23/8.
Note: A worm which is half underground is not fixed or growing nor solidly embedded within the meaning of those terms in the Definition of Loose Impediments.

Q.737
Aidy beats Barney in his semi-final match play and Joel beats Darren in the other. Unfortunately, Joel has been carrying an injury and is unable to compete in the final. The Committee should require that Aidy plays Darren in the final. True or False?
Answer: False. Rule 2-4.
Note: By not being able to play the final Joel has conceded the match to Aidy who is therefore the winner of the competition.

Q.738
In a team competition situation the Committee may permit someone other than the players and their caddies to give advice to any members of the team. True or False?
Answer: True. Note to Rule 8-2.
Note: Any person so appointed must be identified to the Committee before they give advice to any team members during their round.

Q.739
In the play of a particular hole, the Committee may not define an area as in bounds for a stroke from the teeing ground and out of bounds thereafter. True or False?
Answer: True. Decision 33-2a/14.
Note: Under Rule 33-2a a Committee may declare part of an adjoining hole to be out of bounds when playing a particular hole, but they may not make a Local Rule placing an area of the course out of bounds to a stroke played from the teeing ground only.

Q.740
If, by mistake, an opponent in match play claims a higher handicap than he is entitled to, affecting the number of strokes that he receives, he should be disqualified, even after the result has been officially announced. True or False?
Answer: False. Decision 6-2a/5.
Note: Only if the player knew that he was giving wrong information about his handicap may a claim be considered by the Committee after the result of the match has been officially announced.

Q.741
After a player replaces his ball on the green, but before he removes his ball-marker, the wind moves the ball three feet nearer the hole. Unfortunately, he must replace his ball at the marker. True or False?
Answer: False. Decision 20-4/1.
Note: The ball is in play when it is replaced and is at rest, whether or not the object used to

mark its position has been removed. Consequently, the ball must be played from its new position.

Q.742
A Committee is permitted to waive a Rule of Golf to deal with extenuating circumstances. True or False?
Answer: False. Rule 33-8b.
Note: The Committee has no power to waive a Rule of Golf, but it may establish Local Rules for local abnormal conditions if they are consistent with the policy set forth in Appendix I to the Rules of Golf.

Q.743
Items, which in their natural state would be loose impediments, may be transformed into obstructions through processes of construction or manufacturing. True or False?
Answer: True. Decision 23-1.
Note: For example, pieces of wood, which are loose impediments, become obstructions when they are constructed into steps built into a tee box or cut and shaped as stakes for supporting trees.

Q.744
There is no penalty if an opponent stands on an extension of the line of putt or line of play behind the other player's ball while he is making a stroke. True or False?
Answer: True. Rule 14-2b.
Note: However, this action is considered to be bad etiquette. Also, if a player's caddie, partner or partner's caddie stands behind the player's ball during their stroke the player incurs a penalty of two strokes in stroke play or loss of hole in match play.

Q.745
A dropped ball shall be re-dropped, without penalty, if it rolls out of and comes to rest outside a hazard. True or False?
Answer: True. Rule 20-2c.

Q.746
A match referee is an outside agency. True or False?
Answer: True. Definition of Outside Agency.

Q.747
A player may remove loose impediments on his line of putt by brushing them aside with a broom borrowed from a greenkeeper's vehicle standing nearby. True or False?
Answer: True. Rule 16-1a(i).
Note: The player may use anything to remove loose impediments on the green as long as he does not press anything down, but a broom would not be recommended!

Q.748
A player, entitled to drop his ball, marks the outer limit of where his ball is to be dropped with a tee peg. The dropped ball then hits the ground, rolls against the tee peg and is deflected to a place that is still within two club-lengths of where it first hit part of the course and is not nearer the hole. The ball must be re-dropped. True or False?
Answer: False. Decision 20-2a/7 and Definition of Equipment.
Note: A tee peg is a small object and therefore, as per the definition, is not deemed to be the equipment of the player, who must play the ball as it lies. The dropped ball did hit the course within the permitted area before hitting the marker.

Q.749
A player removes a stone from a stone wall on the course that is interfering with his line of play. As the stone is a movable obstruction, there is no penalty. True or False?
Answer: False. Decision 13-2/32.
Note: The wall is an immovable obstruction and all parts of the wall are deemed to be fixed. Players are not allowed to move, bend or break anything growing or fixed that could improve their line of play.

Q.750
The Committee may not make a Local Rule for wintertime play prohibiting removal of the flagstick to reduce traffic around the hole when the putting greens are soft. True or False?
Answer: True. Decision 33-8/10.
Note: The Committee may not introduce a Local Rule that would modify the Rules of Golf.

Q.751
A player lifts his ball, because it is interfering with the play of a fellow competitor's ball, and throws it to his caddie. There is a question whether this action resulted in the ball being cleaned. Any doubt should be resolved against the player. True or False?
Answer: True. Decision 21/3.
Note: Under the Rules a ball may not be cleaned when it is lifted because it is interfering with another player's ball. The person lifting it should take care not to clean it. Any doubt should be resolved against the player.

Q.752
A player may lift his ball to identify it providing he has announced his intention to his opponent or fellow competitor, and given them the opportunity to witness the lift and the replacement. True or False?
Answer: False. The player must also mark the position of his ball before lifting it. Rule 12-2.

Q.753
Ray does not want to play a tricky shot over water to an island green as his ball is caked in mud. He may mark, lift and clean his ball under penalty of one stroke. True or False?
Answer: True. Rule 21.
Note: If a player cleans his ball during play of a hole, except as provided in Rule 21, he incurs a penalty of one stroke and the ball must be replaced.

Q.754
If during a strokes competition a hole becomes irreparably damaged the Committee may make another hole in a similar position. True or False?
Answer: True. Exception to Rule 33-2b.
Note: This is the single exception to the Rule that provides that all competitors in a single round play with each hole cut in the same position.

Q.755
If a player thinks that his ball is completely covered by leaves in a bunker he may carefully remove leaves in order to find it. Once he is able to identify his ball he must then re-cover it, leaving just enough showing to enable him to see it when making his stroke. True or False?
Answer: True. Rule 12-1b.
Note: This is an exception to Rule 12-1, which states that a player is not necessarily entitled to see his ball when making a stroke. If the player moves his ball during the search he incurs a penalty of one stroke under Rule 18-2 and the ball must be replaced.

Q.756
There are 34 Rules of Golf. True or False?
Answer: True.
Note: There are 126 Subsections in the 2012-2015 edition.

Q.757
When there are exceptional reasons the Committee has the authority to reduce the number of holes of a stipulated round once play has commenced for that round. True or False?
Answer: False. Decision 33-1/2.
Note: The Committee does not have the authority to reduce the number of holes of a stipulated round once play has commenced for that round, whatever the circumstances.

Q.758
In golf a threesome is a match in which one plays against two, and each side plays one ball. True or False?
Answer: True. Definition of Forms of Match Play.

Q.759
Following weeks of bad weather, plastic sheeting lining the base of a bunker has come to the surface. In taking his relief from this obstruction a player may, under penalty of one stroke, drop a ball outside the bunker keeping the point where the ball lay directly between the hole and the spot on which the ball is dropped, with no limit to how far behind the bunker the ball may be dropped. True or False?
Answer: True. Rule 24-2b(ii).
Note: However, the player may also avoid a penalty by dropping his ball at the nearest point of relief where there is no interference from the immovable obstruction and is within the bunker.

Q.760
A stroke play competition is closed when the last group has finished the 18th hole and returned their score cards to the Committee. True or False?
Answer: False. Rule 34-1b.
Note: A competition is closed when the result has been officially announced.

Q.761
A player tops his bunker shot and his ball embeds into a grassy bank in front of the bunker. He is entitled to relief for his embedded ball. True or False?
Answer: False. Decision 25-2/5.
Note: In order to obtain relief the ground in which the ball is embedded must be a closely-mown area.

Q.762
Foursome partners, Jan and Judy, carry all of their clubs, nine each, in one bag. This does not break the Rules as long as they only use their own clubs. True or False?
Answer: True. Decision 4-4a/4.
Note: Each player's clubs must be clearly identifiable.

Q.763
A player may have another player's ball lifted merely because when he takes his stance it catches his eye. True or False?
Answer: True. Decision 22-1.
Note: A player may have another ball lifted if the ball interferes either physically or mentally with his play.

Q.764
The penalty for having more than one caddie at any one time is disqualification. True or False?
Answer: False. Rule 6-4.
Note: Players are limited to one caddie at a time but the penalty in stroke play is two strokes for each hole at which any breach occurred, with a maximum penalty per round of four strokes. In match play, the penalty is one hole for each hole at which a breach occurred, with a maximum deduction per round of two holes.

Q.765
During a match a referee does not have the authority to declare an area as ground under repair, if it was not previously marked. True or False?
Answer: False. Decision 34-2/1.
Note: The decision of a referee appointed by the Committee is final.

Q.766
If a player substitutes a ball when not permitted, that ball is a wrong ball. True or False?
Answer: False. Definitions of Ball in Play and Substituted Ball.
Note: A wrongly substituted ball becomes the ball in play.

Q.767
During suspension of play a player may give or receive advice from other players in the competition without penalty. True or False?
Answer: True. Decision 8-1/20.
Note: The prohibition against giving or asking for advice applies only during a stipulated round. Definition of Advice.

Q.768
The margin of a bunker extends vertically downwards, but not upwards. True or False?
Answer: True. Definition of Bunker.
Note: So, if a ball is lying in a tree over a bunker it is not in the bunker.

Q.769
A large branch has fallen from a tree and part of the branch interferes with a player's swing. He may not move the whole branch because it is too heavy, but he breaks off the part of it that interferes with his swing. There is no penalty. True or False?
Answer: True. Decision 23-1/4.
Note: The branch is a loose impediment so all or part of it, may be removed providing the ball is not moved in the process.

Q.770
Al's ball lies several feet outside of an area marked as ground under repair (GUR) but leaves and branches of a tree that is rooted in the GUR interfere with his intended area of swing. He is still entitled to take free relief. True or False?
Answer: True. Decision 25-1a/1 and Definition of Ground Under Repair.
Note: Any growing thing within the area of GUR is part of the GUR.

Q.771
A Committee may make a Local Rule prohibiting play from an environmentally-sensitive area that has been defined as a water hazard. True or False?
Answer: True. Appendix I, Part B, 2b.
Note: However, the Committee may not define the area as a water hazard unless it is, by definition, a water hazard.

Q.772
A player's ball lies on a runway made by a rabbit, so he is entitled to free relief. True or False?
Answer: True. Definition of Abnormal Ground Conditions.
Note: A player is entitled to relief from a hole, cast or runway made by a burrowing animal, a reptile or a bird, except when the ball is in a water hazard or lateral water hazard.

Open Answer

Q.773
Can a match be won after nine holes without it being conceded?
Answer: Yes. Rule 2-3.
Note: This one is a little tricky! The match may only be won after nine holes if the loser has lost eight of the holes played, lost or halved the other one, and also incurred a penalty whereby the state of the match is adjusted by the deduction of one or two holes. For example, he may have started with more than 14 clubs (Rule 4-4) or had two caddies at the same time (Rule 6-4). He will then have lost 11 and 9, or 10 and 9. In fact, the match can be won during play of the 1st hole if the opponent incurs a penalty of disqualification.

Q.774
Bernard's ball comes to rest wedged in an outlying branch of a tree, high off the ground. Bernard declares his ball unplayable. He has a clear shot to the green from anywhere around the tree, so he decides to exercise the option under Rule 28c to take a drop under penalty of one stroke. Where may he drop his ball under this option?
Answer: Bernard may drop a ball within two club-lengths of the spot directly below where the ball is lodged in the tree. Decision 28/11.
Note: In some circumstances this may allow the player to drop a ball on a putting green.

Q.775
A player submits an entry form for a competition with a current handicap of 11. Before the day of the competition he is notified by his Club that he has been cut one stroke and that his new handicap is 10. On the day of the competition the Committee hands him a score card with a recorded handicap of 11. After the competition has closed and a prize awarded to him it is discovered that he should have played off a handicap of 10. What is the ruling?
Answer: He is disqualified and the prize should be taken back. Decision 6-2b/2.
Note: The decision would have been different if the player had not known that he was playing off a handicap higher than that to which he was entitled prior to the competition closing.

Q.776
The day before his first round match is due to be played Nick looks at the atrocious weather forecast and then calls his opponent to say that he is not prepared to play. The Committee subsequently postpones all matches to the following week because the course is unplayable. When he hears this Nick requests that he be reinstated. Should the Committee reinstate him?
Answer: No. Decision 2-4/20.
Note: The Committee should not reinstate the player, as his concession is irrevocable.

Q.777
What is a rub of the green?
Answer: A rub of the green is when a ball in motion is accidentally deflected or stopped by any outside agency. Definition of Rub of the Green.

Q.778
KK, a seven foot tall basketball player, has a custom-made driver with an extra-long (52 inches) shaft in his bag. As he is leaving the 7th green, his fellow competitor notices that the driver, which KK has not yet used during his round, would appear to be non-conforming. What is the penalty?
Answer: KK incurs a penalty of four strokes. Rule 4-1a and Appendix II – Design of clubs.
Note: The maximum length of any club, other than the putter, is 48 inches. The penalty in stroke play is two strokes for any hole at which the breach occurred, with a maximum

penalty per round of four strokes. If KK had used the non-conforming club he would have been disqualified.

Q.779
Bert's ball lies in a bunker that is completely covered by casual water. In some places, the water is several inches deep. Does Bert have an option for taking relief that does not incur a penalty stroke?
Answer: Yes. Bert may drop the ball, without penalty, inside the bunker at the nearest place, not nearer the hole, where the depth of water is the least. Decision 25-1b/8.
Note: Bert also has two other options, a) drop the ball behind the bunker under penalty of one stroke or b) deem the ball unplayable and proceed in accordance with Rule 28, also under penalty of one stroke.

Q.780
The grip on Brandi's driver has become loose. She asks her caddie to go and get a replacement driver but her opponent, Jess, says that the club is not damaged sufficiently for her to be able to replace it during the round within the Rules. Who is correct?
Answer: Brandi may replace her driver in these circumstances. Note to Rule 4-3a.
Note: A loose grip on a club is sufficient for it to be classified as unfit for play.

Q.781
Ciara plays a poor stroke, hitting the ground inches in front of her ball. She replaces her divot and other divots in the area. Then, as she cannot find her ball, she has to return to the same spot to drop and play a ball under stroke and distance penalty. In these circumstances, does Ciara incur a penalty for improving the area in which she has to drop her ball by replacing the divots?
Answer: No. Decision 13-2/4.5.
Note: When Ciara replaced the divots, she was unaware that she would be required to drop a ball in the area. Therefore, in equity (Rule 1-4), she is not penalised.

Q.782
Ike marks the position of his ball on the putting green and lifts it. When it is his turn to putt he replaces a different ball and lifts the ball-marker. As he is addressing his putt he sees that it is not the ball that he should be playing so he then marks the substituted ball, lifts it, and puts back his original ball. What is the ruling?
Answer: There is no penalty. Ike corrected his error and did not make a stroke at the substituted ball. Decision 15-2/2.
Note: Because the substituted ball effectively marked the position of the original ball when the marker was lifted a penalty under Rule 20-1 is not applicable.

Q.783
During a stroke play round Ivor and his playing partners continually have to wait for the group in front to hole out. To kill some time while waiting for the green to clear, Ivor drops a plastic ball on the fairway and chips it several times around where his ball is at rest. What is the ruling?
Answer: Ivor incurs a penalty of two strokes. Decision 7-2/4.
Note: A player must not make a practice stroke during play of a hole.

Q.784
What is the only situation on the putting green that incurs a penalty of two strokes for the player in stroke play and no penalty in match play?
Answer: When a player's putt from on the putting green hits another ball that is in play and at rest on the putting green. Rule 19-5a.
Note: In match play, there is no penalty. In stroke play, there is a penalty of two strokes.

Q.785
On the putting green Tyrone marks and lifts the ball of a fellow competitor, Davy, without authority. By mistake, he replaces the lifted ball with another ball. Davy subsequently plays a stroke with the substituted ball. What is the ruling?
Answer: There is no penalty. Decision 20-1/5.
Note: When a competitor authorises another person to lift his ball, the competitor is responsible for any breach of the Rules (Rule 20-1). The converse is generally true, so the competitor is not responsible for a breach of a Rule caused by the unauthorised lifting of his ball.

Q.786
In stroke play, while preparing to putt, Holly decides to clear some leaves and debris from her intended line. In doing so, she uses her putter to steady herself while bending to pick up the loose impediments. Without her realising it, her putter rested on the line of her putt and smoothed spike marks along the line. Has Holly incurred a penalty?
Answer: Yes. A penalty of two strokes. Rule 16-1a(i).
Note: Holly may remove loose impediments from her line, providing she does not press anything down. There is no exception for inadvertent actions.

Q.787
Thinking that he may have driven his ball out of bounds, Rex plays a provisional ball to a position short of where the original ball is likely to have come to rest. As he walks up the course he sees his original ball and assumes that it is lying in bounds, so he picks up his provisional ball. He then discovers his original ball is out of bounds. What is the ruling?
Answer: Rex must replace his provisional ball at the spot where he lifted it under penalty of one stroke. Decision 27-2b/8.
Note: Because Rex's original ball was out of bounds, his provisional ball was in play. He is penalised one stroke for lifting his ball in play and must replace it. He will be playing his fifth stroke.

Q.788
During the 1st hole of a match Peggy has her daughter carrying her golf bag and her husband cleaning her ball, holding her glove and umbrella, assisting her to line up her putt and attending the flagstick. Her opponent, Davina, advises her that this is not allowed under the Rules. Peggy finishes the hole and scores six while Davina scores five. What is the status of the match?
Answer: Davina is two up. Rule 6-4.
Note: Peggy lost the hole and, as she had two caddies during play of the hole, there is an adjustment of the status of the match by one hole, making her two holes down after the 1st hole.

Q.789
In stroke play, Zara's ball lies by the side of a fixed, course irrigation box, which interferes with her stance, so she is entitled to free relief under Rule 24-2. She determines her nearest point of relief with her 4-iron, as that is the club she intends to play her next stroke with, and drops the ball within one club-length of that nearest point of relief. However, the ball settles down in the rough and Zara changes her mind and plays the ball with a sand wedge out onto the fairway. What is the ruling?
Answer: Zara incurs no penalty. Decision 24-2b/4.
Note: While the Rule states that a player should use the club with which he intends to make his next stroke it does not say that this club has to be used when the stroke is taken.

Q.790
During a round, Roy, who already has a caddie carrying his clubs, asks his brother Graham to go back to his car and get his wet suit, umbrella and soft drinks from his locker. When

Graham returns it is not raining and so he carries them for six holes until there is another downpour and he helps Roy to change. What is the ruling?
Answer: No penalty has been incurred. Decision 6-4/5.3.
Note: Roy may have a caddie carry his clubs and another person to carry other items for him. In the Rules, Graham is an outside agency and any items carried by him would also be considered outside agencies while in his possession.

Q.791
Under the Rules who may lift a ball?
Answer: The player, his partner or anyone authorised by the player. Rule 20-1.
Note: In match play, if a player or his caddie lifts an opponent's ball without authority, the player incurs a penalty of one stroke and the ball must be replaced. If anyone else lifts it, without authority, including a fellow competitor in stroke play, there is no penalty and the ball must be replaced.

Q.792
May a player whose ball lies in soft, mushy earth take relief without penalty from an abnormal ground condition?
Answer: No. Decision 25/1.
Note: Soft, mushy earth is not casual water unless there is water visible on the surface before or after the player takes his stance. Therefore it is not an abnormal ground condition within the Rules.

Q.793
As Valentina's ball is in motion on the putting green Mena realises that it might be diverted by a twig on the putting line. She moves quickly and removes the twig before Valentina's ball reaches it. What is the ruling?
Answer: Mena incurs a penalty of two strokes in stroke play or loss of hole in match play. Rule 23-1.
Note: Loose impediments that might influence the movement of the ball must not be removed once a ball is in motion.

Q.794
Brian hits his ball into a clubhouse that is not out of bounds and has not been declared an integral part of the course. In order to play it out, he opens a window, claiming that it qualifies as a movable obstruction. What penalty does Brian incur?
Answer: Brian does not incur a penalty. Decision 24-2b/14.
Note: The clubhouse is an immovable obstruction. However, any part of it designed to be movable, such as a window or door, may be moved to any position, if this can be done without undue delay.

Q.795
Mark suspects that his tee shot might be lost or out of bounds, and plays a provisional ball that is struck in the same direction as the original ball. Without any announcement, he then plays a third ball from the tee, which comes to rest in the middle of the fairway. What is the ruling?
Answer: If Mark finds his original ball in bounds he must continue play with that ball without penalty. If the original ball is lost or out of bounds, Mark must continue play with the third ball he played from the tee as, when this ball was played without any announcement, it rendered the provisional ball lost, regardless of the provisional ball's location. Mark would lie five with the third ball played from the tee. Decision 27-2a/4.

Q.796
In the final of a match play competition, without the authority of the two opponents, a spectator removed a gallery control rope. It happened also to be holding back branches of a

tree which, when the rope was removed, worsened the position of a player's ball. May that player re-install the rope?
Answer: Yes. Decision 13-2/15.5.
Note: As it was an outside agency that moved the rope the player is entitled to reinstall the rope to where it was, without penalty.

Q.797
May a player take a free drop from a movable obstruction such as temporary rope poles placed to direct players away from a worn area of the course?
Answer: No. The player may move the movable obstruction and then play their stroke from where the ball lies. Rule 24-1.
Note: If the player's ball is moved during the removal of the obstruction it must be replaced and there is no penalty.

Q.798
Austin's ball lies in a water hazard. Is he entitled to drop a ball in a bunker or another water hazard, when properly taking relief under penalty of one stroke?
Answer: Yes. Decision 26-1/2.

Q.799
Due to course renovations the stipulated round of a Stableford competition has been reduced to 12 holes. Penny's handicap is 15, so she calculates that for 12 holes it should be 10 and wrongly records this as her handicap on her score card. What action should the Committee take?
Answer: The Committee should calculate Penny's Stableford points score for the 12 holes based on a handicap of 10, rather than her true handicap of 15. Decision 6-2b/0.5.
Note: Penny is not disqualified for recording a handicap lower than she is entitled to but her score must be calculated on that lower handicap.

Q.800
In match play, through the green, a player improves the area of his intended swing in the process of making the backward movement of his club for a stroke. What is the penalty?
Answer: There is no penalty. Rule 13-2.
Note: Through the green the player incurs no penalty if the action occurs in making a stroke or the backward movement of his club for a stroke and the stroke is made.

Q.801
After playing three strokes with a ball that he had found earlier in a lake a player declares that it is behaving erratically in flight. He marks and lifts it according to the Rules but can detect no visible damage. He reasons that it must be damaged internally. May he therefore substitute it with another ball?
Answer: No. Decision 5-3/1.
Note: A ball is unfit for play if it is visibly cut, cracked or out of shape. There is no provision in the Rules to substitute a ball that may be internally damaged. He must play out the hole with the ball before changing it.

Q.802
Paddy finds a sand wedge on the course and puts it in his bag, meaning to hand it in to the locker room attendant. However, when his round is over he forgets all about it. While he is playing the 4th hole of a strokes competition the following Saturday he finds the club in his bag and tells his fellow competitors how he came to have 15 clubs in his bag. They say that he must penalise himself but he disagrees saying that it is not his club, he took it off the course as a favour to whoever had lost it, and he has not, and will not use it during the round. What is the ruling?
Answer: Paddy incurs a penalty of four strokes. Rule 4-4a.

Note: A player must not start a stipulated round with more than 14 clubs. The penalty in stroke play is two strokes for each hole at which the breach occurred, with a maximum penalty of four strokes a round.

Q.803
Megan is preparing to play a chip shot from off the putting green when her caddie touches the green with a club to indicate her line of play. What is the ruling?
Answer: Megan does not incur any penalty. Decision 8-2b/3.
Note: However, if Megan's ball had been on the putting green and her caddie touched her line of play she would have incurred a penalty of loss of hole in match play or two strokes in stroke play.

Q.804
In a strokes competition, Cain thinks that he will have a little fun and on the 17th teeing ground he tees up his ball on his wallet, which he has taken from his back pocket, and plays it from there. What is the ruling?
Answer: The fun is over for Cain as he incurs the penalty of disqualification. Rule 11-1.
Note: If a player makes a stroke at a ball on a non-conforming tee or at a ball teed in a manner not permitted by this Rule, they are disqualified.

Q.805
Mannie's ball lies on a bridge over a water hazard and he grounds his club. What is the ruling?
Answer: There is no penalty. Decision 13-4/30.
Note: A bridge is an obstruction. In a hazard, the club may touch an obstruction at address or in the backward movement for the stroke. Touching the bridge prior to address is also permissible, since an obstruction in a water hazard is not ground in the hazard.

Q.806
Rupert and Jordan are playing a match. Rupert addresses his ball and is concentrating on his putt, when Jordan's ball, after a stroke, strikes his ball and moves it. What is the ruling?
Answer: It is not relevant whether Rupert had addressed his ball, he incurs no penalty and must replace his ball. Rule 18-5.
Note: Whenever an agency directly causes a ball to move, the Rule applicable to that agency (e.g. Rule 18-1, 18-2a, 18-3, 18-4 or 18-5) applies.

Q.807
Can the Committee insist that competitors enter their scores into a computer, in order to facilitate the administration of the competition and the correct calculation of handicaps?
Answer: No. Decision 6-6b/8.
Note: However, the Committee may produce a club regulation to this effect and impose a disciplinary sanction, such as not being allowed to enter the next competition, for failure to comply.

Q.808
When the Committee has suspended play of a stroke play competition may a player who has started play of a hole lift his ball or does he have to leave it on the course until play is resumed?
Answer: The player may lift his ball, without penalty. Rule 6-8c.
Note: The player must mark the position of his ball before lifting it.

Q.809
Karen and Mandy have enjoyed an excellent foursome strokes competition and are confident that their good score will win a prize. However, Karen misses a very short putt on the 18th putting green as the ball circles the hole, stopping on the lip. She jokes with the two

fellow competitors as she taps the ball in one-handed. Mandy and a marker complete and sign the score card and return them in the competition box. Why are Karen and Mandy disqualified?
Answer: Karen played out of turn when she tapped the ball into the hole. Rule 29-3.
Note: Normally the side incurs a penalty of two strokes and must correct the error before making a stroke on the next teeing ground. However, in the case of the last hole of the round if the players leave the putting green without declaring their intention to correct the error, they are disqualified.

Q.810
What is the procedure if a player thinks his ball may be damaged to the extent that it is unfit for play?
Answer: He must announce his intention to lift his ball, mark its position, and then lift the ball for inspection. He must give his opponent or fellow competitor, the opportunity to observe the lifting and replacing and to examine the ball. The ball must not be cleaned when lifted. Rule 5-3.

Q.811
What is the mandatory diameter for the holes on putting greens on golf courses?
Answer: Four and a quarter inches (108 millimetres). Definition of Hole.

Q.812
In a strokes competition, Roger wrongly thought that he could take relief for an embedded ball in the rough, picked up his ball, cleaned it and dropped it at the nearest point to where it was embedded. After completing his round he and his marker signed for his score and he returned the score card, which did not include the penalty. Before the competition closed the error was brought to the attention of the Committee. How should they rule?
Answer: The Committee must penalise Roger two strokes for lifting his ball in play and not replacing it (penalty statement under Rule 18). They must also penalise him another two strokes, under the Exception to Rule 6-6d, for failure to include the penalty on his score card that he did not know that he had incurred.
Note: Prior to January 2016 Roger would have been disqualified for not including the penalty that he did not know that he had incurred.

Q.813
What is dormie?
Answer: In match play, when a player/side is as many holes up as there are holes left to play. For example, if a player is two up standing on the 17th tee he is said to be dormie, i.e. he cannot lose the match. Rule 2-1.
Note: When extra holes are used to settle a tie then dormie doesn't apply since the match cannot be halved.

Q.814
Didier takes a new ball from a sleeve of three and unfortunately slices his very next shot into an area designated as environmentally-sensitive. He climbs over the wire fence to retrieve his ball. What is the penalty?
Answer: There is no penalty under the Rules of Golf. Decision 33-8/42.
Note: However, depending on the circumstances Didier may be subject to disciplinary action from the Committee or may even have broken the law. A Committee is not entitled to establish a Local Rule imposing a penalty for entering an environmentally-sensitive area.

Q.815
Trevor shanks his ball into a wooded area and his four-ball partner, Don, immediately sets off to try and find it. Trevor goes to his bag, has a drink from his water bottle and then takes out another ball. He drops it correctly at the place where he played his last stroke, and then

shouts to his partner and opponents, who by this time have walked more than 100 yards, to watch out, as he is going to play a provisional ball. Why is Trevor not permitted to continue playing a provisional ball?
Answer: Trevor may only play a provisional ball if he does so before he or his partner proceeds more than a short distance (approximately 50 yards) towards where the original ball is likely to be Decision 27-2a/1.5.
Note: If Trevor does play another ball, that ball is not a provisional ball and becomes the ball in play under penalty of stroke and distance (Rule 27-1), the original ball is lost under the Rules.

Q.816
In stroke play, Olivia hits her ball out of bounds, but a second or two later sees it coming back over a fence onto the fairway. Assuming that it must have ricocheted around hard surfaces before ending up back on the course, she continues play of the hole with the same ball. After she has teed off at the next hole she is advised that a spectator had seen someone pick the ball up from a garden and throw it back onto the course. Does Olivia incur any penalty?
Answer: No. In equity there would be no penalty for playing a wrong ball even though the ball was at rest out of bounds, providing Olivia was not aware that an outside agency had thrown her ball back. Decision 15/10.
Note: However, if Olivia discovers that her original ball was out of bounds before playing from the next teeing ground, she must go back and proceed under Rule 27-1 for a ball out of bounds.

Q.817
Logan is marking Campbell's card in a stroke play competition. As he is feeling unwell he takes a rest while Campbell plays three holes around the turn. When they resume playing together Logan enquires as to Campbell's scores and marks his score card accordingly. At the end of the round they both sign the completed score cards and return them to the Committee. What is the ruling?
Answer: Campbell is disqualified. Rule 6-6a.
Note: Since Campbell was not accompanied by a marker for three holes of the stipulated round the signed card that he returned is invalid.

Q.818
Chris makes a stroke at his ball in a bunker, moving it a few yards forward into the same bunker. He then rakes smooth the footprints that he made in the sand when he took his original stance. Does he incur a penalty?
Answer: No. Exception 2 to Rule 13-4.
Note: Chris may smooth sand or soil in the hazard, providing this is for the sole purpose of caring for the course and nothing is done to improve the position or lie of his ball, the area of intended stance or swing, or his line of play, with respect to his next stroke.

Q.819
After lifting her ball correctly under the Rules, Aoife tries to replace it on a steep greenside slope, but it will not stay on the spot. Each time she tries to replace her ball it rolls to the bottom of the slope. Aoife is not sure what she should do. What is the correct procedure?
Answer: Aoife must place her ball at the nearest spot where it can be placed at rest, not nearer the hole and not in a hazard. Rule 20-3d.

Q.820
In match play, Titch's tee shot strikes her opponent, Tabatha's, golf trolley and rebounds and hits her own golf bag. What are her options?
Answer: Because her ball struck Tabatha's equipment first Titch may replay her tee shot again, without penalty. Titch may also choose to take the option of playing her ball as it lies,

but if she does will incur a penalty of one stroke because, after striking Tabatha's equipment, her ball then struck her own equipment. Decision 19-3/3.
Note: In stroke play, the player incurs a one stroke penalty and must play the ball as it lies.

Q.821
What is the maximum weight and minimum diameter of a golf ball?
Answer: 1.620 ounces (45.93 grams) and 1.68 inches (42.67 millimetres). Appendix III-2 & 3.

Q.822
Bart is playing a match against Bob and is four holes up with four to play. He is tired and has always had a problem with the long 15th at the course they are playing. He concedes the hole to Bob so that they may proceed straight to the teeing ground of the short 16th. Bob is concerned that they will not be playing the stipulated round and that they may both be disqualified. Who is right?
Answer: Bart's concession of the hole before they even tee off is within the Rules. Rule 2-4.
Note: A player may concede a hole at any time prior to the start or conclusion of that hole.

Q.823
A practical joker sticks the flagstick on the other side of the putting green to where the hole is cut. Naturally, the players play towards the flagstick and not the hole. Do the players have the option to replay their shots?
Answer: No. Decision 1-4/3.
Note: The players must accept the resultant advantage or disadvantage.

Q.824
Old Tom has been using a custom-made chipper for 40 years. It has a straight face for putting on one side and a 12° lofted face on the other. May this chipper be used in official competitions?
Answer: No. Decision 4-1/3.
Note: A chipper clubhead must be plain in shape and have only one striking face. See also Appendix II, 4d.

Q.825
In his match with Dara, on a very rainy day, Jimmy has the honour at the 2nd tee. Because the teeing ground is saturated Jimmy tees his ball at least three club-lengths behind the tee-marker and plays his shot. What are Dara's options?
Answer: There is no penalty, but Dara has the option of requiring Jimmy to cancel his shot and re-tee from within the teeing ground or he may let the stroke stand. Definition of Teeing Ground & Rule 11-4.
Note: The teeing ground is two club-lengths in depth behind the tee-markers. In stroke play, if a player plays from outside the teeing ground there is a penalty of two strokes and the ball must be played again from within the teeing ground.

Q.826
Louise intends to play her ball through trees towards the putting green and takes a practice swing to play a stroke in that direction. In doing so she breaks a branch on her backswing. Louise then decides to play out towards the fairway. The area of her intended swing for a stroke in this new direction has not been improved by the breaking of the branch. If she plays in this new direction does she avoid incurring a penalty?
Answer: No. Decision 13-2/24.
Note: Louise incurs a general penalty, two strokes in stroke play or loss of hole in match play, as soon as she improves the area of her originally intended swing. The penalty is not avoided if she subsequently plays in another direction, even if the breaking of the branch has no effect on the area of the swing for a stroke in the new direction.

Q.827
In a match between Barry and Andy, Barry is one up playing the last hole. Andy is on the green in three strokes but a long way from the hole. Barry plays his third stroke from the edge of the green and it comes to rest about one foot from the hole. Andy goes over and shakes hands with Barry. Does Barry win by one hole or two holes?
Answer: Barry wins one up. Decision 2-3/2.
Note: The handshake between the players is deemed to represent an agreement to concede each player's next stroke.

Q.828
Bob misses a short putt and in his frustration instinctively throws his putter at the ball but misses. Has he incurred a penalty for taking an action to influence the position of his ball?
Answer: No. Bob's instinctive action was not made with the intention to influence the movement of his ball and so there is no penalty if he misses the ball. Rule 1-2.
Note: If the thrown putter had moved the ball, Bob would have incurred a penalty stroke under Rule 18-2, and would be required to replace the ball.

Q.829
A player lifts his ball under the Rules, in order to identify it. He takes the opportunity to clear away several loose impediments that are in the area where his ball came to rest, including a large twig that was resting against it. What is the ruling?
Answer: There is a penalty of one stroke. Decision 23-1/8.
Note: Under Rule 18-2 a player incurs a penalty if he causes his ball to move as a result of moving a loose impediment. It would circumvent this Rule if, before a ball is replaced, it was permissible to remove loose impediments which affected the player's lie before the ball was lifted. In equity (Rule 1-4), the player should be penalised one stroke.

Q.830
In a stroke play competition may a Committee modify the penalty for undue delay or slow play from a two strokes penalty for the first offence?
Answer: Yes. The Committee may modify the penalty for breaches of this Rule to: first offence – one stroke, second offence – two strokes, for a subsequent offence – disqualification. Note 2 to Rule 6-7.

Q.831
What is the procedure if a situation occurs on the golf course which is not covered by the Rules?
Answer: If any point in dispute is not covered by the Rules, the decision should be made in accordance with equity. Rule 1-4.

Q.832
Brian was a carpenter and was kind enough to give his Club 18 flagsticks, on which he had carefully carved the number of each hole down the length of the stick. Why should the Committee refuse to use them for Club competitions?
Answer: The carvings meant that they did not conform to the requirements of the Rules. Definition of Flagstick.
Note: The flagstick must be circular in cross-section.

Q.833
Dan strikes a fairway wood with slice and his ball comes to rest in the back of a moving course maintenance buggy about 30 yards from the green. The greenkeeper does not realise that the ball is in the back of his vehicle and does not stop. How does Dan proceed under the Rules?
Answer: Dan must drop another ball as near as possible to the spot directly under the place

where the ball came to rest in the vehicle. Rule 19-1a.
Note: The maintenance buggy was an outside agency.

Q.834
Lee and Diana are to play Dave and Jacqui in a four-ball match. However Lee has been delayed and arrives after Diana, Dave and Jacqui have teed off at the 3rd hole. Lee may not join the match until they tee off at the 4th hole but he does give advice on club selection and line of putt to Diana during play of the 3rd hole. What is the penalty?
Answer: There is no penalty. Decision 30-3a/2.
Note: Lee is entitled to give advice to Diana even though he may not play a stroke until the commencement of the next hole.

Q.835
Tara's ball is lying just off the green and there is a pool of casual water between her ball and the hole. Is Tara or her caddie, permitted to mop up water on her intended line of putt?
Answer: No. Rule 13-2.
Note: Tara must not improve or allow to be improved, her line of play.

Q.836
Ronan has lost his original ball. Under penalty of stroke and distance he takes another ball from his bag and drops it correctly at the place from where he made his last stroke. He then realises that he has dropped a soft, balata ball by mistake. He claims that as he has not put the substituted ball into play he may lift it and exchange it for a different ball. Is Ronan correct?
Answer: No. The substituted ball is in play. Rule 20-4.
Note: A substituted ball becomes the ball in play as soon as it has been correctly dropped or placed. Ronan does not incur any penalty for changing the type of ball being used after his original ball is lost.

Q.837
After 18 holes in a 36-hole match Martha asks the club professional for help with her chipping as her short game is letting her down. Is she breaching a Rule by obtaining the pro's advice during her match?
Answer: No. Decision 8-1/19.
Note: The Rule on giving or receiving advice only applies during a stipulated round. A 36-hole match consists of two 18-hole stipulated rounds.

Q.838
Harry has been marking Max's score card. Both players sign the completed score card and head for the locker room. Harry gets a message to say that he has to leave urgently for family reasons and leaves with Max's score card in his pocket. At the close of competition all efforts to reach Harry have been unsuccessful. What should the Committee do?
Answer: The Committee should accept verification of the score by someone else who witnessed the round (e.g. a caddie or another fellow competitor). In exceptional cases, when no one other than the marker witnessed the round, the score may be accepted by the Committee without penalty. Decision 6-6b/6.

Q.839
George's ball is lodged in a bush. After considering the situation he takes three clubs out of his bag and swings at the ball with all three, fanned out to minimise his chance of missing it. Does George incur a penalty?
Answer: Yes. George incurs a penalty of loss of hole in match play or two strokes in stroke play. Decision 14-1/7.
Note: The ball must be struck at with the head of the club. The word club is in the singular.

Q.840
Martin plays his ball lying in a water hazard and it comes to rest deep in a different water hazard. He then marks where he took his stroke and retrieves his ball, dropping it in the first water hazard at the original spot. Has Martin proceeded within the Rules?
Answer: Martin has taken his relief within the Rules, incurring a penalty of one stroke. Rule 26-2.
Note: Martin's other options were to play the ball as it lay in the second water hazard, under penalty of one stroke, drop a ball behind the hazard on a line extending from the hole through the last place that the original ball crossed the margin of the second water hazard, or play a ball as nearly as possible at the spot from which the last stroke from outside a water hazard was made.

Q.841
In a tense match Frank, who has taken five strokes, asks Lorcan how many strokes he has taken and receives the answer of four. Frank realises that Lorcan has forgotten to add his second stroke, which was a knockdown with a rescue club. Frank quickly takes his putt without much care and then picks up his ball at rest by the hole claiming the hole because Lorcan has given him wrong information. What is the ruling?
Answer: Frank wins the hole as Lorcan has given him wrong information as to his score and does not correct it before Frank plays his next stroke. Rule 9-2b(ii).
Note: If Lorcan had corrected his score error before Frank made his next stroke he would not have incurred the penalty.

Q.842
Miriam's and Becky's balls are both lying in a bunker in a deep footprint left by a previous player. Miriam's ball is obviously interfering with Becky's next stroke so she marks and lifts it. Becky plays first and obliterates the footprint. What should Miriam do?
Answer: Miriam is required to re-create her original lie as nearly as possible, including the footprint, and place her ball in that lie. Decision 20-3b/1.

Q.843
May a player kick the sand from the side of a bunker in order to raise the level of her left foot to the same as that of her right?
Answer: No. This would constitute building a stance. Decision 13-3/3.

Q.844
As a player demonstrates his athleticism by climbing a tree, so as to play his ball that is resting on a branch, the ball drops to the ground. What is the penalty?
Answer: The player incurs a penalty of one stroke for moving his ball in play. Decision 18-2a/26.
Note: The ball must be replaced on the branch.

Q.845
A ball to be placed under the Rules must be placed by the player or his partner. What is the penalty if a ball is placed by any other person and the error is not corrected?
Answer: The player incurs a penalty of one stroke. Rule 20-3a.

Q.846
What is the status of snow?
Answer: A player may opt to treat snow as either casual water or a loose impediment. Definition of Loose Impediments.

Q.847
Mitch chooses to take relief from a course direction sign that is immovable. He drops his ball correctly under the Rules and plays his stroke. However, on his follow-through his club

clearly brushes the edge of the sign. Does he incur a penalty?
Answer: Yes. A penalty of loss of hole in match play and two strokes in stroke play. Decision 20-2c/6.
Note: Having elected to take relief from the obstruction he must then take full relief.

Q.848
After a frosty night, Hayley and Ann have to wait for the course to open before they may commence their match. After nine holes, with the match all square, they realise that they are both going to be late for appointments if their match goes to the 18th. They agree to halve the next five holes and play the final four for the match. What is the ruling?
Answer: Hayley and Ann are both disqualified. Decision 2-1/1.5.
Note: If players agree to consider a hole halved without either player making a stroke, they should be disqualified under Rule 1-3 for agreeing to exclude the operation of Rule 2-1 by failing to play the stipulated round.

Q.849
In taking relief from a staked tree, from which Local Rules allow free relief, a player drops his ball from his hand at arm's length and from shoulder height. However, the ball lodges in a bush without striking the ground. What is the ruling?
Answer: The ball is in play and may not be re-dropped. Decision 20-2b/1.
Note: The bush counts as part of the course where the applicable Rule requires it to be dropped.

Q.850
Kate damages her ball during play of the 7th hole. Cat, her fellow competitor, agrees that it is unfit for play and so she correctly substitutes another ball. At the 16th hole Kate loses her last good ball in a water hazard and only has the damaged ball left in her bag to continue play of the hole. Is Kate permitted to play the damaged ball, having previously taken it out of play?
Answer: Yes and there is no penalty. Decision 5-3/2.
Note: However, Kate may not declare the ball unfit for play a second time, unless there is new damage.

Q.851
What is the status of any material piled for removal by a greenkeeper?
Answer: Ground under repair. Definition of Ground Under Repair.

Q.852
In stroke play, Raine's ball lies under the hanging branches of a tree. He can only get a good swing at it by kneeling down. As the surrounding area is very wet he takes a towel from his bag and kneels on it to make his stroke. What is the ruling?
Answer: Raine is penalised two strokes. Rule 13-3.
Note: A player must not build a stance in order to make a stroke, even if he is kneeling down.

Q.853
A player's ball is embedded in its own pitch-mark on the fairway. He properly lifts his ball under the Rules but, before dropping it he repairs the pitch-mark. Does he incur a penalty?
Answer: Yes. Decision 13-2/10.
Note: A player is not permitted to improve the area in which his ball is to be dropped by eliminating an irregularity of surface. If his ball rolls back into its own pitch-mark it may be re-dropped.

Q.854
A player may remove leaves from a bunker when his ball lies outside the bunker and he wants to putt through the bunker onto the putting green. True or False?

Answer: True. Decision 13-2/31.
Note: Rule 23-1 permits the removal of a loose impediment in a hazard providing the ball is not lying in the hazard.

Q.855
A player who is playing a course for the first time asks a fellow competitor to putt out of turn, to give him a guide as to how much borrow there is on the green. If the other player does play first, both players should be disqualified. True or False?
Answer: True. Rule 10-2c.
Note: Whilst there is no penalty in stroke play for simply playing out of turn, if competitors agree to do so in order to give one of them an advantage, they are both disqualified.

Q.856
Bev's ball came to rest in water in an area that was clearly part of a water hazard but lay outside of a line taken between two red stakes on either side of her ball. It was obvious that there was a stake missing. Because her ball was technically outside the hazard Bev claimed that she could take free relief from casual water. What is the ruling?
Answer: Bev's ball is within the water hazard and she must proceed by taking one of the options under Rule 26-1. Decision 26/2.
Note: A player is not entitled to take advantage of such an error if her ball obviously lies within the intended boundaries of the hazard.

Q.857
Andrew is playing in a team Stableford competition late in the afternoon. The tee shots on the 16th are right into the setting sun and so he asks another member of the team to stand immediately behind him, to watch the flight of his ball. Is this permitted by the Rules?
Answer: No. Rule 14-2b.
Note: When making a stroke, a player must not allow his caddie, his partner or his partner's caddie to be positioned on or close to an extension of the line of play or the line of putt behind the ball.

Q.858
Within the Rules what is the status of insects?
Answer: Loose impediments. Definition of Loose Impediments.
Note: Loose impediments are all natural objects including insects, worms and the like.

Q.859
Laura and Bernie are fellow competitors in a stroke play competition. Laura plays her second stroke onto the green from the right rough. Bernie plays her second onto the green from the left side of the fairway. As they mark their balls on the putting green they both realise that some time earlier in their round they must have played each other's ball. They cannot work out where they had inadvertently exchanged balls. What is the ruling?
Answer: If it cannot be established that their balls were exchanged during play of a hole Laura and Bernie should be given the benefit of the doubt that their balls were exchanged between play of two holes, in which case no penalty is incurred. Decision 15-1/2.

Q.860
In a Bogey competition Monica is unsure whether she may play her ball from a good lie in ground under repair (GUR). She agrees the facts of the situation with her fellow competitors and decides to complete the hole with two balls, saying that if it is within the Rules she wants the ball that she plays from GUR to count. She went on to score a net par with both balls and so did not think it necessary to report the facts to the Committee before signing and returning her score card. Was this the correct procedure?
Answer: No. Monica must report the facts to the Committee, even though she had the same score with both balls. The penalty for not doing so is disqualification. Rule 3-3a.

Q.861
Paul's ball is perched on the lip of a bunker, which is waterlogged. Taking his natural stance, his feet would be in the water in the bunker and so he is entitled to relief from casual water. What is his procedure for taking relief in these circumstances?
Answer: The procedure is the same as for any ball for which relief is available through the green. Paul must determine the nearest point of relief, not in a hazard and not on a putting green, and drop his ball, without penalty, within one club-length of that point, not nearer the hole. Rule 25-1b.
Note: The nearest point of relief is from the casual water. It could mean that Paul's stance is still in the bunker, in a dry part, or it could be on the fairway. It is a matter of fact where the nearest point of relief is.

Q.862
Kerry's approach shot to the green lands in the middle of a lake within the margins of a water hazard. She declares her ball unplayable and drops another ball as nearly as possible to where she played her last shot. Has she breached the Rules?
Answer: Yes and no! Rule 26-1 and 28.
Note: The Ball Unplayable Rule states that a player may deem their ball unplayable at any place on the course, except when the ball is in a water hazard. However, one of the options under the Relief for Ball in Water Hazard Rule is to play a ball as nearly as possible at the spot from which the original ball was last played. Therefore, Kerry incurred the same penalty of one stroke, even though she invoked the wrong Rule.

Q.863
Pat's tee shot comes to rest under a gorse bush. In measuring the option of taking the two club-lengths relief that she may obtain by deeming her ball unplayable, she accidentally moves her ball with the clubhead of her driver. She then declares her ball unplayable, incurring the penalty stroke under Rule 28, and lifts it. She drops a different ball and plays her next stroke to the green. Has Pat incurred any additional penalty?
Answer: No. There is no additional penalty. Rule 18-6.
Note: There is no penalty if the movement of a ball or ball-marker is directly attributable to the specific act of measuring. Also, there is no penalty for continuing play of the hole with a different ball after taking a penalty under Rule 28, Ball Unplayable.

Q.864
Adrian spends seven minutes searching for his tee shot in the rough before he finds it. By this time his fellow competitors are putting out on the green. However, he plays his ball onto the green and holes his putt. What is the ruling?
Answer: Adrian's ball is lost and therefore he played a wrong ball onto the green. Decision 27/8.
Note: As soon as the five minute period allowed for search had expired Adrian's ball was lost. By playing the ball onto the green he played a wrong ball and incurs a penalty of two strokes. If he does not correct the error by returning to the tee and playing again, before playing from the next teeing ground, he is disqualified.

Q.865
A player believes his ball may be in a bunker and finds a ball there that is almost completely covered with sand. He cannot be certain that it is his ball. How should he proceed within the Rules?
Answer: The player may remove as much sand as necessary to enable identification of the ball, Rule 12-1a. If he cannot identify his ball in a bunker without lifting it he must follow the procedure outlined in Rule 12-2.
Note: Before lifting the ball he must announce his intention to his opponent or fellow competitor, and mark the position of the ball. He may then lift the ball and identify it,

providing that he gives his opponent or fellow competitor an opportunity to observe the lifting and the replacement. When replacing the ball he must re-cover it with sand to the extent that it was prior to the search.

Q.866
On a hot summer's day Mary's ball comes to rest on a steeply sloped area of a green. She marks her ball and awaits her turn to putt. After replacing the ball she takes a couple of steps back to check her line of putt and her ball begins to slowly roll, towards the hole. Has she incurred a penalty and where will she have to play her putt from?
Answer: As Mary had not addressed her ball and did not cause it to move there is no penalty and she must putt from where the ball came to rest. Note to Rule 18-1.
Note: It is likely that blades of grass gave way on the lower side of where the ball was at rest and gravity took over. The ball must be played from where it came to rest, whether that is closer to or farther from the hole.

Q.867
What is the line of putt?
Answer: The line of putt is the line that the player wishes his ball to take after a stroke on the putting green. It includes a reasonable distance on either side of the intended line but does not extend beyond the hole. Definition of Line of Putt.

Q.868
Must lines defining out of bounds be painted white?
Answer: No. Definition of Out of Bounds.
Note: The definition says that stakes or lines used to define out of bounds should be white.

Q.869
While considering his shot from a bunker a player rakes the sand to remove footprints that are between his ball and the hole. What is the penalty?
Answer: He incurs a penalty of two strokes. Rule 13-2.
Note: A player must not improve their line of play by eliminating irregularities of surface.

Q.870
After reaching the putting green, Andrew places his clubs behind the back of the green. His opponent, Rory, accidentally drives his cart over the bag, breaking several clubs. What is the ruling?
Answer: In equity, Andrew may use his clubs in their damaged state, repair them or have them repaired or replace them. Decision 4-3/9.5.

Q.871
Maya elects to take relief from a fixed bench and lifts her ball. She then realises that the only area in which she may drop her ball will give her a more difficult shot than from her original lie. She replaces her ball and plays it from its original position. What is the ruling?
Answer: Maya incurs a penalty of one stroke for lifting her ball in play. Decision 18-2a/12.
Note: When she decided not to take relief from the immovable obstruction, Maya's right to lift the ball was negated.

Q.872
Francis brushes away leaves from behind a hole because he suspects that they may act as a backstop to his opponent, Mitch's putt. Mitch thinks that Francis has breached a Rule by removing the leaves and claims the hole. What is the ruling?
Answer: Francis did not incur a penalty as he is entitled to remove loose impediments. However, in equity (Rule 1-4) Mitch is entitled, but not required, to replace the leaves moved by Francis. Decision 23-1/10.

Q.873
Randy's ball comes to rest in high weeds. After searching briefly, he finds a ball that has his brand and number, but he cannot see his identification mark on it. He tells his four-ball partner that he is going to lift the ball to identify it. He then marks the position of the ball, lifts it, identifies it as his own and replaces it. Has he followed the correct procedure within the Rules?
Answer: No. He must inform a fellow competitor in stroke play or opponent in match play that he is going to lift the ball. Rule 12-2.
Note: It is not sufficient to notify his partner who is playing on his side.

Q.874
In stroke play, before playing a stroke, Cyril lifts a large stone lying next to his ball in a water hazard. The stone has obviously broken away from a nearby stone wall that is located outside the hazard. What is the ruling?
Answer: There is no penalty. Decision 24/6.
Note: The stone is a movable obstruction, not a loose impediment, because it was once part of a man-made wall.

Q.875
What is the procedure regarding continuation of play if the Committee suspends play during a strokes competition?
Answer: If the players in a group are between the play of two holes, they must stop play immediately. If they have commenced play of a hole, they may discontinue play immediately or continue to play out that hole, providing they do so without delay. Rule 6-8b.

Q.876
In taking proper relief from an immovable obstruction, Chloe does not go through the procedure recommended for determining the nearest point of relief. Instead, she lifts her ball and drops it about half a club-length from the nearest edge of the obstruction, not nearer the hole than the ball's original position, and plays it. What is the ruling?
Answer: Chloe does not incur any penalty. Decision 24-2b/2.
Note: Although there is a recommended procedure for determining the nearest point of relief, it is not mandatory that a player follows the procedure, providing her ball is dropped at a spot that satisfies the requirements of the relief permitted under the Rule and it does not roll into a position that requires a re-drop.

Q.877
On a cold winter's morning, Finlay's ball lands next to a thin sheet of natural ice on the fairway, which he will have to stand on to take his next stroke. He wants to take relief from the area saying that the ice is casual water. His fellow competitor, Dec, says that ice is a loose impediment and he will have to remove the ice and play the ball as it lay. Who is right?
Answer: Both Finlay and Dec are right as the Definition of Loose Impediments states that snow and natural ice, other than frost, are either casual water or loose impediments at the option of the player.

Q.878
Which areas of the course are not covered by through the green?
Answer: All hazards and the teeing ground and putting green of the hole being played. Definition of Through the Green.

Q.879
On the fairway, Amy addresses her ball and starts her backswing when her ball moves slightly. She continues her stroke and strikes the ball while it is still moving. What is the ruling if it was certain that Amy did not cause her ball to move?
Answer: Amy does not incur a penalty as she did not cause her ball to move. Rule 18-2.

Note: Amy must play her next stroke from where her ball comes to rest. (This Rule was revised January 2016.)

Q.880
In stroke play, a group of players arrive at a teeing ground and find one tee-marker missing. They determine the area of the teeing ground based on the position of the existing tee-marker and the shape of the tee and play from the place they judge to be the teeing ground. Is this the correct procedure?
Answer: The correct procedure is to discontinue play until the Committee resolves the problem. Decision 11-4b/2.
Note: However, if the Committee is satisfied that the competitors did not gain an advantage by playing from the place they judged to be the teeing ground, it would be appropriate for the Committee, in equity (Rule 1-4), to accept their scores, without penalty.

Q.881
Sandra and Karena hit their second shots into the same area of rough. Both balls are quickly found but, because they are playing new balls of the same brand and number, neither Sandra nor Karena are sure which ball is theirs. What is the ruling?
Answer: Since neither player is able to positively identify their own ball, both balls are deemed lost. Decision 27/10.
Note: It is strongly recommended that players put personal identification marks on their golf balls, as advised in Rule 12-2.

Q.882
What are the three occasions when a player may not clean their ball, which they have properly lifted under the Rules?
Answer: i) To determine if it is unfit for play. ii) For identification, except that it may be cleaned to the extent necessary to identify it. iii) Because it is assisting or interfering with play. Rule 21.

Q.883
Josh and Eric are playing a match. Josh plays from the tee first, when in fact Eric has the honour. Eric requests Josh to cancel his stroke and play another ball in the correct order, after him. However, when Eric plays a good tee shot down the middle of the fairway he tells Josh not to bother playing another ball. What is the ruling?
Answer: Josh may choose whether to play his original ball or play another ball from the tee, as originally requested by Eric. Decision 10-1c/1.
Note: Eric should not have changed his request for Josh to play another ball but there is no penalty for having done so.

Q.884
Kevin has borrowed a new driver from the Club Pro Shop with a view to purchasing it. The Pro has attached adhesive tape to the sole of the clubhead to protect it from damage. May the club be used like this in a competition?
Answer: No. Decision 4-1/5.
Note: Tape added to the clubhead is considered an external attachment, rendering the club non-conforming in breach of Rule 4-1a.

Multiple Choice

Q.885
Rollo and Brett, playing partners in a four-ball strokes competition, are sharing a motorised golf cart. Brett skies a bunker shot and it hits the wheel of the cart, while Rollo is driving it behind the green. What is the penalty?
A) There is no penalty as the cart in motion is an outside agency.
B) There is no penalty as the cart is deemed to be Rollo's equipment while he is driving it and not Brett's.
C) Brett incurs a penalty of one stroke.
D) Brett incurs a penalty of two strokes.
Answer: C) Brett incurs a penalty of one stroke. Decision 19/1.
Note: If a player's ball is accidentally deflected or stopped by himself, his partner, either of their caddies or their equipment, the player incurs a penalty of one stroke. If Brett and Rollo were fellow competitors, rather than partners on the same side, no penalty would have been incurred while Rollo was driving the cart.

Q.886
In a foursome match, Avril, whose turn it is to play, plays from outside the teeing ground. Her opponents immediately require her side to cancel the stroke and play again, this time from within the teeing ground. What is the ruling?
A) Avril must play the next stroke, her side's first stroke.
B) Avril must play the next stroke, her side's second stroke.
C) Avril's partner must play the next stroke, her side's second stroke.
D) Avril and her partner lose the hole.
Answer: A) Avril must play the next stroke, her side's first stroke. Decision 29-1/1.
Note: It is Avril who must replay the stroke. The original stroke does not count. Her opponents could have chosen to let the first stroke stand, even though it was played from outside the teeing ground.

Q.887
In a stroke play competition Adrienne notices that there is a bad spike mark directly on her fellow competitor, Sarah's line of putt. She walks over to it and flattens it with her putter. Sarah watches her without doing anything to stop her and then thanks her. What is the ruling?
A) There is no penalty as Sarah did not ask Adrienne to repair the spike mark.
B) Sarah incurs a penalty of two strokes.
C) Adrienne incurs a penalty of two strokes.
D) Both Sarah and Adrienne incur a penalty of two strokes.
Answer: D) Both Sarah and Adrienne incur a penalty of two strokes. Decision 13-2/36.
Note: Adrienne is penalised under Rule 1-2 for exerting influence on Sarah's ball. Sarah is also penalised because she tacitly sanctioned Adrienne's breach, which was to her advantage.

Q.888
In four-ball stroke play, a side returns a score card with the score of one player omitted for one hole. His partner, whose score is marked, had the higher of the two scores in play of the hole. In a separate column the marker has recorded a better-ball score, based on the lower score that was omitted. What is the ruling?
A) The Committee can accept the lower better-ball score if they can find the players in time to correct the marker's error.
B) The Committee should correct this obvious mistake and allow the better-ball score for the hole as recorded by the marker to stand.
C) The Committee is responsible for the better-ball score, so the partner's higher score

stands as the better-ball score for the hole.
D) The side is disqualified for returning an incorrect score card.
Answer: C) The Committee is responsible for the better-ball score, so the partner's higher score stands as the better-ball score for the hole. Rules 31-3 and 33-5.
Note: The Committee is responsible for the addition of scores and the application of the handicap recorded on the score card. As there was only one gross score recorded on the card this is the score that they must apply.

Q.889
Rick chips his ball from off the putting green and as it slows down near the hole a dog takes it in his mouth and then drops it farther away from the hole. There is no penalty, but where does Rick play his next stroke from?
A) It is a rub of the green and Rick must play the ball from where the dog dropped it.
B) Rick must place the ball as near as possible to the spot where his ball was when the dog picked it up.
C) Rick must play his ball again from the place where he originally made his chip.
D) Rick and his playing partners must agree where the ball would have come to rest and he must place the ball there.
Answer: B) Rick must place the ball as near as possible to the spot where his ball was when the dog picked it up. Decision 19-1/6.
Note: If the moving ball is deflected by the dog (rather than picked up), it has to be played from the place at which it comes to rest.

Q.890
As competitors arrive on the 1st tee the Committee issues them with stroke play score cards containing the date, their name and their handicap. The Committee mistakenly records Sid's handicap as 11 instead of 10 and this affects the number of strokes he receives. The error remains unnoticed until after Sid has signed and returned his card, but before the competition has closed. What is the ruling?
A) The Committee should accept the returned card as it was their fault that the wrong handicap was applied.
B) Sid's correct handicap should be applied to his score by the Committee.
C) Sid should be disqualified if he returned his card knowing that it had the wrong handicap.
D) Sid should be disqualified, whether he knew of the mistake on his handicap or not.
Answer: D) Sid should be disqualified, whether he knew of the mistake on his handicap or not. Decision 6-2b/3.5.
Note: It is Sid's responsibility to ensure that his correct handicap is recorded on his score card before he signs it and returns it to the Committee.

Q.891
In stroke play, Doreen removes the flagstick and places it on the putting green near the hole. As she putts and her ball nears the hole, a fellow competitor, Joan, moves the flagstick, fearing that the ball might strike it. What is the ruling?
A) There is no penalty.
B) Doreen incurs a penalty of two strokes.
C) Joan incurs a penalty of one stroke.
D) Joan incurs a penalty of two strokes.
Answer: A) There is no penalty. Rule 24-1.
Note: The flagstick and any player's equipment are specific exceptions in this Rule that obstructions that might influence the movement of a ball in motion must not be moved.

Q.892
In match play, Hugo and Simpson find that they have exchanged their balls during play of the hole, but they cannot work out who played the wrong ball first. What is the correct procedure?

A) Hugo and Simpson should play out the hole with the balls exchanged.
B) Hugo and Simpson halve the hole.
C) Hugo and Simpson should replay the hole from the teeing ground.
D) Hugo and Simpson should both be disqualified.
Answer: A) Hugo and Simpson should play out the hole with the balls exchanged. Rule 15-3a.
Note: When it cannot be determined where the balls were exchanged the hole must be played out with the balls exchanged.

Q.893
In stroke play, Lottie's tee shot strikes a tree and her ball rebounds back and comes to rest within the area of the teeing ground. With her foot she presses down some grass growing behind her ball before she plays. What is the ruling?
A) There is no penalty.
B) Lottie incurs a penalty of one stroke.
C) Lottie incurs a penalty of two strokes.
D) Lottie incurs a penalty of one stroke and must take her tee shot again.
Answer: A) There is no penalty. Decision 13-2/2.
Note: Lottie is entitled to eliminate irregularities of surface on the teeing ground, whether or not her ball is in play.

Q.894
Robbie and Dan both lose their balls in the same area of a lateral water hazard and therefore it is not known which ball is farther from the hole. However, Dan's ball last crossed the hazard margin farther from the hole than Robbie's ball. What is the order of play for their next strokes?
A) The ball to be played first should be decided by lot.
B) Robbie must play first.
C) Dan must play first.
D) Whichever player's ball is farther from the hole after they have both dropped their balls under Rule 26 must play first.
Answer: A) The ball to be played first should be decided by lot. Decision 10-3.
Note: A Note to 10-1b and 10-2c says that when a ball may be played from a spot other than where the previous stroke was made, the order of play is determined by the position where the original ball came to rest. As this is unknown in this situation the order must be decided by lot.

Q.895
In a match, Ronan, who has already holed out for four, gives advice to his opponent, Eamon, who is about to putt for a four. What is the ruling?
A) Ronan loses the hole for giving advice.
B) There is no penalty for giving advice to an opponent and Eamon must take his putt.
C) The hole is halved.
D) Ronan incurs a penalty of one stroke.
Answer: C) The hole is halved. Decision 2-2/1.
Note: When a player has holed out and his opponent has been left with a stroke for the half, if the player subsequently incurs a penalty, the hole is halved.

Q.896
In foursomes match play, Anne, whose turn it is to play, plays first from the tee. Then absent-mindedly, Bonnie, her partner, plays from the tee as though it is a four-ball event. What is the ruling?
A) The side is lying two and Bonnie's ball is in play.
B) The side is lying three and Bonnie's ball is in play.
C) The side is lying three and Anne's ball is in play.

D) Anne and Bonnie lose the hole.
Answer: B) The side is lying three and Bonnie's ball is in play. Decision 29-1/9.
Note: As Bonnie plays a stroke at another ball from the spot at which the original ball was properly played by Anne, she is deemed to have proceeded under penalty of stroke and distance.

Q.897
A ball is embedded in an orange lying under an orange tree. What is the ruling?
A) As the orange is a loose impediment the player should mark the position of the ball, remove the ball from the orange, and replace the ball.
B) As the orange is a loose impediment the player should mark the position of the ball, remove the ball from the orange, and drop the ball at the mark.
C) The player must play the ball as it lies.
D) The player must play the ball as it lies or declare it unplayable.
Answer: D) The player must play the ball as it lies or declare it unplayable. Decision 23/10.
Note: Since the orange was adhering to the ball, it was not a loose impediment.

Q.898
A player's ball lies in a bunker covered by leaves. He probes with his club to remove enough leaves to enable him to see part of the ball. As he prepares to make his stroke, he touches some of the leaves with his club. What is the ruling?
A) There is no penalty for using his club to remove leaves to see part of the ball or touching leaves with his club in preparing for his stroke.
B) There is a penalty for using his club to remove leaves to see part of the ball but not for touching leaves with his club in preparing for his stroke.
C) There is a penalty for touching leaves with his club in preparing for his stroke but not for using his club to remove leaves to see part of the ball.
D) There are penalties both for using his club to remove leaves to see part of the ball and touching leaves with his club in preparing for his stroke.
Answer: C) There is a penalty for touching leaves with his club in preparing for his stroke but not for using his club to remove leaves to see part of the ball. Rules 12-1 & 13-4.
Note: The player is allowed to remove, by probing or raking with a club, as many loose impediments as will enable him to see a part of the ball. However, once he has identified his ball, he may not touch or move a loose impediment lying in or touching the hazard.

Q.899
Keith's ball is oscillating on the putting green due to the windy conditions. To ensure that it does not move after he addresses it Keith firmly presses the ball into the surface of the green and then holes out. What is the ruling?
A) Keith incurs no penalty.
B) Keith incurs a penalty of one stroke.
C) Keith incurs a penalty of loss of hole in match play or two strokes in stroke play.
D) Keith incurs total penalties of loss of hole in match play or three strokes in stroke play.
Answer: C) Keith incurs a penalty of loss of hole in match play or two strokes in stroke play. Decision 1-2/9.
Note: In altering the surface of the putting green, Keith has breached Rule 1-2 by intentionally taking action to influence the movement of a ball in play and to alter physical conditions that affect the playing of the hole. The ball must be played as it lies.

Q.900
Which is correct regarding a player taking relief without penalty under the obstruction Rule?
A) If his ball lies on a bridge over a hollow, through the green, he may drop the ball within two club-lengths of the bridge.
B) If his ball lies on a bridge over a hollow, through the green, he may drop the ball within one club-length of the point on the ground directly beneath where it lay.

C) If his ball lies on a folding chair, through the green, he may drop the ball within one club-length of the point on the ground directly beneath where it lay.
D) If his ball lies on a folding chair, through the green, he may lift the chair and place the ball on the spot directly beneath where it lay.
Answer: B) If his ball lies on a bridge over a hollow, through the green, he may drop the ball within one club-length of the point on the ground directly beneath where it lay. Decision 24-2b/11.
Note: In determining the nearest point of relief vertical distance is disregarded. In the two cases where the ball was lying on a folding chair, the ball may be lifted and the obstruction removed. The ball must then be dropped as near as possible to the spot directly under the place where the ball lay in or on the obstruction, but not nearer the hole.

Q.901
In a Stableford competition, Rolf marks Colin's gross scores correctly and also calculates his points accurately, using Colin's correct handicap, which he knows because they often play together. Both he and Colin sign the score card and return it to the Committee. However Colin had forgotten to record his handicap on his score card. What is the ruling?
A) There is no penalty as the gross scores and Stableford points have been entered correctly.
B) There is no penalty if Colin can be contacted to verify his handicap before the competition closes.
C) Colin is penalised two strokes for failing to record his handicap on his score card.
D) Colin is disqualified from the competition.
Answer: D) Colin is disqualified from the competition. Rule 6-2b.
Note: If no handicap is recorded on the score card before it is returned, the competitor is disqualified.

Q.902
In stroke play, Arthur's caddie practises on the 18th putting green of the course 15 minutes before Arthur is due to tee off. What is the penalty?
A) There is no penalty.
B) Arthur incurs a penalty of two strokes.
C) Arthur is disqualified.
D) Arthur must find another caddie or play without one.
Answer: A) There is no penalty. Decision 7-1b/5.
Note: A competitor is responsible for the actions of his caddie only during a stipulated round, not before the round.

Q.903
In a stroke play competition, John's ball is lying just outside a bunker. Lying in the bunker and on his line of play is a large branch of a tree that had blown down overnight. John proceeds to remove the branch from the bunker saying that it is a loose impediment. What is the ruling?
A) John incurs a penalty of two strokes for removing a loose impediment from a bunker and has to replace the branch.
B) John incurs a penalty of two strokes for removing a loose impediment from a bunker but does not have to replace the branch.
C) John does not incur any penalty because the branch is a movable obstruction, which can be removed anywhere on the course.
D) John does not incur any penalty because a player may remove a loose impediment from a bunker if his ball does not lie in that bunker.
Answer: D) John does not incur any penalty because a player may remove a loose impediment from a bunker if his ball does not lie in that bunker. Rule 23-1.
Note: Loose impediments may be removed from a hazard providing the ball does not lie in that hazard.

Q.904
In stroke play, Marion incurs a disqualification penalty in a play-off. Is she disqualified from the whole competition?
A) No, the disqualification applies only to the play-off.
B) Yes, the play-off is an integral part of the competition.
C) The Committee must decide, according to the circumstances.
D) The matter should be decided by lot.
Answer: A) No, the disqualification applies only to the play-off. Decision 3/1.

Q.905
Sally replaces her ball on the putting green and it is at rest. Just as she starts to address the ball a sudden gust of wind blows it farther from the hole. What is the ruling?
A) Sally plays her ball from its new position and there is no penalty.
B) Sally plays her ball from its new position and incurs a penalty of one stroke.
C) Sally replaces her ball where she thinks it was at rest before the wind moved it and there is no penalty.
D) Sally replaces her ball where she thinks it was at rest before the wind moved it and incurs a penalty of one stroke.
Answer: A) Sally plays the ball from its new position and there is no penalty. Decision 18-1/12.
Note: Wind is not an outside agency. Definition of Outside Agency. So, Rule 18-1, relating to a ball at rest moved by outside agency, does not apply.

Q.906
In stroke play, Dave's ball lies within the margin of a water hazard. During a practice swing he moves small stones, twigs and loose earth and also touches the ground in the hazard. He then bends back some reeds with his club, improving the area of his intended swing. What penalty or penalties does he incur?
A) Dave does not incur any penalty as it was only a practice swing.
B) Dave incurs a penalty of two strokes.
C) Dave incurs total penalties of three strokes.
D) Dave incurs total penalties of four strokes.
Answer: D) Dave incurs total penalties of four strokes. Decision 13-4/28.
Note: Dave's single act of moving loose impediments and grounding the club in a hazard during his practice swing incurs a single penalty of two strokes. However, he also incurs a penalty of two strokes for improving the area of his intended swing by bending growing reeds.

Q.907
After a week of heavy rain, Sharon finds her ball at the base of a large tree. She realises that she cannot play her natural right-handed stroke because of the position of her ball against the tree. She decides to take a left-handed stance but then finds that in order to do this she will be standing in casual water. She wants to take relief from the casual water as an abnormal ground condition. Which of the following is correct?
A) Sharon's only option, without incurring a penalty, is to play her ball as it lies.
B) Sharon may take relief, without penalty, but if she does she must play her next stroke left-handed.
C) Sharon may take relief, without penalty, and may play her next stroke either right or left-handed.
D) Sharon must declare her ball unplayable and incur a penalty of one stroke.
Answer: C) Sharon may take relief without penalty and may play her next stroke either right or left-handed. Rule 25-1b and Decision 25-1b/3.
Note: If a player's line of play is improved when she takes proper relief it is her good fortune.

Q.908
During a match with Donal, Cian thins his bunker shot and it sails over the putting green and comes to rest on Donal's towel that is lying by the side of his bag on the apron. Cian decides to play the ball from where it has come to rest on the towel, chips onto the green and holes his putt for a four. Donal scores a five. Before leaving the putting green Donal makes a claim concerning Cian playing his ball from his towel. What is the result of the hole?
A) Cian's procedure was correct and he wins the hole.
B) Donal's claim is valid and he wins the hole.
C) Donal's claim is valid, but Cian incurs a penalty of one stroke so the hole is halved.
D) Cian may drop his ball at the spot where it came to rest on the towel and play out the hole from there, without penalty.
Answer: B) Donal's claim is valid and he wins the hole. Rule 19-3.
Note: Because the ball came to rest on an opponent's equipment, it must be dropped as near as possible to the spot directly under the place where it was at rest on the article, not nearer the hole. However, when Cian found that his ball was lying on Donal's towel he could have chosen to cancel the stroke and play a ball, without penalty, as nearly as possible to the spot from which he had played his original ball.

Q.909
Which of the following statements is incorrect regarding a ball played from off the green?
A) The player incurs a penalty of two strokes if her ball hits the unattended flagstick in the hole.
B) The player incurs a penalty of loss of hole if her ball hits the flagstick held by her opponent.
C) The player incurs a penalty of two strokes if her ball hits her fellow competitor who is attending the flagstick.
D) The player incurs a penalty of two strokes if her ball hits the flagstick lying on the putting green beside the hole.
Answer: A) The player incurs a penalty of two strokes if her ball hits the unattended flagstick in the hole. Rule 17-3.
Note: Unless the player plays her ball from on the putting green or asks for the flagstick to be attended, there is no penalty for her ball hitting the flagstick.

Q.910
In stroke play, Brian looks into Tom's golf bag to determine which club Tom used for his last stroke. What is the ruling?
A) Brian incurs a penalty of one stroke.
B) Brian incurs a penalty of two strokes.
C) Brian is disqualified.
D) There is no penalty.
Answer: D) There is no penalty. Decision 8-1/10.
Note: Information obtained by observation is not advice. However, a player is prohibited from obtaining such information through a physical act, such as moving a towel covering the clubs.

Q.911
April and Sadie start their match at 9.00am. After they had played seven holes, they were told that the course had been closed since 7.30am, but that no notice to this effect had been put up. What is the ruling when the course reopens?
A) Their match should be resumed at the 8th hole.
B) Their match should be replayed entirely.
C) Both April and Sadie are disqualified.
D) The result of the holes played should stand and if their match was all square it should be decided by lot.

Answer: B) Their match should be replayed entirely. Decision 33-2d/4.
Note: Play on a course that is closed is null and void.

Q.912
In a stroke play competition, Liam mistakenly tells a fellow competitor, Brian, who was not his marker that he has holed out in six strokes, when in fact he has taken seven strokes. What is his penalty?
A) There is no penalty.
B) Liam is penalised one stroke.
C) Liam is penalised two strokes.
D) Liam is disqualified.
Answer: A) There is no penalty. Decision 9-3/1.
Note: In stroke play, there is no penalty for mistakenly giving wrong information to another fellow competitor as to the number of strokes taken. However, after each hole the marker should check the score with the competitor and record it. If a score is returned that is lower than was actually taken the player is disqualified.

Q.913
Hilary's tee shot comes to rest in a fairway bunker. She walks into the bunker to survey the situation. Staying several yards behind her ball she digs in her feet, simulating how she intends to make her stroke, without a club. She returns to her bag outside the bunker to select a club. Without being asked, Hilary's caddie then rakes her footprints in the bunker, without touching or moving any loose impediments and nowhere near where she will be taking her stance or on her line of play. Hilary then plays out of the bunker to just short of the green. She chips on and makes the putt. What is her score for the hole?
A) Four strokes.
B) Five strokes.
C) Six strokes.
D) Eight strokes.
Answer: A) Four strokes. Decision 13-4/0.5 and Exception 2 to Rule 13-4.
Note: Hilary's digging into the sand with her feet several yards from where her ball lies to simulate her stance does not constitute testing the condition of the bunker. As her caddie was raking her footsteps solely for the purpose of caring for the course no penalty was incurred for this action either. Hilary has therefore played four strokes.

Q.914
In stroke play, Ewan's ball is at rest within the course boundaries but is lodged in a hollow between three branches of a tree that is rooted out of bounds. Ewan gets help to climb onto the boundary wall and into the tree and manages to play his ball towards the green. Which of the following is correct?
A) The ball is out of bounds and Ewan incurs a stroke and distance penalty.
B) The ball is in bounds and Ewan incurs no penalty.
C) Ewan incurs a penalty of two strokes for receiving assistance in taking his stance.
D) Ewan incurs a penalty of two strokes for climbing onto a boundary wall.
Answer: B) The ball is in bounds and Ewan incurs no penalty. Definition of Out of Bounds.
Note: An out of bounds line extends vertically upwards and downwards. There is no penalty for a player receiving assistance in getting into position to play a stroke.

Q.915
Paulo is attending the flagstick for his opponent, Luigi. After Luigi has taken his putt and his ball is in motion, Paulo removes the flagstick and lays it on the putting green. He then realises that Luigi has putted his ball too far right of the hole and that it may hit the flagstick lying on the green. He quickly picks it up and holds it until Luigi's putt comes to rest. What is the penalty?
A) There is no penalty.

B) Paulo loses the hole.
C) Luigi loses the hole.
D) The hole is halved.
Answer: A) There is no penalty. Rule 24-1.
Note: When a ball is in motion, the only obstructions that may be moved if they might influence the movement of the ball, are the equipment of any player, or the flagstick when attended, removed or held up.

Q.916
In match play, Debbie requests her opponent, Martha, to lift her ball because it is interfering with her play. Instead of lifting, Martha plays her ball. Debbie claims the hole. What is the ruling?
A) Debbie wins the hole because Martha played out of turn.
B) There is no penalty, Martha's stroke stands and it is Debbie's turn to play.
C) There is no penalty but Martha must replace her ball and play again.
D) Debbie may let Martha's stroke stand or she may require her to replay her stroke in the correct order.
Answer: D) Debbie may let Martha's stroke stand or she may require her to replay her stroke in the correct order. Rule 10-1c.
Note: There is no penalty, but the opponent may immediately require the player to cancel the stroke so made and, in correct order, play a ball as nearly as possible at the spot from which the original ball was last played.

Q.917
In stroke play, Ger is playing with two others and all three of their balls are on the putting green. He putts badly and his ball bounces off one of his fellow competitor's balls onto the other, moving them both. The fellow competitors' balls are replaced where they were at rest before being moved. What is Ger's penalty?
A) There is no penalty.
B) Ger incurs a penalty of one stroke.
C) Ger incurs a penalty of two strokes.
D) Ger incurs penalties totalling four strokes.
Answer: C) Ger incurs a penalty of two strokes. Decision 1-4/12(1).
Note: A single penalty is applied for a single act resulting in one Rule being breached more than once.

Q.918
In stroke play, Olga's ball is covered in sand in a bunker. She removes sand by raking it aside with her club and soon finds her ball, moving it slightly. What is her penalty?
A) There is no penalty.
B) Olga incurs a penalty of two strokes.
C) Olga incurs total penalties of three strokes.
D) Olga incurs total penalties of four strokes.
Answer: A) There is no penalty. Rule 12-1a.
Note: Olga may remove as much sand as will enable her to see a part of the ball by probing or raking with a club or otherwise. There is no penalty if she moves her ball while searching for it in the sand but it must be replaced and the lie re-created.

Q.919
Robbie is an early starter in a stroke play competition and completes his round before midday. As he enters the locker room his friend, Charles, says that he has strained his back and asks Robbie if he will carry his clubs for his round. Robbie agrees to caddie for Charles and does so for nine holes, after which he has to leave. Has there been any breach of Rules?

A) Charles is disqualified as Robbie is not permitted to caddie for him, having already played the course that day.
B) Both Charles and Robbie are disqualified from the competition.
C) Robbie is entitled to caddie for Charles and no penalty is incurred.
D) At the end of the round Charles is penalised a maximum of four strokes from his total score.
Answer: C) Robbie is entitled to caddie for Charles and no penalty is incurred. Decision 6-4/8.
Note: The fact that Robbie has already played the course is irrelevant, as a competitor is responsible for the actions of his caddie only during a stipulated round.

Q.920
Freddie's third stroke on the 12th hole is from a bunker and he watches as the ball flies over the boundary wall. Trying to compose himself, as he was doing well in the Saturday medal competition, he carefully rakes over the area of his stance and stroke. He then drops another ball at where he had played his last stroke, playing it close to the hole, from where he taps in. What is his score on the hole?
A) Five strokes.
B) Six strokes.
C) Seven strokes.
D) Eight strokes.
Answer: B) Six strokes. Decision 13-4/37.
Note: Freddie played five strokes, and incurred the stroke and distance penalty for ball out of bounds, but no penalty for smoothing the sand. Exception 2 to Rule 13-4 states that if a ball is outside the hazard after the stroke, the player may smooth sand or soil in the hazard without restriction.

Q.921
During a stroke play competition Ernie finds that his area of swing is impeded by a fence, which is not a boundary fence. He removes a part of the fence that is easily removable, so that he may get a better swing. What is the ruling?
A) Ernie incurs a penalty of one stroke for removing part of something fixed.
B) Ernie incurs a penalty of two strokes for removing part of something fixed.
C) There is no penalty for removing part of a fence that is not a boundary fence.
D) There is no penalty for removing part of a fence if the part is easily removable.
Answer: B) Ernie incurs a penalty of two strokes for removing part of something fixed. Decision 13-2/32.
Note: A fence is an immovable obstruction and all parts of the fence are deemed to be fixed.

Q.922
In stroke play, during play of the 4th hole, Bill's ball comes to rest on the fringe of the 6th green. Even though his ball does not lie on the 6th green, Bill will have to stand on the putting green to play the ball. Unsure as to whether he is allowed to play the ball from such a position, Bill announces that he will play two balls (the original as it lies and a second ball dropped away from the putting green so as to remove his stance from the green) and that he would like to score with the original ball played as it lies. He scores four with each ball and returns his score card to the Committee, without reporting to them that he had played two balls. What is the ruling?
A) Bill's score for the hole is four.
B) Bill's score for the hole is five.
C) Bill's score for the hole is six.
D) Bill is disqualified.
Answer: D) Bill is disqualified. Rule 3-3a.
Note: When a player who is doubtful of his rights or the correct procedure, plays two balls

under the Rules, it is mandatory that he reports the facts of the situation to the Committee before returning his card.

Q.923
A player's ball lies in a bunker. While he is assessing his stroke, a member of the greenkeeping staff rakes the bunker, improving his line of play. Which statement is correct?
A) If the staff member's actions were not on the instructions, but were with the sanction of the player, there is no penalty.
B) If the staff member's actions were on the instructions of the player, there is no penalty.
C) If the staff member's actions were not on the instructions nor with the sanction of the player, there is no penalty.
D) The player incurs a penalty of two strokes.
Answer: C) If the staff member's actions were not on the instructions nor with the sanction of the player, there is no penalty. Decision 13-2/4.
Note: If the staff member raked the bunker on the instructions or with the sanction of the player, the player incurs a penalty of two strokes in stroke play or loss of hole in match play.

Q.924
Gerry has a habit of teeing his ball very close to one of the tee-markers, which at his club are straight, wooden logs about 18 inches long. He does this so that the marker gives him a guide for his line of swing. In a stroke play competition he walks onto the 17th tee and finds that he cannot tee his ball in his customary manner, close to the left hand tee-marker, because a fence impedes his stance. He moves the tee-marker two feet closer to the other one to give himself room. What is the penalty?
A) There is no penalty.
B) Gerry incurs a penalty of one stroke.
C) Gerry incurs a penalty of two strokes.
D) Gerry is disqualified.
Answer: C) Gerry incurs a penalty of two strokes. Decision 11-2/2.
Note: A player is penalised the general penalty if he moves a tee-marker for the purpose of avoiding interference with his stance, the area of his intended swing or his line of play. However, if he moves either of the tee-markers because in his view they are too close together, too far back, aimed in the wrong direction or some similar reason he is disqualified under Rule 33-7.

Q.925
In stroke play, Dylan plays a provisional ball from the teeing ground. He discovers his original ball out of bounds but cannot find his provisional ball. What is the ruling?
A) Dylan must return to the tee where he will be playing his third stroke.
B) Dylan must return to the tee where he will be playing his fourth stroke.
C) Dylan must return to the tee where he will be playing his fifth stroke.
D) Dylan may drop a ball where he thinks the provisional ball was lost under penalty of a further stroke.
Answer: C) Dylan must return to the tee where he will be playing his fifth stroke. Decision 27-2c/4.
Note: As the original ball was out of bounds the provisional ball became Dylan's ball in play. When the provisional ball could not be found the only option was for him to return to the tee to play a third ball, his fifth stroke.

Q.926
George replaces his ball where he had marked it, on the downslope of a putting green, about 18 inches from the hole, and the ball stays at rest for several seconds. As he is about to address the ball, it rolls down into the hole. What is the ruling?
A) George is required to replace the ball where it was marked.
B) George is required to replace the ball where it was marked and must add a penalty stroke

to his score.
C) George is deemed to have holed out with his previous stroke.
D) George is deemed to have holed out with his previous stroke but must add a penalty stroke to his score.
Answer: C) George is deemed to have holed out with his previous stroke. Decision 20-3d/1.
Note: In this situation the ball was definitely at rest before it started to roll. If it was not at rest then George must replace it where it was marked.

Q.927
Cian leaves his ball on the course when play is suspended, due to lightning in the area. When play resumes he notices that there is mud adhering to the underside of his ball. Without stating his intention he marks his ball, lifts it, cleans off the mud and replaces it at the mark. What is the ruling?
A) Cian incurs a penalty of one stroke for lifting his ball without announcing his intention.
B) Cian incurs a penalty of one stroke for cleaning his ball.
C) Cian incurs a penalty of two strokes for lifting his ball without announcing his intention and then cleaning it.
D) Cian incurs no penalty.
Answer: D) Cian incurs no penalty. Rule 6-8d(ii).
Note: Following a discontinuance of play ordered by the Committee, either before or when play is resumed, players are permitted to mark, lift, and clean their ball in play and then replace the original or a substitute ball on the spot at which the original ball was marked.

Q.928
Tom's tee shot comes to rest on a steep downslope inside a water hazard. He decides to play the ball as it lies, but does not move it with his stroke. Embarrassed and agitated he steps away from his ball and cleans his club in the water in the water hazard. He takes a deep breath and plays his next shot onto the putting green. At this point how many does Tom lie on this hole?
A) Three strokes.
B) Four strokes.
C) Five strokes.
D) Six strokes.
Answer: C) Five strokes. Rule 13-4b.
Note: One stroke off the tee, one fresh air, a penalty of two strokes and the stroke from the hazard onto the putting green. When his ball lies inside the margin of a water hazard a player may not touch water in the hazard with his hand or a club, other than during a stroke.

Q.929
Kay starts a stroke play round with 13 clubs. During the front nine she breaks her putter in anger. After finishing the 9th hole she quickly goes into the Pro Shop and buys a new putter, which she then uses for the rest of the round. What is the ruling?
A) Kay incurs a penalty of two strokes.
B) Kay incurs a penalty of two strokes at each hole where she uses the new putter.
C) Kay incurs the maximum penalty of four strokes, deducted from her score at the end of her round.
D) There is no penalty.
Answer: D) There is no penalty. Decision 4-3/8.
Note: Since Kay started her round with only 13 clubs, she is entitled to add another club during her round.

Q.930
Which is correct regarding a player's ball being embedded?
A) If he takes relief under the embedded ball Rule but the ball embeds again when dropped and re-dropped, he is entitled to place it as near as possible to the spot where it embedded

after the second drop.
B) If he plays a stroke at his ball, which lies on a steep bank in a closely-mown area through the green, and hits it straight into the bank without it ever being airborne, he is entitled to relief without penalty for an embedded ball.
C) If his ball is embedded in ground under repair in a closely-mown area through the green he must take relief from ground under repair.
D) If his ball is embedded in a closely-mown pathway from the teeing ground to the fairway he is not permitted to take relief.
Answer: A) If he takes relief under the embedded ball Rule but the ball embeds again when dropped and re-dropped, he is entitled to place it as near as possible to the spot where it embedded after the second drop. Decision 25-2/2.5.
Note: In B) the ball was not embedded in its own pitch-mark as it was never airborne. In C) as the area was closely-mown he is entitled to take relief but does not have to. In D) he may take relief.

Q.931
Bunnie's ball enters a rabbit hole, the opening of which is in bounds but very close to a boundary fence. The rabbit hole slopes steeply down below the fence, so that her ball is at rest on the far side of the boundary line. What is the ruling?
A) Bunnie must drop a ball, without penalty, within one club-length of the nearest point of relief to the rabbit hole, an abnormal ground condition.
B) Bunnie must drop a ball, under penalty of one stroke, within one club-length of the nearest point of relief to the rabbit hole.
C) Bunnie must drop a ball, under penalty of two strokes, within one club-length of the nearest point of relief to the rabbit hole.
D) Bunnie must proceed under penalty of stroke and distance as her ball is out of bounds.
Answer: D) Bunnie must proceed under penalty of stroke and distance as her ball is out of bounds. Decision 25-1b/24.
Note: The ball is out of bounds because it came to rest outside of the boundary of the course, the margins of which are vertically upwards and downwards.

Q.932
In order to identify her ball Jasmine lifts it without marking its position, and without announcing her intention to her match play opponent. She then cleans her ball thoroughly with a towel from her bag. What is the ruling?
A) Jasmine incurs a penalty of one stroke.
B) Jasmine incurs a penalty of two strokes.
C) Jasmine incurs total penalties of three strokes.
D) Jasmine loses the hole.
Answer: A) Jasmine incurs a penalty of one stroke. Decision 21/4.
Note: Although Jasmine has breached three Rules, each of which incur a penalty of one stroke, the Exception under Rule 21 means that a second or third penalty is not justified.

Q.933
In stroke play, Louisa's ball lies in a flowerbed and she is uncertain if she is entitled to relief. She announces that she will play a second ball under the Rules. She plays the original ball as it lies and then the second ball, taking relief under the ground under repair Rule. However, she fails to declare in advance with which ball she wishes to score. The Committee confirms that there is a Local Rule defining the flowerbed as an area of ground under repair from which play is prohibited. What is the ruling?
A) Since the first ball was not played according to the Rules, the score with the second ball counts without penalty.
B) Since the first ball was not played according to the Rules, the score with the second ball counts with a penalty of two strokes.

C) Since Louisa did not declare in advance which ball she would score with, the score with the original ball counts with a penalty of two strokes.
D) Louisa is disqualified for not fully complying with the correct procedure for playing a second ball.
Answer: A) Since the first ball was not played according to the Rules, the score with the second ball counts without penalty. Rule 3-3b.
Note: If the competitor fails to announce in advance which ball she wishes to count, the score with the original ball counts providing it has been played in accordance with the Rules.

Q.934
In match play, Sam's opponent, Tim, has already made par on the hole. Sam's birdie putt appears to stop on the lip of the hole. He walks up to the hole and waits for 25 seconds, willing his ball to drop in to win the hole. To his great relief it does. What is the ruling?
A) Sam has holed out with his putt and wins the hole.
B) Sam is penalised one stroke and halves the hole.
C) Sam incurs the general penalty of loss of hole.
D) Sam incurs a penalty of two strokes for undue delay.
Answer: B) Sam is penalised one stroke and halves the hole. Rule 16-2.
Note: In this situation the player is allowed enough time to reach the hole without unreasonable delay and an additional 10 seconds to determine whether the ball is at rest. If the ball subsequently falls into the hole, the player is deemed to have holed out with his last stroke and must add a penalty stroke to his score for the hole.

Q.935
Whilst making a stroke, Gerry bends the shaft of his 4-iron against a tree. In attempting to repair the club he breaks the shaft in half, rendering it unfit for play. What is the ruling?
A) Gerry may not repair or replace his 4-iron.
B) Gerry is penalised two strokes for attempting to change his 4-iron's playing characteristics.
C) Gerry may repair his 4-iron or replace it with another 4-iron.
D) Gerry may repair his 4-iron or replace it with any club he chooses.
Answer: D) Gerry may repair his 4-iron or replace it with any club he chooses. Decision 4-3/3.
Note: As the club was damaged in the normal course of play, Gerry was entitled to repair it and, having damaged it further, have it repaired or replaced with any club.

Q.936
Alice and Charlotte are playing in a Stableford competition on a nine hole course. Due to bad weather the play is delayed and when they finish nine holes they have a wait of 30 minutes before they can continue at the 10th. The practice facilities are nearby and Alice uses her driver in the driving bay while Charlotte putts on the practice putting green. Do they incur any penalties?
A) Both Alice and Charlotte are disqualified.
B) Both Alice and Charlotte incur a penalty of two strokes.
C) There is no penalty for Charlotte but Alice incurs a penalty of two strokes.
D) There is no penalty for Alice but Charlotte incurs a penalty of two strokes.
Answer: C) There is no penalty for Charlotte but Alice incurs a penalty of two strokes. Rule 7-2.
Note: While players are allowed to practice pitching and putting near the putting green of the hole last played or on a practice putting green, the Rule does not permit players to practice driving.

Q.937
Jacque's and Ollie's shots have come to rest within an inch of each other inside the boundary of a water hazard, but not in the water. They both elect to play their shots from the

hazard. Jacque's ball lies in Ollie's line of play and they agree that it should be lifted, noting the ground condition and lie of his ball. Jacque then marks and lifts his ball. What is the ruling?
A) Jacque and Ollie are both disqualified for agreeing to waive a Rule.
B) Jacque is penalised one stroke for lifting his ball in play contrary to the Rules.
C) Jacque is penalised two strokes for lifting his ball from a hazard.
D) There is no penalty as Jacque and Ollie have acted correctly to this point.
Answer: D) There is no penalty as Jacque and Ollie have acted correctly to this point. Rule 22-2.
Note: Jacque's ball must be replaced back in the water hazard in the nearest lie most similar to his original lie that is not more than one club-length from the original lie and not nearer the hole (Rule 20-3b). Jacque must not clean his ball during this procedure.

Q.938
On the 1st hole of a strokes competition, James realises that he has left his putter at home and asks Marty if he will lend him his putter while someone goes to get it for him. Marty agrees and they share his putter until the 4th green when James is handed his own. What is the penalty?
A) James incurs a penalty of two strokes.
B) James incurs penalties totalling four strokes.
C) Both James and Marty are disqualified.
D) Both James and Marty incur penalties totalling four strokes.
Answer: B) James incurs penalties totalling four strokes. Decision 4-4a/12.
Note: Borrowing a club that has been selected for play by any other person on the course is not permitted. James incurs a penalty of two strokes for each hole at which any breach occurred with a maximum penalty per round of four strokes.

Q.939
In stroke play, on the 1st tee a very nervous Sheila misses her ball completely. She bends down and pushes her tee deeper into the ground and prepares to make another stroke at her ball. What is the ruling?
A) Sheila incurs a penalty of one stroke.
B) The ball was not yet in play and so no penalty is incurred.
C) Sheila incurs a penalty of stroke and distance.
D) Sheila incurs a penalty of two strokes.
Answer: C) Sheila incurs a penalty of stroke and distance. Decision 18-2/1.
Note: When Sheila had her 'fresh air' her ball was in play. By pushing her tee further into the ground, she moved the ball, incurring a penalty of one stroke under Rule 18-2 and was required by that Rule to replace it. However, as she did not replace her ball she was effectively playing her next stroke under penalty of stroke and distance (Rule 27-1a). It will therefore be her third stroke.

Q.940
Zoe's ball is within the margins of a water hazard resting against a brick, which has a large pine cone lying on top. What are her options?
A) Zoe must play her ball as it lies.
B) Zoe may remove the pine cone and the brick but must then replace the pine cone.
C) Zoe may remove the pine cone and the brick providing she does not touch the pine cone.
D) Zoe may drop her ball within one club-length of the nearest point of relief from the brick.
Answer: B) Zoe may remove the pine cone and the brick but must then replace the pine cone. Decision 1-4/5.
Note: Zoe may remove the brick, which is an obstruction, as permitted under Rule 24-1. As the loose impediment will also be moved in the process, in equity the player incurs no penalty and must replace the loose impediment as near as possible to where it lay.

Q.941
The greenkeeper had sanded many of the fairways on the morning of a strokes competition. On the 2nd hole Rod's tee shot lies on the fairway with a clump of sand lying where he wants to ground his club to address his ball. Rod brushes the sand away with his loose glove. What is the ruling?
A) There is no penalty.
B) Rod incurs a penalty of one stroke for brushing away the sand.
C) Rod incurs a penalty of one stroke for using his glove to brush away the sand.
D) Rod incurs a penalty of two strokes for brushing away the sand.
Answer: D) Rod incurs a penalty of two strokes for brushing away the sand. Rule 13-2.
Note: Sand and loose soil are loose impediments only on the putting green.

Q.942
Darrell's tee shot on a par 3 hole comes to rest on a closely-mown area sloping towards the putting green. He carefully removes some grass clippings from two feet behind where his ball is at rest doing nothing that could cause his ball to move. The ball subsequently rolls down the slope onto the putting green coming to rest three feet from the hole. He holes the putt for an apparent two. Before leaving the putting green, he is advised by a fellow competitor that he should have replaced the ball on the slope rather than putting it from where it rolled to. Darrell replaces a ball back at the spot on the slope where his tee shot came to rest. He holes out in two more strokes. After reporting the facts to the Committee, what is Darrell's score for the hole?
A) Two strokes.
B) Three strokes.
C) Four strokes.
D) Six strokes.
Answer: A) Two strokes. Rule 23-1.
Note: Darrell's removal of the loose impediments in no way caused his ball to move. Thus, it was proper to play the ball from its new position without penalty, even though the ball had rolled closer to the hole.

Q.943
Nils and Gustav are partners in a four-ball Stableford competition. During the play of the 10th hole they realise that they exchanged balls during play of the 9th hole. What is the ruling?
A) There is no penalty as Nils and Gustav have already put their balls in play at the 10th hole.
B) Nils and Gustav incur a penalty of two strokes at the 9th hole.
C) Nils and Gustav are disqualified from the 9th hole.
D) Nils and Gustav are disqualified from the competition as they did not finish out the 9th hole with their original balls.
Answer: C) Nils and Gustav are disqualified from the 9th hole. Decision 32-2b/1.
Note: Nils and Gustav score no points at the hole at which they exchanged balls.

Q.944
Marion purposely steps on spike marks that are on the line of putt of her fellow competitor, Norah, so as to improve her line. What is the ruling?
A) There is no penalty.
B) Norah incurs a penalty of two strokes.
C) Marion incurs a penalty of two strokes.
D) Both Marion and Norah incur a penalty of two strokes.
Answer: C) Marion incurs a penalty of two strokes. Decision 1-2/1.
Note: A player must not take any action to influence the position or the movement of a ball except in accordance with the Rules. If Marion's action damaged Norah's line of putt, in equity she may restore it to its previous condition.

Q.945
Imelda drives her ball into a fairway bunker that is filled with water. After probing the water she finds her ball at the front of the bunker. How may she proceed?
A) Imelda may drop a ball in the bunker without penalty at the nearest point, not nearer the hole, where the depth of the casual water is least.
B) Imelda may drop a ball outside the bunker, keeping the point where the ball lay directly between the hole and the spot where the ball is dropped, under penalty of one stroke.
C) Imelda may deem the ball unplayable and, under penalty of one stroke, proceed in accordance with Rule 28.
D) All of the above.
Answer: D) All of the above. Rule 25-1b(ii).

Q.946
Barak is having a bad day in the Saturday strokes competition. After his tee shot on the 15th hole he plays a wrong ball into a difficult area under a tree. His next shot is a fresh air and then he manages to move it a few yards onto the fairway. He then realises that he has played a wrong ball with his second stroke. How many strokes does Barak lie if he finds his original ball?
A) Three strokes.
B) Four strokes.
C) Five strokes.
D) Six strokes.
Answer: A) Three strokes. Rule 15-3b.
Note: Strokes made with the wrong ball do not count, but Barak incurs a penalty of two strokes and has to find his original ball or return to the teeing ground to play another ball, which would be his 5th stroke.

Q.947
Having addressed his ball on the fairway, Chip starts his stroke and is on his downswing when it starts to move. He continues his stroke, moving the ball just 20 yards forward. What is the ruling if it is known or virtually certain that Chip did not cause his ball to move?
A) Chip must play the ball from where it comes to rest, without penalty.
B) Chip must play the ball from where it comes to rest and incurs a one stroke penalty.
C) Chip must retrieve his ball and drop it at the point where he made the stroke, without penalty.
D) Chip must retrieve his ball and drop it at the point where he made the stroke and incurs a one stroke penalty.
Answer: A) Chip must play the ball from where it comes to rest, without penalty.
Note: As Chip did not cause his ball to move he did not incur a penalty and must play his next stroke from where it came to rest. Rule 18-2, revised January 2016.

Q.948
On a dog-leg hole Brad plays a good 7-iron over the trees thinking that his ball is going to be very close to the hidden putting green. However, when he reaches the area in which he presumes his ball should be, he cannot find it. His opponent, Larry, points out that there is a dog running around that may have picked it up. How should Brad proceed?
A) Brad has to play another ball from where he last played under penalty of stroke and distance.
B) Brad may drop another ball at the place that he and Larry agree the ball would have come to rest, without penalty.
C) In equity, Brad may replay his stroke from where he last played, without penalty.
D) Brad loses the hole as he cannot finish the hole with the same ball that he started with.
Answer: A) Brad has to play another ball from where he last played under penalty of stroke and distance. Decision 27-1/2.5.

Note: If it is not known or is virtually certain that the ball has been moved by an outside agency, the player must put another ball into play under Rule 27-1, Stroke and Distance

Q.949
In a four-ball match, Perry walks onto the green and by mistake marks and lifts an opponent's ball. What is the ruling?
A) There is no penalty.
B) Perry incurs a penalty of one stroke.
C) Perry and his partner each incur a penalty of one stroke.
D) Perry and his partner lose the hole.
Answer: B) Perry incurs a penalty of one stroke. Rule 18-3b.
Note: The ball must be replaced by either of the opponents or Perry.

Q.950
In four-ball match play, Todd putts away from the hole to a spot near his partner, Bobbie's ball-marker, but farther from the hole. Then, Todd putts towards the hole. He does this so that he may give a line to Bobbie for his putt. What is the ruling?
A) There is no penalty.
B) Todd is disqualified for the hole.
C) Todd and Bobbie lose the hole.
D) Todd is disqualified from the match.
Answer: C) Todd and Bobbie lose the hole. Decision 30-3f/6.
Note: Since Todd's action assisted Bobbie, the partners both incur the penalty and lose the hole. Such action is contrary to the spirit of the game and the ruling is made under Rule 1-4, equitable decisions on points not covered by the Rules, and Rule 30-3f.

Q.951
In a strokes competition, Dale and Jennie play their approach shots to the 5th green. They then agree to take their tee shots for the 6th hole before putting out at the 5th, so that they do not have to walk back up the hill to the 6th tee, and also to save time. What is the ruling?
A) There is no penalty as they are playing out all the holes in the stipulated round.
B) They are both disqualified.
C) They both incur a penalty of one stroke.
D) They both incur a penalty of two strokes.
Answer: B) They are both disqualified. Rule 3-2.
Note: In stroke play, competitors must complete the play of each hole before making a stroke from the next teeing ground. In match play, the players would also be disqualified for agreeing to play other than the stipulated round.

Q.952
Which of the following is not a wrong ball, when played by a competitor?
A) A ball substituted for a ball that has been lifted on the putting green.
B) An abandoned ball in a water hazard.
C) Another player's ball at rest in a bunker.
D) The player's own ball played from an out of bounds lie.
Answer: A) A ball substituted for a ball that has been lifted on the putting green. Definition of Wrong Ball.
Note: A wrong ball is any ball other than the player's ball in play. Ball in play includes a ball substituted for the ball in play, whether or not the substitution is permitted under the Rules.

Q.953
In stroke play, Raj putts his ball just as a gust of wind blows a paper bag in front of the hole. He quickly moves forward and removes the bag to stop the ball hitting it. What is the penalty?
A) There is no penalty.

B) Raj incurs a penalty of one stroke.
C) Raj incurs a penalty of two strokes and his putt stands.
D) Raj incurs a penalty of two strokes and must replay his putt.
Answer: C) Raj incurs a penalty of two strokes and his putt stands. Rule 24-1.
Note: Once a ball is in motion, the only obstructions that may influence the movement of the ball that a player may remove are equipment of a player and the flagstick.

Q.954
In equity, under what circumstance may Rowena take relief, without penalty?
A) When her ball comes to rest in a patch of stinging nettles.
B) When her ball comes to rest in a gull's nest.
C) When her ball comes to rest in a prickly cactus.
D) All of the above.
Answer: B) When her ball comes to rest in a gull's nest. Decisions 1-4/9 and 1-4/11.
Note: It is unreasonable to expect Rowena to play from a bird's nest and unfair to require her to incur a penalty stroke. However, unpleasant lies in conditions that may normally be encountered on a golf course are a common occurrence, which players must accept.

Q.955
In stroke play, Padraig practises putting on the 18th green immediately after finishing the first round of a 36-hole event scheduled over consecutive days. What is the ruling?
A) There is no penalty.
B) Padraig incurs a penalty of one stroke.
C) Padraig incurs a penalty of two strokes.
D) Padraig is disqualified.
Answer: A) There is no penalty. Decision 7-2/8.
Note: Rule 7-2 permits practice putting or chipping on or near the putting green of the hole last played and this applies, even though technically in this case the practice was between rounds, not during a round.

Q.956
In stroke play, Aran's ball lies deep in a bush. Having identified it as his ball he declares it unplayable and decides to drop a different ball within two club-lengths of where it lay not nearer the hole. What is the ruling?
A) Aran incurs no penalty.
B) Aran incurs a penalty of one stroke.
C) Aran incurs a penalty of two strokes for substituting a ball for the ball in play.
D) Aran must drop a ball at the spot from which he last played under penalty of stroke and distance.
Answer: B) Aran incurs a penalty of one stroke. Rule 28.
Note: Providing a player has identified a ball as his ball he may deem it unplayable at any place on the course except in a water hazard. When taking one of the three options under Rule 28, all of which incur a penalty of one stroke, he does not have to continue with the same ball.

Q.957
Matt's ball is lost in a tree growing in an area marked as ground under repair (GUR). What is the ruling?
A) Matt must proceed as though his ball is lost incurring a stroke and distance penalty.
B) Matt must proceed by taking one of the three options for ball unplayable.
C) Providing he finds his ball, Matt is entitled to take relief, without penalty, from an abnormal ground condition.
D) Matt is entitled to take relief, without penalty, from an abnormal ground condition even if he cannot find his ball.
Answer: D) Matt is entitled to take relief, without penalty, from an abnormal ground condition

even if he cannot find his ball. Decision 25/10.
Note: As the tree is rooted in GUR the ball is considered to be lost in GUR and Matt is entitled to relief, without penalty.

Q.958
During a round, Sarah realises that she is carrying 15 clubs in her bag. She tells her opponent, Maya, who refuses to apply the penalty for this breach of the Rules and they continue to play out their match. How should the Committee rule?
A) That the result of the match should stand.
B) Adjust the result of the match by penalising Sarah two holes, the maximum penalty for this breach of Rules.
C) Disqualify Sarah.
D) Disqualify both Sarah and Maya.
Answer: D) Disqualify both Sarah and Maya. Rule 1-3.
Note: As the players agreed to waive the known penalty, they are disqualified.

Q.959
In a strokes competition, Tom is acting as caddie for two players, Sheila and Maria. After they have played nine holes, Maria's friend, Alison, says that she will pull her trolley for her for the rest of her round. Tom continues to give Maria advice on club selection and line of putts for the rest of the round. Has any penalty been incurred?
A) Both players are disqualified as two players may not share a caddie.
B) Maria is disqualified for having two caddies at the same time.
C) Maria incurs a penalty of two strokes for having two caddies at the same time.
D) Maria incurs a maximum penalty of four strokes for having two caddies at the same time.
Answer: D) Maria incurs a maximum penalty of four strokes for having two caddies at the same time. Rule 6-4.
Note: A player is limited to having only one caddie at any one time. The penalty in stroke play is two strokes for each hole during which the breach occurred, with a maximum of four strokes per round.

Q.960
In a match, Sarah has played three strokes and Eva has holed out for five. Sarah putts and her ball apparently comes to rest, but is overhanging the hole. Within five seconds, Eva concedes Sarah's next stroke and knocks her ball away. What is the ruling?
A) Because Eva has infringed Sarah's rights she loses the hole.
B) Because Eva has infringed Sarah's rights she loses the match.
C) Eva incurs a penalty of one stroke for moving a ball at rest and the ball must be replaced by Sarah without penalty.
D) The concession stands and the hole is halved.
Answer: A) Because Eva has infringed Sarah's rights she loses the hole. Decision 16-2/2.
Note: Sarah is allowed a reasonable time to reach the hole and an additional 10 seconds to determine whether her ball might drop in the hole. As Eva has infringed Sarah's rights by knocking the ball away before the 10 seconds has expired, in equity (Rule 1-4), Eva loses the hole.

Q.961
In match play, Rees cannot determine whether his ball is lost in casual water, overflowing outside the margins of a water hazard or the water hazard itself. How should he proceed?
A) Assume that the ball is in casual water and take free relief.
B) Assume that the ball is in the water hazard and take one of the relief options under penalty of one stroke.
C) Replay his last stroke, without penalty.
D) Play out the hole with two balls and report to the Committee at the end of the round to ascertain which score will stand.

Answer: B) Assume that the ball is in the water hazard and take one of the relief options under penalty of one stroke. Decision 1-4/7.
Note: In equity, the player must proceed under the water hazard Rule.

Q.962
Boo strikes his ball from a water hazard onto an adjacent teeing ground where Jim, a competitor in another group, is making a practice swing, accidentally strikes it. Boo's ball comes to rest in a bunker. What is the ruling?
A) The ball must be replaced where it was when Jim struck it.
B) The ball must be played as it lies in the bunker.
C) Boo must replay his stroke from the water hazard.
D) Boo can choose whether to replay his stroke from the water hazard or play his next stroke from the bunker.
Answer: B) The ball must be played as it lies in the bunker. Decision 19-1/2.
Note: Jim is an outside agency so Boo's next stroke has to be played from where his ball came to rest.

Q.963
In match play, Rory holes out and tells George, his opponent, that he has scored a five. George, having already played five strokes, picks up assuming he has lost the hole. Rory then realises that he had actually scored a six. He immediately informs George. What is the ruling?
A) George wins the hole as Rory incurs a penalty for giving wrong information.
B) Rory wins the hole as George effectively conceded the hole in picking-up his ball.
C) The hole is halved as George cannot possibly score better than Rory's six.
D) George must replace his ball, without penalty, and has a putt to halve the hole.
Answer: C) The hole is halved as George cannot possibly score better than Rory's six. Decision 9-2/6.
Note: Under Rule 9-2 Rory would normally lose the hole for giving wrong information. However, since Rory had already holed out for no worse than a half, the hole is halved. (Rule 2-2).

Q.964
Several people are searching for Randy's ball in long grass when a spectator says that he has trodden on a ball by mistake pressing it into the ground. Having identified it as his ball Randy is unsure how to proceed. What is the ruling?
A) Randy must play the ball where it lies after being trodden on.
B) Randy must place the ball as near as possible to where it lay in the rough without penalty.
C) Randy must drop the ball as near as possible to where it lay in the rough without penalty.
D) Randy must drop the ball as near as possible to where it lay in the rough and he incurs a penalty of one stroke.
Answer: C) Randy must drop the ball as near as possible to where it lay in the rough without penalty. Decision 20-3b/5.
Note: As it is impossible for Randy to determine the original lie of his ball, which has been altered due to the ball being trodden on, he must drop it in the long grass as near as possible to where it lay.

Q.965
While play is suspended, wind moves Erica's ball that she left on the course after her tee shot. What is the ruling?
A) When play resumes Erica must replace her ball on the spot where it was marked, without penalty.
B) When play resumes Erica must play her ball from its new position without penalty.
C) When play resumes Erica must replace her ball and she incurs a penalty of one stroke.

D) Erica is disqualified for leaving her ball unattended on the course during suspension of play.
Answer: A) When play resumes Erica must replace her ball on the spot where it was marked, without penalty. Rule 6-8d(iii).
Note: If the spot where the ball is to be placed is impossible to determine, it must be estimated and the ball placed on the estimated spot. The provisions of Rule 20-3c do not apply.

Q.966
Carl is playing with Alan in a stroke play competition. After Alan plays from the 2nd tee, but before Carl plays his own tee shot, Carl discovers that he has two putters in his bag and has carried 15 clubs from the start of his round. What is the ruling?
A) There is no penalty as Carl did not use one of the putters on the 1st hole and he can now declare the second putter out of play.
B) Carl incurs a penalty of two strokes.
C) Carl incurs total penalties of four strokes.
D) Carl is disqualified.
Answer: B) Carl incurs a penalty of two strokes. Decision 4-4a/11.
Note: In stroke play, the penalty for starting a round with more than 14 clubs is two strokes for each hole at which any breach occurs. As Carl had not played a stroke from the second tee he is not penalised for that hole.

Q.967
In stroke play, Tammy's ball lies under a bush and it is clearly impracticable for her to play any stroke at it. However, her ball lies against a mound made by burrowing animals. What is the ruling?
A) Tammy may take relief, without penalty, from the abnormal ground condition even if this also gives her relief from the bush.
B) Tammy may take relief from the abnormal ground condition and then decide whether to play her ball or follow the procedure for ball unplayable, incurring a penalty of one stroke.
C) Tammy must take relief from both the abnormal ground condition and the bush, within two club-lengths of where her ball lies, incurring a penalty of two strokes.
D) Tammy must either play her ball as it lies or follow the procedure for ball unplayable, incurring a penalty of one stroke.
Answer: D) Tammy must either play her ball as it lies or follow the procedure for ball unplayable, incurring a penalty of one stroke. Decision 25-1b/19.
Note: Tammy is not entitled to relief from the mound made by burrowing animals because it is clearly impracticable for her to play a stroke due to interference by the bush. See Exception to Rule 25-1b.

Q.968
Miko's ball comes to rest in a hole left by a yellow water hazard stake that had been removed by an earlier player and has not been replaced. What is the Rule?
A) The stake hole is a hole made by a greenkeeper and Miko may take free relief under Rule 25-1, Abnormal Ground Condition.
B) The hole is within the water hazard and so Miko is not entitled to free relief. He must proceed under one of the options of Rule 26-1 Relief for Ball in Water Hazard.
C) If he cannot play the ball Miko has to declare the ball unplayable and take one of the three options under Rule 28.
D) Miko may choose to replay his ball from where he last played it, without penalty.
Answer: B) The hole is within the water hazard and so Miko is not entitled to free relief. He must proceed under one of the options of Rule 26-1 Relief for Ball in Water Hazard. Decision 25/18.
Note: Although the hole falls within the definition of a hole made by a greenkeeper, there is no relief from abnormal ground conditions in water hazards.

Q.969
In stroke play, David's ball lies through the green on a steep slope, so he does not ground his club. As David is about to putt, the ball moves and comes to rest against his club. He removes his club and the ball rolls farther away. What is the ruling?
A) David incurs a penalty of one stroke and the ball must be replaced at the point where he stopped it.
B) David incurs a penalty of one stroke and the ball must be played from where it rolled to.
C) David incurs a penalty of two strokes and the ball must be replaced at the point where he stopped it.
D) David incurs a penalty of two strokes and the ball must be played from where it rolled to.
Answer: A) David incurs a penalty of one stroke and the ball must be replaced at the point where he stopped it. Decision 19-2/1.5.
Note: A further penalty for moving a ball at rest would not be appropriate in the circumstances, providing the player replaces the ball.

Q.970
In stroke play, Jason's ball lies on the putting green. Before playing his stroke he taps down spike marks in the vicinity of the hole but not on his line of putt. What is the ruling?
A) Jason incurs a penalty of one stroke.
B) Jason incurs a penalty of two strokes.
C) Jason incurs a penalty of two strokes only if the act assists with his subsequent play of the hole.
D) Jason incurs no penalty.
Answer: B) Jason incurs a penalty of two strokes. Decision 16-1c/4.
Note: The repair of spike marks in the vicinity of a hole might assist a player in his subsequent play of the hole. For example, if he putts wide of or past the hole.

Q.971
In stroke play, who is responsible for the correctness of the gross scores recorded for each hole?
A) The competitor.
B) The marker.
C) The Committee.
D) All of the above.
Answer: A) The competitor. Rule 6-6b.
Note: After completion of the round, the competitor should check his score for each hole and settle any doubtful points with the Committee.

Q.972
In stroke play, during the first round of a 36-hole event, a player incorrectly substitutes a ball on a putting green, but a member of the Committee advises him that there is no penalty. He completes his round and returns his score card. During play of the second round, the Committee realises a mistake has been made and adds two penalty strokes to the player's first round score. What is the ruling?
A) The Committee has ruled appropriately.
B) The Committee should stand by the initial decision made by one of its members.
C) The Committee should disqualify the player for an incorrect score card.
D) The Committee member should be sacked!
Answer: A) The Committee has ruled appropriately. Decision 34-3/1.
Note: The Committee may correct an incorrect ruling and impose or rescind a penalty providing that no penalty is imposed or rescinded after the competition has closed.

Q.973
In match play, both Des and his four-ball partner, Malachy, have played their balls onto the putting green. Des is first to putt and his ball rolls past the hole and hits Malachy's ball at

rest. What is the ruling?
A) Des incurs a one stroke penalty and Malachy has to play his ball from where it was moved to.
B) Des incurs a one stroke penalty and Malachy has to replace his ball where it was.
C) There is no penalty, Des plays his ball from where it came to rest and Malachy must replace his ball where it was.
D) There is no penalty and both players have to play their balls from where they came to rest.
Answer: C) There is no penalty, Des plays his ball from where it came to rest and Malachy must replace his ball where it was. Rule 19-5a.
Note: In match play, there is no penalty if a player's ball in motion after a stroke on the putting green is deflected or stopped by another ball in play and at rest on the putting green. The player must play his ball as it lies, whereas the other ball must be replaced where it was.

Q.974
Having spent a few minutes searching for his tee shot in deep undergrowth, Robin takes the lonely walk back to the tee box and tees up another ball. Just as he is about to start his backswing, and four and a half minutes from when he started to look for his ball, he hears a shout from his playing partner that he has found his ball. What is the ruling?
A) Having teed his ball Robin must proceed with that ball and consider the original ball lost.
B) If Robin can get back and identify his original ball within five minutes he must proceed with that ball.
C) Robin must play the original ball, even if he does not identify it within five minutes of starting to search for it.
D) Robin must play out the hole with both balls and report the situation to the Committee.
Answer: C) Robin must play the original ball, even if he does not identify it within five minutes of starting to search for it. Decision 27/5.5.
Note: The teed ball was not in play when the original ball was found and the player is allowed enough time to reach the area in order to identify it, even if the five minute search period has passed.

Q.975
A player may mark and lift his ball if he thinks that it might assist another player ...
A) Only at the request of another player.
B) At any time providing both balls are at rest.
C) Only if his own ball is at rest on the putting green.
D) Only if both balls are at rest on the putting green.
Answer: B) At any time providing both balls are at rest. Rule 22-1.
Note: Except when a ball is in motion, if a player considers that a ball might assist any other player, he may lift his ball or have any other ball lifted.

Q.976
In a strokes competition, Howard hits his par 3 tee shot into rough at the edge of the putting green. He decelerates on his tricky chip shot and hits the ball twice. He then makes a good recovery by holing out the long putt. What is his gross score for the hole?
A) Three strokes.
B) Four strokes.
C) Five strokes.
D) Howard is disqualified from the competition unless he drops a ball back in the rough at the place where he played his second stroke from before he tees off at the next hole.
Answer: B) Four strokes. Rule 14-4.
Note: When Howard hit his ball twice he must count the stroke and add a penalty stroke, making two strokes, plus his tee shot and putt.

Q.977
In a four-ball match, Maeve and Niall are playing Judy and Gerald. Maeve reaches the putting green first and marks and lifts Judy's ball. She does this without Judy's authority. What is the ruling?
A) Maeve incurs a penalty of one stroke.
B) Both Maeve and Niall incur a penalty of one stroke.
C) Maeve is disqualified from the hole.
D) Maeve and Niall lose the hole.
Answer: A) Maeve incurs a penalty of one stroke. Decision 30-3f/10.
Note: A ball to be lifted under the Rules may be lifted by the player, her partner or another person authorised by the player. Accordingly, Maeve incurs a penalty of one stroke but the penalty does not apply to her partner, Niall.

Q.978
All of the area surrounding a hole on a putting green is covered with casual water and the hole itself is filled with water. What is the ruling?
A) In match play competition only, the Committee may relocate the hole.
B) In stroke play competition only, the Committee may relocate the hole.
C) In all forms of competition, the Committee may relocate the hole.
D) In all forms of competition, the Committee is prohibited from relocating the hole.
Answer: A) In match play competition only, the Committee may relocate the hole. Rule 33-2b.
Note: In a stroke play competition all competitors in a single round must play with the holes cut in the same position.

Q.979
Noel and Frank have both played their tee shots onto the fairway when they realise they are playing balls with identical markings. Noel knows which ball is his and to avoid possible confusion, marks and lifts his ball, substitutes another ball with different markings, and plays out the hole. What is the ruling?
A) There is no penalty.
B) Noel incurs a penalty of one stroke for touching his ball in play.
C) Noel incurs a penalty of two strokes for playing an incorrectly substituted ball.
D) Noel incurs total penalties of three strokes.
Answer: C) Noel incurs a penalty of two strokes for playing an incorrectly substituted ball. Decision 15/6.5.
Note: Noel incurs the general penalty of two strokes for incorrectly substituting a ball, under Rule 18, but there is no additional penalty for lifting the ball without authority (see penalty statement under Rule 18).

Q.980
Davis is standing too close to his ball when he makes a clumsy practice swing on the fairway and accidentally moves the ball with the toe-end of his club. What is the ruling?
A) Davis has made a stroke and must play the ball as it lies, without penalty.
B) Davis incurs a penalty of one stroke and must replace the ball.
C) There is no penalty but Davis must replace the ball.
D) Davis incurs a penalty of one stroke and must play the ball as it lies.
Answer: B) Davis incurs a penalty of one stroke and must replace the ball. Decision 18-2a/20.
Note: There is no stroke unless the player intends to move the ball (Definition of Stroke) so the player incurs a penalty stroke for causing their ball in play to move, which must then be replaced.

Q.981

Donald hits his second shot into deep rough and then, presuming that it may be lost, plays a provisional ball to the edge of the green. He and his fellow competitors search for his original ball for four minutes and then he says, "Leave it guys, it's lost, I'll play my provisional ball". However, after he has addressed his provisional ball a shout goes up that his original ball is found. Which statement is correct?
A) Donald must play his provisional ball as he has announced his intention that he is going to play it.
B) Donald must play his provisional ball as he has addressed it.
C) Donald must play his original ball providing it is found within five minutes of the search commencing and he has not put another ball in play.
D) Donald must play his provisional ball if he is not able to identify his original ball within five minutes of the search commencing.
Answer: C) Donald must play his original ball providing it is found within five minutes of the search commencing and he has not put another ball in play. Decision 27-2b/6.
Note: The original ball remains the ball in play since it was found within five minutes after search for it had begun and Donald had not played a stroke with the provisional ball from nearer the hole than where the original ball was thought to be.

Q.982
In singles match play, Charlie, a caddie, is carrying both bags. Prior to her stroke, Cindy asks Charlie what club her opponent used from about the same position. What is the ruling?
A) Cindy incurs no penalty.
B) Cindy incurs a penalty of one stroke.
C) Cindy incurs a penalty of two strokes.
D) Cindy is disqualified.
Answer: A) Cindy incurs no penalty. Decision 8-1/12.
Note: Cindy is entitled to seek any information from her caddie that he might possess. It does not matter that he is also the caddie for her opponent.

Q.983
Part of a boundary fence is bowed towards the course so that it is inside the out of bounds line formed by the inside points of fence posts at ground level. Art's ball comes to rest against this part of the fence. Which of the following statements is correct?
A) Art may push back the bowed section of the fence to obtain a better stroke at his ball.
B) Art may take relief from the immovable boundary fence.
C) Art must play the ball as it lies.
D) Art must play the ball as it lies or deem his ball unplayable.
Answer: D) Art must play the ball as it lies or deem his ball unplayable. Decision 13-2/18.
Note: Art may not improve the position or lie of his ball or the area of his intended stance or swing, by moving or bending objects defining out of bounds.

Q.984
Rhys lifts his ball without marking its position on the putting green. Corey, his opponent, then lifts his ball without marking its position and claims the hole, because he thinks that Rhys has already incurred a loss of hole penalty. What is the ruling?
A) Corey's claim is correct and Rhys incurs the loss of hole penalty.
B) Corey's claim is not valid and both he and Rhys incur a penalty of one stroke for lifting without marking.
C) Corey's claim is not valid and he must replace his ball without penalty. Rhys incurs a penalty of one stroke for lifting without marking.
D) Corey's claim is not valid and he is therefore deemed to have conceded the hole to Rhys.
Answer: B) Corey's claim is not valid and both he and Rhys incur a penalty of one stroke for lifting without marking. Rule 20-1.
Note: A ball must be marked on the green before it is lifted. The penalty for not marking the ball is one stroke, and therefore at this stage the hole had not been lost by either player.

Q.985
Mark's ball comes to rest on a bridge that is within the margins of a water hazard. Which of the following options is correct?
A) Mark must play the ball from the bridge without grounding his club.
B) Mark may play the ball as it lies and ground his club on the bridge or he may take relief from the water hazard under penalty.
C) Mark may take relief from the bridge, without penalty, as the bridge is an immovable obstruction.
D) Mark may play off the bridge or declare his ball unplayable under penalty of one stroke.
Answer: B) Mark may play the ball as it lies and ground his club on the bridge or he may take relief under penalty. Decision 13-4/30.
Note: A bridge is an obstruction. In a hazard, the club may touch an obstruction at address or in the backward movement for the stroke. Grounding the club on the bridge is also permissible, since an obstruction in a water hazard is not ground in the hazard. A player may not deem their ball unplayable when it lies within the margin a water hazard.

Q.986
In a Stableford competition, Paige played from the wrong tees and her ball came to rest out of bounds. She prepares to play her next stroke from within the correct teeing ground. Which is correct?
A) Paige is penalised stroke and distance for the ball out of bounds as well as two strokes for playing from outside the teeing ground. Her next stroke will be her fifth.
B) Paige is penalised two strokes for playing from outside the teeing ground. Her next stroke from the tee will be her third.
C) Paige is penalised two strokes for playing from outside the teeing ground and another stroke for hitting her ball out of bounds. Her next stroke from the tee will be her fourth.
D) Paige is disqualified for playing from the wrong place.
Answer: B) Paige is penalised two strokes for playing from outside the teeing ground. Her next stroke from the tee will be her third. Decision 11-4b/6.
Note: Paige is only penalised two strokes as the ball played from outside the teeing ground was not in play. Therefore, the fact that it came to rest out of bounds was irrelevant.

Q.987
Naomi is standing close to the flagstick as Zoe, her partner in a four-ball better-ball competition, chips onto the green. After Zoe makes her stroke Naomi realises that the ball may strike the flagstick and so she grabs it out of the hole so that the ball will not hit it. What is the ruling?
A) Naomi incurs a penalty of one stroke.
B) Naomi incurs a penalty of two strokes.
C) Both Naomi and Zoe incur a penalty of one stroke.
D) Neither Naomi nor Zoe incurs any penalty.
Answer: D) Neither Naomi nor Zoe incurs any penalty. Note to Rule 17-1.
Note: If the flagstick is in the hole and anyone stands near it while a stroke is being made, they are deemed to be attending the flagstick. In these circumstances if Naomi had not removed the flagstick at the last minute, and Zoe's ball had hit it, Zoe would have incurred a penalty of two strokes as when a flagstick is being attended it must be removed before the ball hits it.

Q.988
Art does not realise that, following a hooked shot from the teeing ground, his ball is lying out of bounds and he plays a good shot onto the putting green. His fellow competitor saw what happened and said that he must go back to the teeing ground to play again. What is the ruling?

A) Art must play his next stroke from the teeing ground and it will be his third stroke.
B) Art must play his next stroke from the teeing ground and it will be his fifth stroke.
C) Art may play his next stroke from the putting green and it will be his fifth stroke.
D) Art is disqualified for playing his ball that was lying out of bounds.
Answer: B) Art must play his next stroke from the teeing ground and it will be his fifth stroke. Decision 15/6.
Note: A ball lying out of bounds is no longer in play and so Art played a wrong ball. He incurs a penalty of two strokes and must proceed under the Rule for lost ball, incurring a stroke and distance penalty.

Q.989
Which statement is correct?
A) The margin of ground under repair extends vertically downwards and upwards.
B) The margin of ground under repair extends vertically downwards but not upwards.
C) The margin of ground under repair extends vertically upwards but not downwards.
D) The margin of ground under repair extends neither vertically downwards nor upwards.
Answer: B) The margin of ground under repair extends vertically downwards but not upwards. Definition of Ground Under Repair.

Q.990
In a four-ball stroke play event, Jonjo accidentally touches the putting green in pointing out the line of putt for Christie, his partner. The spot that Jonjo touches is also on his own line of putt. What is the ruling?
A) There is no penalty as there was no advantage to either player.
B) Jonjo incurs a penalty of two strokes.
C) Christie incurs a penalty of two strokes.
D) Both Jonjo and Christie incur a penalty of two strokes.
Answer: D) Both Jonjo and Christie incur a penalty of two strokes. Decision 30/2.5.
Note: Rule 8-2b states that a player's partner may, before but not during the stroke, point out a line of putt, but in so doing the putting green must not be touched, so Christie incurs the penalty. Because Jonjo also touched his own line of putt he also incurs the penalty under Rule 16-1a.

Q.991
Scott and Jock are all square in their match as they approach the 17th green. Scott arrives at the green first and sees that Jock's ball is on his line of putt and closer to the hole. He walks up to Jock's ball, marks and lifts it. Which of the following statements is correct?
A) Because Scott lifted Jock's ball it must be him that replaces it after he has taken his putt.
B) Scott incurs a penalty of one stroke for lifting Jock's ball without permission.
C) Scott loses the hole for lifting Jock's ball without permission.
D) Scott has acted within the Rules and there is no penalty.
Answer: B) Scott incurs a penalty of one stroke for lifting Jock's ball without permission. Decision 20-1/2.
Note: A player's ball may only be lifted by his opponent with his authority. If Scott had asked Jock's permission before lifting the ball there would have been no penalty.

Q.992
Sonya's caddie is attending the flagstick while she chips from just off the green. After making the stroke, her caddie has difficulty in pulling the flagstick out of the hole and in her panic she pulls out the hole liner, and the ball rolls into the unlined hole. What is the ruling?
A) Sonya incurs no penalty and the ball is holed.
B) Sonya is penalised one stroke.
C) Sonya is penalised two strokes.
D) Sonya has to replace her ball and play her stroke again.

Answer: A) Sonya incurs no penalty and the ball is holed. Decision 17/7.
Note: A hole need not contain a lining. Definition of Hole.

Q.993
In stroke play, Maura's ball lies near the hole in a position to assist Ruby, whose ball lies off the green. Maura advises Ruby that she wants to lift her ball. However, Ruby says, "No, leave it there" and then takes her putt before Maura has an opportunity to lift it. What penalty does Ruby incur?
A) There is no penalty.
B) Ruby incurs a penalty of one stroke.
C) Ruby incurs a penalty of two strokes.
D) Ruby is disqualified.
Answer: D) Ruby is disqualified. Decision 3-4/1.
Note: A competitor is disqualified if they refuse to comply with a Rule affecting the rights of another competitor.

Q.994
Mohammed chips his ball towards the hole from just off the putting green. Without having been asked, his opponent, Asif, removes the flagstick and lays it on the green. Mohammed's ball goes straight over the hole and comes to rest three feet away. Mohammed claims the hole. What is the ruling?
A) There is no penalty.
B) Asif is penalised one stroke for unauthorised removal of the flagstick.
C) Asif loses the hole.
D) There is no penalty but Mohammed may choose to take his putt again with the flagstick left in.
Answer: C) Asif loses the hole. Decision 17-2/2.
Note: If, without the player's authority or prior knowledge, an opponent attends the flagstick while the ball is in motion and that act might have influenced the movement of the ball, the opponent or fellow competitor incurs the applicable penalty.

Q.995
Esther takes out a handheld anemometer during her round to help her determine the strength of the wind on a winter's day. What is the ruling?
A) There is no penalty.
B) Esther incurs a penalty of one stroke.
C) Esther incurs a penalty of two strokes.
D) Esther is disqualified.
Answer: D) Esther is disqualified. Rule 14-3b.
Note: A device that is used for the purpose of gauging wind conditions is considered to be an artificial device and may not be used during a round.

Q.996
Noah's ball comes to rest in a bunker near some wooden steps that interfere with the area of his intended swing. What are his options, without incurring a penalty?
A) There is no relief from the wooden steps, he must play his ball as it lies.
B) Noah may drop his ball in the bunker within one club-length of the nearest point of relief, not nearer the hole.
C) Noah may drop his ball in the bunker within two club-lengths of where the ball lay, not nearer the hole.
D) Noah may drop his ball outside the bunker, keeping the point where the ball lay directly between the hole and the spot on which the ball is dropped.
Answer: B) Noah may drop his ball in the bunker within one club-length of the nearest point of relief, not nearer the hole. Rule 24-2b.

Note: The player is entitled to take relief from an immovable obstruction, without penalty, by following this procedure.

Q.997
Serge putts his ball past the hole and it comes to rest in a deep footprint in a bunker. He declares his ball unplayable. Which of the following procedures may he follow for a penalty of one stroke?
A) Drop a ball outside of the bunker within two club-lengths of the place where the ball crossed the margin of the bunker.
B) Drop a ball outside the bunker anywhere on an extension of the line from the hole and where the ball came to rest in the bunker.
C) Drop a ball anywhere in the bunker that is not nearer the hole.
D) Place a ball on the putting green at the spot where he took his last stroke.
Answer: D) Place a ball on the putting green at the spot where he took his last stroke. Rule 28a.
Note: A player may deem his ball unplayable anywhere on the course except when it lies in a water hazard. One of the options for a ball unplayable is to play a ball as nearly as possible at the spot from which the original ball was last played, under penalty of one stroke.

Q.998
Which is correct regarding ground under repair?
A) Deep cracks in the earth are not always ground under repair.
B) Grass cuttings piled for removal are not always ground under repair.
C) Tractor ruts through the green are always ground under repair.
D) Areas of ground under repair are designated by a red line.
Answer: A) Deep cracks in the earth are not always ground under repair. Decision 25/12.
Note: However, players would be justified in asking the Committee to declare the cracks to be ground under repair, but if they are not so marked then no relief is available.

Q.999
What is the maximum retail value of a prize that an amateur golfer is permitted to accept, other than for a hole-in-one?
A) £500 / $750 or the equivalent.
B) £1,000 / $1,500 or the equivalent.
C) £2,000 / $3,000 or the equivalent.
D) £5,000 / $7,500 or the equivalent.
Answer: A) £500 / $750 or the equivalent. Rules of Amateur Status 3-2a.
Note: There is no limit to the prize for a hole-in-one made while playing a round of golf. Rules of Amateur Status 3-2b.

INDEX

abnormal ground condition, aeration holes	see: aeration holes								
abnormal ground condition, burr'ng animal	see: burrowing animal								
abnormal ground condition, casual water	see: casual water								
abnormal ground condition, definition	94	106	137	267	276	468	705	772	792
abnormal ground condition, GUR	see: ground under repair								
abnormal ground condition, miscellaneous	128	137	143	451	455	690	705	967	
adhering	see: ball, adhering								
aeration holes	434	441							
addressing the ball	88	118	145	207	268	364	407	434	508
	539	565	612	879	898	905			
advice, caddie	167	466	586	640	803	982			
advice, captain	732	738							
advice, club selection	103	193	419	581	664	704	834	910	
advice, definition	45	239	252	290	335	359	717	767	
advice, line of putt	109	119	396	430	586	640	788	895	
advice, public information	18	220	252	359	436	446			
advice, rules	45	239	290	335	524				
advice, stroke	112	171	333	516	717	837			
altered lie	see: lie, altered								
alteration, score card	see: score card, alteration								
amateur status, prize	538	999							
area of intended stance	38	169	188	413	450	550	679	37	169
area of intended swing	450	457	462	526	578	600	608	623	636
	711	769	770	796	800	826	906	921	941
	983								
artificial device	see: assistance, artificial device								
assistance, artificial device	54	55	198	234	269	360	449	490	620
	631	645	995						
assistance, caddie	501	639							
assistance, flagstick	422	592							
assistance, line of play	56	291	454	685	744	857			
assistance, line of putt	43	56	165	173	291	372	396	454	639
	685	744	855	887	950				
assistance, partner	165	294	547						
assistance, physical protection	148	501	649						
bad weather	332	444	545	560	703	776			
ball, adhering	52	114	296	502	897				
ball, addressing	see: addressing the ball								
ball, assisting play	51	405	597	975	882	993			
ball, borrowing	160								
ball, changing between holes	509								
ball, cleaning	see: cleaning ball								
ball, deflected by another ball	205	391	610	681	784	973			
ball, deflected by fellow comp's equipment	655								
ball, deflected by opponent	179	222							
ball, deflected by opponent's equipment	820	908							
ball, deflected by outside agency	22	63	279	473	648	715	889	962	
ball, deflected by player or their caddie	101	969	624						

ball, deflected by player's equipment	101	194	305	314	377	431	603	655	820
	885								
ball, dropping and re-dropping	see: dropping and re-dropping								
ball, embedded	122	615	658	761	812	853	897	930	
ball, exert influence on	209	432	828	887	891	944			
ball, fairly struck	29	154	225	246	260	308	443	839	
ball, falling off tee	84	207	337	407					
ball, holed	75	576	595	715	926				
ball, identifying	68	89	113	151	263	372	513	534	647
	662	668	686	701	752	755	829	865	873
	881	882	932						
ball, in hazard	44	53	77	79	118	124	127	215	216
	229	274	292	302	317	435	469	483	485
	505	510	515	542	548	569	614	619	622
	651	676	805	818	842	865	869	894	918
	923	928	945	985					
ball, in motion	417	678	793	915	947	953	994		
ball, in play	120	161	205	438	714	766	836	871	939
	952	974							
ball, in tree	477	682	768	774	844	914	957		
ball, interfering with play	626	670	751	763	882	916	937		
ball, lifting and marking	see: lifting and marking ball								
ball, moved by another ball	242	806	917						
ball, moved by gravity	819	866	926	942	969				
ball, moved by opponent	286	577	701	949	991				
ball, moved by outside agency	16	440	456	491	503	833	964		
ball, moved by player or their caddie	46	88	105	108	111	152	219	273	292
	298	300	306	355	496	512	602	629	653
	682	692	719	844	871	899	939	980	
ball, moved by player's equipment	311	351	425	537	573				
ball, moved by wind	440	491	508	539	741	866	905	965	
ball, moved in measuring	300	311	596	863					
ball, moves after address	539	719	806	879	947				
ball, moves, definition	434	482							
ball, out of bounds	72	251	256	263	272	415	613	617	659
	726	787	795	816	920	925	931	988	
ball, overhanging hole	23	288	432	934	960				
ball, pitch mark	39	203	266	282	313	324	536	604	697
	707	853							
ball, placing and replacing	see: placing and replacing								
ball, played while moving	337	533	879						
ball, played within water hazard	see: water hazard, ball played within								
ball, seeing when playing	38	90	166	265	310	662	755	898	
ball, struck more than once	168	582	976						
ball, substitute	26	316	484	495	529	598	668	724	766
	782	785	801	836	850	927	952	956	972
	979								
ball, touched by player	40	43	89	145	196	253	355	410	434
	460	496	513	534	614	638	871	969	984
ball, unfit for play	1	27	247	296	379	511	638	801	810
	850	882							

ball, unplayable	183	221	375	495	497	531	621	650	656
	665	682	774	862	863	956	967	997
ball, weight and size	706	821
ball mark	see: ball, pitch mark
ball-marker	31	61	199	206	289	313	356	425	493
	555	657	866	708	741
boundary	see: out of bounds, boundary
breach of rules, caddie	see: caddie, breach of rules
breach of rule, ignore	see: match play, ignore breach of rule
breach of rule, multiple	see: multiple breach of rule
bridge, water hazard	see: water hazard, bridge
building stance	see: stance, building
bunker, definition	13	86	92	121	233	336	378	418	768
bunker, grounding club	485	505	569	622	676
bunker, loose impediment	21	127	215	229	239	240	292	510	547
	755	854	898
bunker, miscellaneous	68	77	126	227	231	259	329	331	341
	451	579	759	779	861	865	903	945	996
	997
bunker, rake	44	358	512	619	644	755	818	869	913
	918	920	923
bunker, stance	79	118	843	920
bunker, test condition	53	79	317	469	548	669	699
burrowing animal	128	197	276	468	712	772	931	967
caddie, assistance	see: assistance, caddie
caddie, breach of rules	480	580	692	701	803	902	913
caddie, definition	167	343	369	397	632	696	919
caddies, multiple	461	561	663	764	788	790	959
casual water, definition	106	381	558	689	792
casual water, putting green	428	552	731	835	978
casual water	106	177	196	208	212	319	357	374	381
	428	455	552	558	587	668	689	731	779
	792	835	846	856	861	877	907	945	961
	978
claim, match play	see: match play, claim
cleaning ball	6	52	82	197	253	259	306	502	594
	647	751	753	882	927	932
club, add	78	195	250	293	929
club, conforming	210	449	518	637	778	824	884
club, foreign material	20	164
club, fourteen	62	64	78	116	195	213	250	293	574
	637	734	802	929	938	958	966
club, grounding	41	77	88	124	268	302	483	505	508
	515	548	565	612	652	729	805	928	985
club, playing characteristics	64	297	518
club, repair and replacement	64	463	518	780	870	935
club, share	116	762	938
clubhead	12	29	154	210	225	313	824	884
committee	74	178	220	288	390	412	427	471	478
	506	560	564	571	583	599	620	633	661
	667	672	677	688	691	697	709	728	731

	737 738 739 742 750 754 757 799 807
	812 814 830 860 880 888 890 922 942
	972 978
competition closed	740 760 775 812 890 904 972
competitor, definition	9 70 285
concession, hole	280 382 532 575 641 687 822 827
concession, match	737 776 827
concession, stroke	66 140 280 294 590 960
course closed	911
course, care of	619 818 913
dew	see: loose impediment, dew, frost, snow and ice
discontinue play	176 241 332 348 395 444 545 560 703
	709 875 927 880
dormie	295 813
doubt as to procedure	416 471 520 860 922 933
dropping and re-dropping ball	35 83 91 149 150 201 217 236 270
	284 323 352 406 523 556 570 593 621
	650 722 745 748 798 849 930 964
embedded ball	see: ball, embedded
environmentally-sensitive area	771 814
equipment, cart	142 178 377 397 885
equipment, definition	31 142 377 577 605 714 748
equipment, golf bag	209 305 314 377 820
equidistant, order of play	see: order of play, equidistant
equity	104 259 292 294 435 488 517 536 541
	585 644 781 816 823 829 831 870 880
	940 954 960 961
etiquette	see: serious breach of etiquette
flagstick, assistance	see: assistance, flagstick
flagstick, attended removed or held up	47 139 249 277 362 417 437 580 675
	678 730 891 909 915 987 994
flagstick, definition	725 832
flagstick, miscellaneous	17 34 200 252 384 725 823 891 909
	915 992
four-ball	19 57 109 116 119 165 254 447 454
	466 547 599 625 692 815 834 873 885
	888 943 950 973 977 987 990
four-ball, order of play	see: order of play, four-ball and foursome
foursome	80 83 116 262 322 429 466 606 646
	666 762 809 886 896
foursome, order of play	see: order of play, four-ball and foursome
fourteen clubs	see: clubs, fourteen
forms of match play	see: match play, forms of
forms of stroke play	see: stroke play, forms of
frost	see: loose impediment, dew, frost, snow and ice
general penalty	7 488
ground under repair	93 94 258 267 281 349 361 504 567
	593 613 765 770 851 933 957 989 998
ground under repair, material for removal	361 504 851
grounding club	see: club, grounding
grounding club in bunker	see: bunker, grounding club

group	583
growing thing	38 50 136 147 169 219 226 265 274
	299 423 462 472 515 526 542 550 567
	600 652 770 826 893
handicap, player	see: player, handicap
handicap, score card	see: score card, handicap
hazard, definition	121 378 878
hole and holed, definition	75 85 811 992
hole halved, match play	see: match play, hole halved
hole out	66 200 288 934 951
hole, damaged	546 667 697 754
hole, made by greenkeeper	41 709 968
honour	see: order of play, honour
ice	see: loose impediment, dew, frost, snow and ice
identifying ball	see: ball, identifying
immovable obstruction	see: obstruction, immovable
improving lie	see: lie, improving
improving line of play	see: line of play, improving
improving teeing area	see: teeing area, improving
indexes, match play	see: match play, indexes
information, public	see: advice, public information
information, wrong	563 735 740 841 912 963
insect	see: loose impediment, insect
intended stance	see: area of intended stance
intended swing	see: area of intended swing
lateral water hazard, definition	123 175 245 677 729
lateral water hazard, relief	98 433 487 630 680 722
lie, altered	259 842 899 964
lie, improving	459 781 853 893 899 923
lifting and marking ball	40 59 61 113 199 206 253 255 289
	300 306 313 356 373 404 455 493 633
	638 656 701 708 724 752 753 782 785
	791 829 927 932 949 977 984 991
line of play, assistance	see: assistance, line of play
line of play, improving	214 358 363 371 423 536 604 699 749
	835 854 869 903 907
line of play, miscellaneous	96 133 189 396 522 524 559 640 723
	803
line of putt, advice	see: advice, line of putt
line of putt, assistance	see: assistance, line of putt
line of putt, definition	158 474 867
line of putt, touching	24 39 95 202 218 282 309 320 324
	365 394 414 428 519 546 565 733 747
	786 835 970 990 143 144
local rule	189 215 248 258 270 281 312 441 490
	498 521 554 620 623 739 742 750 771
	814 849
location of ball, order of play	see: order of play, location of ball
loose impediment, definition	48 52 110 187 287 733 736 743
loose impediment, dew, frost, snow & ice	381 394 476 551 589 846 877
loose impediment in bunker	see: bunker, loose impediment

loose impediment, insect	114	392	435	589	858			
loose impediment, miscellaneous	10	33	73	95	99	202	240	312	320
	324	414	460	489	502	602	607	710	736
	743	747	769	781	786	793	829	872	897
	898	903	906	940	942				
loose impediment, natural thing	21	49	50	99	127	136	217	226	229
	366	411	467	547	653	654	733		
loose impediment, sand and loose soil	8	287	315	330	340	365	448	654	941
loose impediment, stones and rocks	403	589	607						
loose soil and sand	see: loose impediment, sand and loose soil								
lost ball, definition	11	170	271	881					
lost ball, provisional ball	15	72	170	256	263	272	415	453	494
	716	787	815	981					
lost ball, stroke and distance	25	81	244	251	256	271	497	568	617
	659	781	815	836	864	931	948	988	
marker	155	427	442	486	527	616	627	635	817
	838	888	901	912	971				
match play, claim	506	532	687	740	841	908	916	984	994
match play, forms of	80	758							
match play, hole halved	430	702	848	895	963				
match play, waive breach of rule	628	672							
match play, indexes	478								
match play, order of play	see: order of play, match play								
match play, winner	672	737	773	827	848	911			
movable obstruction	see: obstruction, movable								
move, definition	105	434	482	719					
multiple breaches of rule(s)	41	292	651	652	906	917	928	932	946
natural thing	see: loose impediment, natural thing								
nearest point of relief	212	270	319	409	412	552	556	587	588
	593	759	789	861	876				
nearest point of relief, definition	28	156	177	357	557	712			
obstruction, definition	42	115	125	238	298	325	327	341	345
	380	450	554	698	743				
obstruction, immovable	6	28	42	96	133	188	189	261	298
	299	380	386	409	439	489	498	499	522
	549	554	559	588	623	634	695	711	749
	759	789	794	847	871	876	900	921	985
	996								
obstruction, movable	46	48	97	115	125	126	152	159	186
	187	217	224	231	257	261	307	325	327
	345	410	424	450	512	554	578	579	684
	749	794	796	797	874	908	940	953	
order of play, equidistant	543	894							
order of play, four-ball and foursome	57	262	646	666	809	886	896		
order of play, honour	100	153	243	321	367	464			
order of play, match play	30	153	211	223	228	237	283	465	532
	883	916							
order of play, provisional ball	100	230	514						
order of play, stroke play	76	102	228	264	420	528	643	855	
out of bounds, ball	see: ball out of bounds								

out of bounds, boundary	33 37 81 135 238 298 578 613 695 698 739 868 931 983
out of bounds, definition	58 81 135 180 370 398 553 578 613 727 868 914
out of bounds, wrong ball	see: wrong ball, out of bounds
outside agency, ball	see: ball, outside agency
outside agency, ball deflected by	see: ball, deflected by outside agency
outside agency, ball moved by	see: ball, moved by outside agency
outside agency, definition	65 318 440 467 491 632 696 710 726 746 905
outside agency, miscellaneous	473 686 777 790 796 816 948
outside teeing ground	see: teeing ground, playing from outside
overhanging hole	see: ball, overhanging hole
partner, definition	172 326
physical protection, assistance	see: assistance, physical protection
pitch mark	see: ball, pitch mark
placing and replacing ball	173 255 644 741 819 842 845 926 937 964 965
play suspended	395 560 642 767 776 808 875 927 965
player, handicap	243 275 321 346 354 385 464 478 606 671 687 713 740 775 799 890 901
player responsibilities, rules	see: rules, player responsibilities
player, start time	19 383 390 643 688 834
playing from wrong place	see: wrong place, playing from
practice swing	41 111 449 457 515 629 636 651 826 906 980
practice, before or between rounds	353 399 445 470 507 530 562 669 902 919 955
practice, during round	182 232 488 609 660 694 783 936
provisional ball, definition	15 162 181 204 716
provisional ball, lost ball	see: lost ball, provisional ball
provisional ball, miscellaneous	15 72 100 162 170 181 204 230 256 263 272 415 453 494 514 531 535 673 795 925 981
provisional ball, order of play	see: order of play, provisional ball
public information	see: information, public
putting green, casual water	see: casual water, putting green
putting green, definition	132 613 878
putting green, pitch mark	see: ball, pitch mark
putting green, test surface	82 140 507 601
putting green, wrong	60 192 481 922
rake	see: bunker, rake
referee	368 637 746 765
refusal to comply with a rule	993
responsibility, score card	see: score card, responsibility
re-tee	32 84 207 251 407 629 825
rub of the green, definition	22 63 473 777
rules of golf - definition	174 376 720 742 750 756 831
rules, player responsibilities	97 480 735
rules, waive	4 373 420 525 628 672 702 742 848 855 951 958

score card, alteration	387	408	442	486	572	616		
score card, handicap	275	346	385	458	564	606	627	775	799
	890	901						
score card, miscellaneous	426	427	478	807	817			
score card, responsibility	155	458	564	661	691	888	971	
score card, sign	388	447	527	635	700	838	901	
score card, wrong score		117	342	540	599	661	812	888
sand and loose soil	see: loose impediment, sand and loose soil							
search for ball	11	108	138	147	196	204	219	300	310
	311	328	349	494	535	576	642	673	693
	702	815	864	865	918	964	974	981
second ball	416	471	520	728	860	922	933	
serious breach of etiquette	74	389	571	633	728			
slow play	566	830						
snow	see: loose impediment, dew, frost, snow and ice							
spike mark	218	324	707	786	887	944	970	
stableford	3	185	342	347	367	458	574	
stakes	37	144	175	186	238	245	248	270	325
	338	398	450	578	613	623	680	743	849
	856	868	968					
stance	5	33	38	87	216	225	364	413	481
	492	508	519	539	550	587	593	612	679
	689	727		789	792	861	907	922	924
stance, area of intended	see: area of intended stance							
stance, building	184	492	618	843	852			
stance, bunker	see: bunker, stance							
start time	see: player, start time							
stones and rocks	see: loose impediments, stones and rocks							
stipulated round, definition	157	683	757	822	848	951		
stroke play, forms of	3	254	322	347	426	904		
stroke play, order of play	see: order of play, stroke play							
stroke, definition	67	71	120	146	246	273	301	400	500
	800	980						
substitute ball	see: ball, substitute							
suspended play	see: play suspended							
tee, ball falling off	see: ball, falling off tee							
tee, definition	107	129	421	804				
teeing ground, definition	87	303	402	475	479	825		
teeing ground, improving teeing area	401	472	492	551	608	679	893	
teeing ground, miscellaneous	5	32	71	120	131	141	153	161	251
	393	452	459	739	878	880	939	
teeing ground, playing from outside	14	344	438	825	886	986		
teeing ground, wrong	163	235	544					
tee-marker	130	452	584	721	880	924		
test surface	see: putting green, test surface							
through the green, definition	393	588	878					
touching line of putt	see: line of putt, touching							
undue delay	10	138	176	241	278	566	607	611	830
waive rules	see: rules, waive							
water hazard, ball played within	227	257	840	937	985			
water hazard, bridge	622	711	805	900	985			

water hazard, definition	36	121	186	191	245	338	378	477	674
	856							
water hazard, miscellaneous	41	106	124	183	190	216	257	274	302
	375	379	411	415	424	453	585	652	693
	716	726	771	856	906	928	961		
water hazard, relief	26	69	128	329	334	568	798	840	856
	862	961	968						
winner, match play	see: match play, winner
wrong ball, definition	718	766	952
wrong ball, miscellaneous	11	134	227	301	304	331	339	350	382
	595	617	625	641	659	782	816	859	864
	892	943	946	988					
wrong ball, substitute ball	598	617	766	952	979
wrong information	see: information wrong
wrong place, playing from	149	244	304	412	521	570	591	728
wrong putting green	see: putting green, wrong
wrong score	see: score card, wrong score
wrong teeing ground	see: teeing ground, wrong

The answers to questions in this book refer to;
1) Rules of Golf 2016, ©2015 R&A Rules Limited and The United States Golf Association. All rights reserved.
2) Decisions on the Rules of Golf 2016-2017, ©2015 R&A Rules Limited. All rights reserved.

The R&A and USGA review and make revisions to the Rules of Golf every four years. The last revision was effective 1st January 2016.

The questions, answers and explanations to the questions in this book are the author's interpretation and understanding of the 34 Rules of Golf and do not carry the official approval of either the R&A or USGA.

Whilst every attempt has been made to ensure the accuracy and reliability of these questions and answers on the Rules of Golf, I am human and have been known to be wrong! I shall not be held responsible for any loss or damage of any sort caused by reliance upon the accuracy or reliability of such information. Readers should refer to the full text of the Rules and Decisions, as published in the official publications of the R&A (www.randa.org) and the USGA (www.usga.org).

Barry Rhodes, www.rhodesrulesschool.com.

Printed in Great Britain
by Amazon